Environmental Aesthetics

Environmental Aesthetics

Crossing Divides and Breaking Ground

EDITED BY

Martin Drenthen and Jozef Keulartz

Fordham University Press | *New York 2014*

Fordham University Press has no responsibility for the persistence or accuracy of URLs for external or third-party Internet websites referred to in this publication and does not guarantee that any content on such websites is, or will remain, accurate or appropriate.

Fordham University Press also publishes its books in a variety of electronic formats. Some content that appears in print may not be available in electronic books.

Library of Congress Cataloging-in-Publication Data is available from the publisher.

Printed in the United States of America
16 15 14   5 4 3 2 1
First edition

Contents

Preface

The field of environmental philosophy has its base primarily in North America, and many of its central topics and approaches clearly reflect a North American perspective on environmental issues, for instance regarding the importance of the concept of wilderness, a concept the relevance of which is not obvious in Old World contexts such as Europe.

Since 2004, the *International Society for Environmental Ethics* and the *International Association for Environmental Philosophy* organize their annual joint meeting in Allenspark, USA, in the heart of the Colorado Rocky Mountains. The Rockies are a beautiful location for an environmental philosophy conference, but locations tend to direct the attention to certain issues while ignoring others. Therefore, in 2010 it was decided that henceforth, the meeting should be held biannually on alternating locations.

The intended establishment of a European Network for Environmental Ethics in 2011 provided an excellent opportunity for us to volunteer and organize the 2011 joint meeting in The Netherlands. We hoped the conference would result in a stronger involvement of European environmental philosophers to the field. The central theme of the conference was "Old World and New World Perspectives on Environmental Philosophy."

Luckily, the choice for Europe as a location did not put off many US-based scholars. On the contrary, the location proved to be one of the factors that made this into one of the largest and most diverse environmental philosophy conferences of the last few years.

The city of Nijmegen, in the Netherlands, is over two thousand years old and lies close to the German border at the borders of the

Rhine River. The venue itself, "De Holthurnse Hof," is a former estate that is surrounded by a centuries-old cultural landscape with a mix of farmland and woods, and a designated Natura 2000 area. The hilly terrain was formed by a glacial moraine in the last ice age and contains many signs of history: ancient Roman clay pits; roads and aqueducts; remnants of mediaeval castles and villages; signs of nineteenth-century romanticism; and remains of the Second World War, when one of the biggest WWII battles, Operation Market Garden, took place in these surroundings.

The venue provided a perfect location to discuss a wide variety of topics in their real-life context. The program featured site visits to a demonstration project of the "Dutch Society for the Conservation of the Cultural Landscape" (showing how landscapes can be improved making use of traditional land use practices) and to an experimental rewilding project along the borders of the Rhine: "new wilderness." The conference program contained sessions on topics ranging from rewilding in old European cultural heritage landscapes to animal ethics and environmental virtue ethics, but also dealt with the new challenges posed by rapid changes in the world: ethics of climate change, land grab, fresh water ethics, and environmental justice.

The conference program features three themed sessions on environmental aesthetics and one session about the relation between nature and art. The essays in this book are reworked versions of these papers, and some additions.

Environmental Aesthetics

Introduction

Martin Drenthen and Jozef Keulartz

Environmental aesthetics has a long history. During the period of Enlightenment and early Romanticism, nature was seen as *the* paradigm of aesthetic experience and judgment. This gradually changed in the nineteenth century when the focus of philosophical aesthetics gradually shifted from nature to art. This changed again in the late 1960s when environmental aesthetics emerged as a new discipline in reaction to the growing popular and political concerns over environmental degradation and destruction.

Empirical Versus Speculative Aesthetics

However, from the start the new discipline of environmental aesthetics displays a split personality, a Janus face with an empirical and a philosophical side that seem to be in constant disagreement. Initially, in the first decades, empirical research developed much faster than philosophical reflection. "Speculative" aesthetics was looked upon by empirical aesthetics with some disdain as arm chair discipline that takes place in a study or in a library.

A case in point is psychologist Daniel Berlyne, who developed a very influential theory of landscape perception and appreciation.[1] Berlyne sees "speculative" aesthetics as limited by the subjective analyses of its adherents. "Its conclusions may reflect elitist and idiosyncratic ideas about what aesthetic interpretations, values and norms *ought* to be. The scientific researcher, on the other hand, is *objective* and detached from the research process. Consequently, the concrete facts which result from the research are less prone to bias and interference."[2]

Douglas Porteous' comprehensive book *Environmental Aesthetics: Ideas, Politics and Planning* from 1996 still doesn't fully recognize the contribution of philosophy to the discipline of environmental aesthetics. According to Porteous, "very few modern aesthetic philosophers have cared to venture beyond the art gallery."[3] Ronald Hepburn is briefly mentioned as an exception, but then again, only "few philosophers have followed Hepburn's attempt to come to grips with environmental aesthetics."[4] Porteous concludes that the philosophy of aesthetics leaves us empty-handed and that we have to turn to empirical and experimental research to understand our reactions to our environment.

In the second half of the 1970s, philosophers started to fight back and to criticize empirical research designed to map public landscape preferences by assessing and measuring responses to environmental stimuli. Most empirical work takes place in a laboratory or quasi-experimental setting in which environmental stimuli are presented in simulated form such as photographs or color slides. The most prominent pioneering work was performed by Elwood Shafer and his associates in the United States, who developed a "Landscape Preference Model" for quantifying and predicting public preferences by means of measuring formal aspects of photographs.[5]

Allen Carlson has taken Shafer and his coworkers to task not only for their obsession with the idea of quantifying aesthetic value but also for their exclusive reliance on photographs, which is typical for what Carlson calls the "scenic cult" or the "landscape cult."[6] This cult encourages perceiving and appreciating the natural environment as if it were a landscape painting, that is, as a certain kind of scene observed from a specific viewpoint. It requires us to view the environment as if it were a static representation which is essentially two dimensional. "It requires the reduction of the environment to a scene or view. But what must be kept in mind is that the environment is not a scene, not a representation, not static, and not two dimensional."[7]

Nature Versus Art

Carlson blames mainstream empirical aesthetics for obscuring the differences between the natural environment and works of art. As Hepburn has already argued, the aesthetic appreciation of nature differs in at least three crucial ways from the appreciation of artworks.[8]

First, the degree to which the spectator is involved in the natural aesthetic situation is usually greater than in art appreciation. The spectator of a landscape is surrounded by and immersed in that landscape in a way in which the spectator of a landscape painting is not in that painting. The natural environment impinges upon a broader range of senses than is commonly the case with artworks. Movements in the natural environment (of wind and water, for instance) and the spectator's movements—Hepburn mentions the movement of a glider-pilot—may have an important impact on aesthetic experience: The dichotomy between subject and object collapses and the spectator also becomes actor. In Hepburn's own words: "We have here not only a mutual involvement of spectator and object, but also a reflexive effect by which the spectator experiences *himself* in an unusual and vivid way."[9]

Second, traditional artworks are "framed" in a way that natural objects and landscapes are not. Hepburn uses the notion of "frame" not only in the literal sense of the physical boundaries of pictures but in a much broader sense—as the totality of devices employed in different arts to set art objects apart from natural objects and from artificial objects without aesthetic interest. The natural world, in contrast, is "frameless." This may seem like a disadvantage because the absence of frames precludes the recognition of the formal completeness and stability characteristic of art objects; it makes natural objects more indeterminate and unpredictable. But, on the other hand, this makes room for perceptual surprises and a sense of adventurous openness, and challenges the appreciator of a natural environment to come up with his or her own "framing."

Lastly, unlike works of art, the meaning of natural environments is not determined by a designer and a design. There are no guides to interpretation built in by some creator. But again this lack of artistic intent can enhance aesthetic experience and offer scope for the exercise of creativity and for imaginative play.

Hepburn argues that it is important to recognize these differences between art objects and natural objects and the types of aesthetic experience they provide:

> Supposing that a person's aesthetic education fails to reckon with these differences, supposing it instils in him the attitudes, the tactics of approach, the expectations proper to the appreciation of artworks only, such a person will either pay very little aesthetic heed to natural objects or else will heed them in the wrong way. He will look—and of course look in vain—for what can be found and enjoyed only in art. Furthermore, one cannot

be at all certain that he will seriously ask himself whether there might be other tactics more proper and more fruitful for the aesthetic appreciation of nature.[10]

Such failure will have negative ramifications for the protection of the environment because "a sound natural aesthetics is crucial to sound conservation policy and management."[11]

Outline of This Volume

By stressing the difference between an aesthetic appreciation of nature and an appreciation of artworks, philosophical aesthetics has distanced itself self-confidently from its empirical counterpart in environmental aesthetics that still seems to overlook this crucial difference. In the first decade of this century, this emancipation from empirical aesthetics was followed by a gradual expansion of the scope of the field of environmental aesthetics from natural environments to the mixed or modified environments of gardens, environmental and land art, and everyday environments, including built environments.[12] With this broadening, environmental aesthetics has finally been coming of age, reminding us of the heydays of philosophical aesthetics in the eighteenth century when natural beauty was the paradigm object of aesthetic experience and judgment.

Coming of Age

The volume's first part sketches this coming of age of environmental aesthetics. It is kicked off by Allen Carlson, who provides a historical backdrop for this volume by outlining "Ten Steps in the Development of Western Environmental Aesthetics," briefly describing some of the main contributions to the field that have been made at each stage. The chapter begins with Ronald Hepburn's seminal 1966 essay "Contemporary Aesthetics and the Neglect of Natural Beauty" and ends with what Carlson calls the "Coming of Age" of environmental aesthetics, which is marked by the proliferation of new monographs, anthologies, reference volume entries, and introductory textbooks that have been published in the field since the turn of the century. He then adds a coda concerning environmental aesthetics beyond the West.

Next, Yuriko Saito discusses some important "Future Directions for Environmental Aesthetics." Her chapter starts where Carlson's chapter ends: the broadening of environmental aesthetics' scope from natural environments to mixed environments such as gardens, agricultural landscapes, urban environments, and its further expansion to include what Saito has called "everyday aesthetics" (i.e., all those ingredients that constitute our spatial environments, namely artefacts, human activities, and social relationships). At the end of her chapter, Saito also considers Carlson's very last (eleventh) step that goes beyond Western environmental aesthetics, and argues that many non-Western traditions such as Taoism and Japanese aesthetics provide rich insight into environmental aesthetic issues. Learning from their often time-honored thoughts and practices may very well enrich the environmental aesthetics discourse.

Finally, in his chapter "European and American Approaches to Environmental Aesthetics," Jonathan Maskit advocates yet another (twelfth) step—we should not only encourage a dialogue between Western and Eastern perspectives on environmental aesthetics but also engage in a dialogue between New World and Old World perspectives.[13] Maskit challenges the "standard view" that the most important division in contemporary aesthetics is that between cognitivists (those who believe that concepts, usually scientific concepts, are essential for the aesthetic appreciation of nature) and noncognitivists (those who do not so believe). If we confront New World with Old World perspectives, an alternative distinction comes to the fore—that between universalism and cultural historicism. Universalism, the dominant approach of the field, generally holds that culture and history are—ultimately—unimportant when trying to figure out how people should appreciate nature aesthetically. Cultural historicism, by contrast, holds a pluralist or relativist position and believes that one's culture and history are crucial to working out one's environmental aesthetic, and rejects the universalist idea of there being only one correct way to appreciate an environment appropriately.

Rethinking Relationships

The widening of scope that characterized the coming of age of environmental aesthetics involves a continual rethinking of relationships, which is the subject of the volume's second part. This part opens with a chapter by Arnold Berleant, who is known for his "aesthetics of engagement" that stands in sharp contrast to the traditional contemplative model, which isolates aesthetic objects from the rest of life and requires an attitude of disinterestedness.[14] In "The Cultural Aesthetics of Environment," Berleant attempts to reconcile the need for cooperative environmental action in the face of environmental degradation and destruction with the existence of cultural and historic differences. In his 2005 book *Aesthetics and Environment*, Berleant tries to narrow the gap between universalism and relativism (the topic of Maskit's chapter) by introducing the notion of "generality," suggesting a degree of extent and allowing variability. In this volume, he argues that an ecological perspective can narrow the gap between the traditional Western view of the environment as separate and independent from humans, and thus as an object of control and manipulation, and the view of many Eastern cultures of living in harmony with nature.

While Berleant's chapter is about the relationship between universalism and cultural-historicism, and between Western and non-Western approaches, in Dennis Dumas' "Towards an Aesthetics of Respect" the focus is on the relationship between environmental ethics and environmental aesthetics, two philosophical disciplines that emerged at about the same time.[15]

Dumas turns to Kant's third critique—the *Critique of the Power of Judgment*—to obtain an aesthetics of respect for nature. Strictly speaking, the one and only object of our respect ("Achtung") is the moral law. Respect means the awareness of the free and voluntary subordination of our will to the moral law. According to Kant, respect for a person is, in fact, only respect for the law. In this way, Kant extends the notion of respect to humans. Dumas examines another extension of this notion, an extension of the second degree, from respect for humanity to respect for the aesthetic value of natural environments. Along these lines, Dumas arrives at an indirect duty of environmental protection which avoids the pitfalls and problems of non-anthropocentrism that proclaims direct ethical respect for nature.

In "From Theoretical to Applied Environmental Aesthetics," Yrjö Sepänmaa discusses yet another interrelationship, that between the theory and practice of environmental aesthetics. After reviewing the historical development of the field, Sepänmaa suggests that its future lies in moving outside the academy through a new kind of professional aesthetic activity and through engagement with the public. Environmental aestheticians should combine or complement their role as analysts with the role of guides, acting as experts in beauty in cooperation with researchers from other disciplines, practical workers, policymakers, and the wider public. The need for a close cooperation between various parties as a consequence of the transition from theoretical to applied environmental aesthetics poses intricate problems of communication across boundaries between different and sometimes divergent disciplines and audiences. As an important way to tackle these problems, Sepänmaa points to a series of seven prestigious international congresses on environmental aesthetics that took place in Finland from 1994 to 2009 under his direction. This series has been a major force in the unification of the discipline, in crossing borders between the natural sciences and the humanities, in finding a common language for exchanging information and ideas across boundaries, and in linking activities of players from different fields (see also Carlson in this volume).

Nature, Art, and the Power of Imagination

The third part is devoted to yet another relationship that needs rethinking, the relationship between nature and art. In "Environmental Art and Ecological Citizenship," Jason B. Simus discusses and dismisses the criticism put forward by Allen Carlson that some, if not most, environmental artworks constitute an "aesthetic affront to nature."[16] Carlson claims that whether an environmental artwork constitutes an affront depends only on aesthetic qualities apart from any relationship to its social, moral, and ecological qualities. Simus rejects his claim and argues that the aesthetic qualities of a work should not be divorced from these other qualities; instead we should aim at a comprehensive evaluation that takes all the work's qualities into consideration when the question is whether an environmental artwork is an affront. Simus also criticizes Carlson's idea that real nature is pristine, untouched by humans, as based on an outdated ecological theory. If humans are not seen as part of nature but apart from nature, environmental artworks are almost by definition an affront to nature. Simus' central thesis is that environmental artworks have the same democratic potential as restoration projects if participation in their creation, appreciation, and criticism encourages deliberation about aesthetic, social, moral, ecological, and all other community-regarding values.

In "Can Only Art Save Us Now?," David Wood discusses the well-known problem that little has been done until now to address global environmental change, especially climate change, that threatens life as we know it. We humans are shortsighted, unwilling to act in our long-term interest. Reason alone will not inspire us to act in the interest of future generations; we also need the power of imagination to overcome our indifference and indolence. If our inability to act responsibly is indeed a failure of the imagination, art might be an eminent resource to steer us in the right direction. Hence Wood's question: Can only art save us now? Can art bridge the imagination gap, to make our potentially catastrophic future vividly plausible, and to open up space for alternative, less "toxic," forms of living and dwelling? To answer this question, Wood turns to Heidegger, and especially to his essay "The Origin of the Work of Art," drafted between 1935 and 1937. Following in the footsteps of Heidegger, Wood considers art as an event of disclosure or uncovering that might open onto modes of dwelling that are less destructive than the current ones. Art can make us aware of our present suboptimal habits and patterns of behavior that are ruining the earth; it can also encourage us to transform or displace them by habits and patterns that are necessary to "save the earth."

Irene Klaver takes the baton from Wood in exploring the power of imagination for the environment. In "Landscapes of the Environmental Imagination: Ranging from NASA and Cuyahoga Images to Kiefer and O'Keeffe Paintings," Klaver sketches the rise of what she calls "environmental imagination," with special attention to the work of two modern painters, Georgia O'Keeffe and Anselm Kiefer. Klaver sketches a conceptual framework of the environmental imagination through the work of philosophers and social theorists, such as Benedict Anderson, Edward Said, Arjun Appadurai, and Maurice Merleau-Ponty, who all developed a notion of the imagination beyond the mental faculties of the individual. She shows how an unexpected commonality emerges from the perspective of an environmental imagination between two radically different painters—Georgia O'Keeffe and Anselm Kiefer.

Wind Farms, Shopping Malls, and Wild Animals

The last part of the volume is illustrative of Yrjö Sepänmaa's claim about the new relation between theory and practice, typified by the emergence of practical applications from theoretical studies and the use of concrete examples and case studies. In "Beauty or Bane: Advancing an Aesthetic Appreciation for Wind Turbine Farms," Tyson-Lord Gray discusses the landscape effects of windfarms. Gray begins his chapter by looking at declining wind turbine sales during the years 2007–2010. In an attempt to locate a reason for this decline, he evaluates two claims: (1) that windfarms reduce property value and (2) that windfarms ruin the beauty of nature. For the first claim, he looks at three studies conducted on residential property sales located near wind farms. For the second claim, he engages in a comparison of Immanuel Kant's *Critique of the Power of Judgment*, which defends purely emotional aesthetic evaluations, and John Dewey's *Art as Experience*, which provides an understanding that views beauty as an integration of both emotional and cognitive judgments. According to Gray, Dewey's aesthetic can help to push the conversation beyond the purely emotional response of many windfarm opponents.

In "Thinking Like a Mall," Steven Vogel examines the history of the City Center Mall (1989–2009) in Columbus, Ohio, asking whether the same sorts of consideration that led Aldo Leopold to call for humans to "think like a mountain" might suggest that we should also learn to think like a mall. The moral considerability of natural entities such as mountains is often claimed to derive from their autonomy or independence from human beings, where autonomy is understood either narrowly in terms of a teleology internal to the entities that human action might modify or frustrate, or more broadly in terms of a liability to forces that operate beyond human control. But Vogel claims malls, too, exhibit "autonomy" in both those senses, as do all humanly built structures. The commercial failure of City Center itself shows this, revealing it to have been subject to an ecology of commerce that escaped human understanding and prediction. Human artifacts, Vogel concludes, are as marked by "otherness" from humans as so-called natural objects are; we cannot "identify" with our artifacts, we do not "see ourselves reflected" in them, they do not exist on the other side of an ontological divide from natural entities, and so forth. We live in one world, not two; if we are to let mountains be, we should let malls be as well.

In "Aesthetic Value and Wild Animals," Emily Brady discusses a subject long neglected in environmental aesthetics. Animals are commonly featured in our aesthetic experience, from our interactions with companion animals to the attention given to iconic species and "charismatic" megafauna. Mammals, birds, insects, and marine life are part of our everyday and not-so-everyday lives, in the flesh and featuring as subjects in the arts and media. Given the significance of animals in these domains, it is surprising how neglected they are in debates in environmental aesthetics. On what grounds do we ascribe aesthetic value to wild animals? Recently, Glenn Parsons has argued that this value is grounded in the "fitness" of animals in relation to their form, behavior, and traits.[17] Brady contends that Parsons' "functional beauty" approach overlooks the important role played by expressive qualities in our aesthetic experience of animals. Drawing on expressive theories of music and discussions of expressive qualities in nature, Brady examines the distinctive character and basis of these qualities in sentient nonhuman creatures. She then addresses potential moral problems and objections, in particular, how aesthetic appreciation of expressive qualities is related to or distinct from sentimental, trivial, and anthropomorphic responses to wild animals.

This volume clearly shows that the field of philosophical environmental aesthetics has reached maturity and at the same time has diversified considerably over the past few decades. Environmental aesthetics today harbors a wide range of perspectives and crosses several commonly recognized divides, notably between analytic and continental philosophical traditions, Eastern and Western cultural worldviews, universalizing and historicizing understandings of aesthetic experience, aesthetics and ethics, and theoretical and practical concerns. This volume sets out to show how these different approaches and perspectives can be brought into conversation with one another, lending environmental aesthetics a degree of coherence, while reinforcing the diversity of positions that it displays.

PART

I

Coming of Age

CHAPTER

1

Ten Steps in the Development of Western Environmental Aesthetics

Allen Carlson

Introduction

In 1967 Richard Rorty published a seminal collection of essays called *The Linguistic Turn*.[1] The volume has a masterful introduction in which Rorty told the story of the obsession with language that had developed within Western analytic philosophy over the previous thirty years or so. However, Rorty's introduction is no simple historical account. Rather Rorty focused on the interrelationships among the major figures, the key publications, and the accompanying theoretical commitments that gave shape to the linguist turn, thereby making evident how it was not simply a series of philosophical Ideas and theories but rather a movement within philosophy. I intend the following observations to help make clear in a similar, although much more modest and simplistic manner, the way in which the development of environmental aesthetics within Western analytic aesthetics over the last forty years has likewise not been just a series of ideas about aesthetic appreciation, but rather a progression of stages in the growth of an area of research that has gradually evolved into an important subdiscipline of philosophical aesthetics. I identify and discuss ten such stages.

The Neglect of Natural Beauty

The first step in the development of Western environmental aesthetics is Ronald Hepburn's classic 1966 essay, "Contemporary Aesthetics and the Neglect of Natural Beauty," for this article helped to set the agenda for much of the later work in the field.[2] Hepburn was the first to bring attention to the extent to which analytic aesthetics had virtually ignored the aesthetic appreciation of the natural world throughout the twentieth century, essentially reducing the discipline of aesthetics to the philosophy of art. Moreover, he noted that although the aesthetic appreciation of art frequently provides misleading models for the appreciation of nature, there is nonetheless, in the aesthetic appreciation of nature, as in the appreciation of art, a distinction between appreciation that is only trivial and superficial and that which is serious and deep. He furthermore suggested that for nature, such serious appreciation may require new and different theoretical approaches that can accommodate not only nature's indeterminate and varying character but also both our multisensory experience and our diverse understanding of it. By focusing attention on natural beauty, Hepburn thereby demonstrated that there could be significant philosophical investigation of the aesthetic experience of the world beyond the world of art. In this way, he not only generated interest in the aesthetics of nature, he also laid the foundations for environmental aesthetics in general.

Issues with Empirical Environmental Aesthetics

Hepburn's essay can be seen as the first philosophical move in the development of environmental aesthetics. However, the next stage in that development had a slightly different starting point. Although, as Hepburn had observed, philosophical aesthetics continued to ignore the aesthetic appreciation of nature in the second half of the twentieth century, the same was not true beyond the siloed world of academic philosophy, where there was a growing public concern about the apparent aesthetic degeneration of the environment. The initial response to this concern was a proliferation of empirical research designed to identify and thereby make possible the preservation and the management of "environmental aesthetic quality." As a result, the next stage of environmental aesthetics focused on the theoretical problems generated by this new interest in the aesthetic quality of environments. In the first half of the 1970s, theoretical problems were addressed in general terms in two groundbreaking articles by philosophers Francis Sparshot and Mark Sagoff.[3] At the same time, geographer Jay Appleton argued that the empirical work in particular was being conducted in what he called a "theoretical vacuum."[4] These critical discussions were followed by a series of articles by Allen Carlson in which he argued that the aesthetic quality assessment and management approaches developed in the empirical research were not only obsessed with the idea of quantifying aesthetic value but also—in part due to being unduly influenced by traditions such as that of picturesque landscape appreciation—fixated on scenery, "scenic beauty," and formal aesthetic properties, while overlooking expressive and other kinds of aesthetic properties.[5] This critical work made clear that if progress is to be made in addressing the aesthetic degeneration of the environment, what is required is not only empirical research but also the kind of philosophical attention to the aesthetic experience of the natural world that Hepburn had called for a decade earlier. Needless to say, since the 1970s progress has been made concerning the pressing aesthetic problems of both natural and human environments, in part because the empirical work on the aesthetic appreciation of environments has become increasingly more sophisticated, effective, and constructive, due to some extent to the sustained consideration of it by environmental aestheticians.

Science and the Aesthetics of Nature

In the third step of the development of environmental aesthetics, Carlson built on both his previous critique of empirical research and Hepburn's insights. Although he continued to argue that certain art-influenced models of the aesthetic appreciation of nature—such as that based on the idea of the picturesque—are misleading, he also held, as Hepburn had pointed out, that there is a fundamental similarity between the aesthetic appreciation of nature and that of art in that in both there is a distinction between appreciation that is superficial and that which is serious. He therefore suggested that the aesthetic appreciation of nature should be understood as analogous to that of art and, consequently, that art appreciation can show some of what is required in appropriate aesthetic appreciation of nature. In the case of art, appropriate aesthetic appreciation is informed by art history and art criticism. For example, appropriate appreciation of a work such as Picasso's *Guernica* (1937) requires that we experience it as a cubist painting. Thus Carlson argued that, since in serious, appropriate aesthetic appreciation of works of art, it is essential that they be experienced as what they are and in light of knowledge of their true natures, the same is the case for serious, appropriate aesthetic appreciation of natural environments. However, since nature is nature and not art, although the knowledge given by art criticism and art history is relevant to art appreciation, in nature appreciation the relevant knowledge is that provided by natural history, by the natural sciences, especially geology, biology, and ecology. This position that appropriate aesthetic appreciation of nature requires that it be appreciated as it is characterized by science, although initially labelled the natural environmental model, later became known as scientific cognitivism.[6] Carlson also argued that the position is conceptually related to the view called positive aesthetics, the idea that untouched natural environments have only, or at least mainly, positive aesthetic properties.[7]

The Aesthetics of Engagement

The next pivotal stage in the development of environmental aesthetics jelled in the early 1990s with the publication of two books by Arnold Berleant—*Art and Engagement* and *The Aesthetics of Environment*, the latter of which articulated another major position in the area of research.[8] Berleant had published several essays on environmental aesthetics prior to this time, but it was with the appearance of these volumes that his position attracted general attention.[9] In the former volume, Berleant developed his position in regard to works of art and in the latter applied it directly to environments. Consequently, the position, which is known as the aesthetics of engagement, has relevance not only for nature but also for art. In developing this position, Berleant rejected much of traditional aesthetic theory, arguing that the concept of disinterestedness, for example, involves a mistaken analysis of aesthetic experience and that this is most evident in the experience of natural environments. According to the engagement approach, disinterested appreciation, with its isolating, distancing, and objectifying gaze, is out of place in the aesthetic experience of nature, for it wrongly abstracts both natural objects and appreciators from the environments in which they properly belong and in which appropriate appreciation is achieved. Thus Berleant stressed the contextual dimensions of nature and our multisensory experience of it. Viewing the environment as a seamless unity of places, organisms, and perceptions, he challenged the importance of traditional dichotomies, such as that between subject and object, beckoning appreciators to immerse themselves in the natural environment and to reduce to as small a degree as possible the distance between themselves and the natural world. In short, appropriate aesthetic experience is held to involve the total "sensory immersion" of the appreciator in the object of appreciation. Berleant's work, like Carlson's, helped to advance environmental aesthetics as a discipline in that it articulated an explicit position on the aesthetic appreciation of environments that became a focus of discussion and debate by other researchers in the area.

The International Conferences on Environmental Aesthetics

Like the work of Berleant and Carlson, the fifth step in the development of environmental aesthetics did much to help weave the diverse strands of research on the aesthetic appreciation of environments into a discipline of its own. The step was due to the initiative of Finnish aesthetician Yrjö Sepänmaa. Sepänmaa's first major contribution to the field was the publication of his doctoral dissertation, *The Beauty of Environment: A General Model for Environmental Aesthetics*, which was published in Finland in 1986, making it the first book-length treatment of environmental aesthetics to appear since Hepburn first brought attention to this area of research. However, Sepänmaa's wide-ranging and important investigation of the topic did not attract general attention until it was reprinted in the Environmental Ethics book series in 1993.[10] Shortly after its North American publication, Sepänmaa launched his second major contribution to the discipline, which was the first of what was to become a series of prestigious international congresses on environmental aesthetics. The first of these, known as the Koli conference, was officially titled The First International Conference on Environmental Aesthetics and took place in Koli, Finland, in June of 1994. The conference was especially significant in regard to building the discipline in that it was the first time that early researchers in the field—such as Hepburn, Carlson, Berleant, and Sepänmaa—all came together to exchange ideas and debate the major issues, both with each other and with more recent North American contributors, such as Cheryl Foster, Marcia Eaton, Mara Miller, Holmes Rolston, Yuriko Saito, and Barbara Sandrisser, as well as with scholars from Europe and as far away as Korea. The Koli conference was followed by six other international conferences on environmental aesthetics organized by Sepänmaa, each focusing on a different dimension of the subject: forests, bogs and peat lands, water, agricultural landscapes, rock and stone, and skies and space. Over the fifteen years of their tenure, these conferences, as well as the sumptuously illustrated proceedings volumes that followed them, have been a major force in the development and the unification of the discipline. During this time, development and unification was also promoted by an increasing number of sessions on environmental aesthetics at other conferences, especially the meetings of the American and the Canadian Societies of Aesthetics.

The Cambridge Volume and Some New Positions

The next step in the growth of environmental aesthetics was another major publication, which, like the North American publication of Sepänmaa's volume, appeared in 1993. This was the first collection of essays in the field, Salim Kemal and Ivan Gaskell's *Landscape, Natural Beauty and the Arts*, which appeared in the prestigious Cambridge series, Studies in Philosophy and the Arts.[11] The volume has a forty-two page introduction to the field; position papers by Hepburn, Berleant, and Carlson; and essays by other scholars who had previously contributed to the area, such as T. J. Diffey, Yi-Fu Tuan, Stephanie Ross, and Donald Crawford, as well as by some new contributors, such as Noël Carroll. Carroll's essay was especially important since it presented another major position on the aesthetic appreciation of nature, what is called the arousal model. Carroll held that we may appreciate nature simply by opening ourselves to it and being emotionally aroused by it, which he contended is a legitimate way of aesthetically appreciating nature without invoking any particular knowledge about it.[12] In addition to Kemal and Gaskell's collection, the early 1990s also saw the publication of the first major reference volume entry on environmental aesthetics, in David Cooper's *A Companion to Aesthetics*.[13] Following quickly on this activity in the now increasingly recognized discipline of environmental aesthetics were two other significant developments: the publication of Stan Godlovitch's influential "Icebreakers" essay and prominent environmental philosopher Holmes Rolston's first essay explicitly addressing issues in environmental aesthetics. Godlovitch's view, sometimes called the mystery model of nature appreciation, constituted another new position in the field. He contended that neither knowledge nor emotional involvement yields appropriate appreciation of nature, for nature itself is ultimately alien, aloof, and unknowable, and thus the appropriate experience of it is a state of appreciative incomprehension involving a sense of mystery.[14] Rolston, by contrast, supported a position endorsing the importance of both scientific knowledge and emotional engagement in appropriate aesthetic appreciation of natural environments, a view that has affinities with those of both Carlson and Berleant.[15] Godlovitch's and Rolston's contributions were especially significant in being among the first to bring attention to the connections among environmental aesthetics, environmental ethics, and environmentalism.

The JAAC Special Issue and Some Additional Positions

The publication of another important collection of essays constituted the next stage in the development of environmental aesthetics. This step marked the formal recognition of the area within the discipline of analytic aesthetics, since it was a special issue of the mainstream *Journal of Aesthetics and Art Criticism*, the 1998 Special Issue on Environmental Aesthetics.[16] The special issue was edited by Berleant and Carlson and contained ten original essays by both old and new contributors to the field. Previous contributors Foster, Eaton, Godlovitch, Rolston, Saito, and Sandrisser were joined by Emily Brady, John Andrew Fisher, Sally Schauman, and Kevin Melchionne. Concerning the aesthetic appreciation of natural environments, this volume brought a number of important issues to the fore. For example, Brady introduced a new position that emphasizes the role of imagination in the appreciation of nature and, by appealing to the notion of "imagining well," responded to concerns that imagination introduces subjectivity.[17] Brady's view was challenged by Eaton who argued that in aesthetic appreciation of nature, we must carefully distinguish between facts about nature and fictions, since while knowledge of the former is necessary for appropriate aesthetic appreciation, the latter can often lead us astray and pervert appreciation.[18] Saito further developed her view, which emphasizes, in addition to factual knowledge, other kinds of information and contends that appreciating nature "on its own terms" may involve experiencing it in light of various local, folk, or historical traditions.[19] A more subjective-leaning position was defended by Fisher, who, focusing on the sounds of nature, argued that, unlike the case with art, many of the most significant aesthetic dimensions of natural environments are extremely relative to conditions of observation, and thus the aesthetic appreciation of nature allows for considerable freedom.[20] A more conciliatory position was defended by Foster who attempted to find a middle ground between what she called the narrative and the ambient approaches to environmental aesthetics, essentially cognitive positions such as Carlson's and less cognitive ones such as Berleant's.[21] The essays in the *JAAC* Special Issue that addressed the aesthetic appreciation of natural environments were later included, along with others, in the anthology *The Aesthetics of Natural Environments*, edited by Carlson and Berleant in 2004.[22]

The Aesthetics of Human Environments

Much of the most significant work in environmental aesthetics published during the first thirty years of its development focused on natural environments. The next significant stage in its evolution was the broadening of this focus to include human-influenced and human-constructed environments. Like other developments in the field, the aesthetics of human environments was initially explored by some authors before it was generally acknowledged as a central area of environmental aesthetics. For example, a few of the essays in the 1993 Kemal and Gaskell collection touched on this area, and three of the articles in the 1998 *JAAC* Special Issue discussed the aesthetics of human environments, those by Melchionne, Sandrisser, and Schauman.[23] In addition, earlier than either of these collections, Berleant had published several essays that focused explicitly on the urban environment, such as his "Aesthetic Participation and the Urban Environment," which appeared in 1984.[24] Likewise, Carlson had published an essay on the aesthetic appreciation of agricultural landscapes in 1985.[25] Moreover, in the 1990s a somewhat more traditional area of aesthetics that at least boarders on the aesthetics of human environments, the aesthetics of architecture, was addressed in articles collected in two volumes edited by Michael Mitias.[26] Similarly, another related area, the aesthetics of gardens, was examined in the 1990s in two monographs—Miller's *The Garden As Art* and Ross's *What Gardens Mean*.[27] However, in spite of this research, the aesthetics of human environments was seemingly not generally recognized as an integral part of environmental aesthetics until the publication of two books that explicitly joined this area of research with earlier work on natural environments. The first was Berleant's 1997 *Living in the Landscape: Toward an Aesthetics of Environment*, which includes a number of his essays treating the aesthetic appreciation of urban as well as other kinds of human environments.[28] The second volume was Carlson's 2000 *Aesthetics and the Environment: The Appreciation of Nature, Art and Architecture*, the first part of which focuses on the aesthetic appreciation of nature and the second part on the appreciation of architecture, gardens, and other human manipulations of the landscape.[29] Carlson followed up the publication of this volume with an article unequivocally noting the significance of the aesthetics of human environments in its title, the 2001 essay "On Aesthetically Appreciating Human Environments."[30] And in 2007 Berleant and Carlson brought together a number of essays in this area of research in the anthology, *The Aesthetics of Human Environments*.[31]

Everyday Aesthetics

The ninth stage in the development of the discipline of environmental aesthetics involved a further broadening of its focus, this time beyond both natural and human environments to all of the items, activities, and events that inhabit such environments. This subject area is appropriately called everyday aesthetics or the aesthetics of everyday life and examines the aesthetic appreciation of the world in which we live on a day-to-day basis. The area of research has roots outside of mainstream analytic aesthetics, such as the writings of John Dewey, and later those of thinkers such as Tuan.[32] However, it became solidly positioned within contemporary environmental aesthetics mainly due to the work of Saito, who, although she had previously written primarily about the aesthetic appreciation of natural environments, in 2001 published a short but definitive essay called simply "Everyday Aesthetics."[33] There had been significant sorties into this area of study before this time, such as Sandrisser's research on the aesthetic appreciation of the ordinary and the commonplace, especially in Japan; Berleant's work on what he calls "social aesthetics"; and Carolyn Korsmeyer's 1999 volume *Making Sense of Taste: Food and Philosophy*.[34] However, it was Saito's 2001 essay that set the general character of the area of research. She followed up her initial essay with a major volume, her 2007 *Everyday Aesthetics*.[35] Another contributor to this area is Thomas Leddy, who had published essays on this topic in the 1990s.[36] Moreover, Leddy became a major contributor to the field with his substantial introductory essay "The Nature of Everyday Aesthetics," which is published in Andrew Light and Jonathan Smith's 2005 anthology *The Aesthetics of Everyday Life*.[37] Needless to say, the Light and Smith collection contains a number of other important contributions to everyday aesthetics, ranging over topics such as food, sports, film, weather, and even human relationships.³⁸ The aesthetics of everyday life, together with the aesthetics of human environments, has also been actively investigated by contemporary Finnish aestheticians, not only Sepänmaa but also Pauline von Bonsdorff and Arto Haapala as well as other scholars associated with the International Institute of Applied Aesthetics in Lahti, Finland.³⁹

Coming of Age: New Books, Anthologies, Reference Volume Entries, and Introductory Texts

These contributions to the aesthetics of everyday life, such as Light and Smith's collection and Saito's volume, bring the discipline of environmental aesthetics to its major developments in the new century. This tenth stage can be called its "coming of age" as a discipline, since it is marked by a proliferation of new books, major anthologies, numerous encyclopedia and reference volume entries, and textbooks. The new books include, in addition to Saito's 2007 monograph on everyday aesthetics, Malcolm Budd's *The Aesthetic Appreciation of Nature*, Brady's *Aesthetics of the Natural Environment*, Ronald Moore's *Natural Beauty: A Theory of Aesthetics Beyond the Arts*, Glenn Parson and Carlson's *Functional Beauty*, and two volumes by Berleant, *Aesthetics and Environment: Variations on a Theme* and *Sensibility and Sense: The Aesthetic Transformation of the Human World*.⁴⁰ In addition to Light and Smith's 2005 everyday aesthetics collection and the two anthologies edited by Berleant and Carlson on the aesthetics of natural and human environments, published in 2004 and 2007, respectively, major anthologies published since 2000 include two collections of original essays, Berleant's *Environment and the Arts: Perspectives on Environmental Aesthetics* and Sven Arntzen and Brady's *Humans in the Land: The Ethics and Aesthetics of the Cultural Landscape* as well as an anthology edited by Carlson and Sheila Lintott, *Nature, Aesthetics, and Environmentalism: From Beauty to Duty*.⁴¹ As the title suggests, the latter collection focuses on some of the relationships among environmental aesthetics, environmental ethics, and environmentalism. Another sign of the coming of age of a discipline is the appearance of dictionary, encyclopedia, and reference volume entries on the subject, and environmental aesthetics has been treated in almost all of such volumes that have been published within the last twenty years. In addition to the earlier entry in Cooper's 1992 *A Companion to Aesthetics*, articles on environmental aesthetics and/or the aesthetics of nature have appeared in, to mention only some of the relevant volumes, the *Encyclopedia of Aesthetics*, the two editions of the *Routledge Companion to Aesthetics*, the *Blackwell Guide To Aesthetics*, the *Oxford Handbook of Aesthetics*, the *Routledge Encyclopedia of Philosophy*, the second edition of *The Encyclopedia of Philosophy*, *The Stanford Encyclopedia of Philosophy*, and the new second edition of *A Companion to Aesthetics*.[42] Last but not least, two textbooks have been recently added to the growing assortment of resources available in environmental aesthetics, Parsons's *Aesthetics and Nature* and Carlson's *Nature and Landscape: An Introduction to Environmental Aesthetics*.[43] In addition to these significant and positive developments in environmental aesthetics, the first decade of the new century also brought the unfortunate passing of the founder of the discipline. Ronald Hepburn died on December 23, 2008.

Environmental Aesthetics Beyond Western Environmental Aesthetics

The title of this chapter is "Ten Steps in the Development of Western Environmental Aesthetics." However, it would be remiss if I did not also take note of the recent developments in environmental aesthetics that have taken place beyond the confines of Western thinking on this subject. Throughout the development of Western environmental aesthetics, a few scholars have focused on the aesthetic appreciation of natural and human environments within other cultures, most notably Saito and Sandrisser, both of whom published articles about aesthetic appreciation in Japan.[44] Since the turn of the century, however, there has been a rapidly growing interest in environmental aesthetics within major countries in the East, especially China, Japan, and Korea. Articles and books by Western aestheticians, such as Berleant, Carlson, and Sepänmaa, have been translated into different eastern languages, and numerous major articles and books have been published by scholars from these countries. An important recent event highlighting this interest was the International Conference on Ecological Aesthetics and Environmental Aesthetics in Global Perspective, held in October of 2009 and hosted by Shandong University in Jinan, China. The conference focused on topics such as the emergence of ecological aesthetics in China, the development of environmental aesthetics in the West and its relationship to Eastern ecological aesthetics, the traditional Chinese sources of eco-wisdom, and the connections between ecological aesthetics and ecocriticism. The conference was well attended by scholars from both the East and the West. More recently, in August of 2010, China hosted the Eighteenth International Congress of Aesthetics at Peking University in Beijing. Environmental aesthetics was well represented at the Congress, and those who work in this area of research, including, along with many others, Zeng Fanren, Xue Fuxing, and Cheng Xiangzhan from China and Berleant, Carlson, Saito, and Sepänmaa from the West, participated in sessions at the congress.[45]

CHAPTER

2

Future Directions for Environmental Aesthetics

Yuriko Saito

The Formative Years of Environmental Aesthetics

Within the Western philosophical discourse, environmental aesthetics is a relatively new, but now firmly established, discipline. It
started with the late Ronald Hepburn's 1966 essay on the neglect of
natural beauty in contemporary aesthetics. This essay ushered in a
new chapter of twentieth-century Western aesthetics that had been
dominated by discussion of art.[1] Around the same time, Arnold
Berleant was exploring the phenomenologically oriented aesthetics
through the notions of aesthetic field and aesthetic engagement,
focusing on the interaction between us and the object of our aesthetic experience. These works by the founding fathers of environmental aesthetics paved the way for the next generation of
environmental aestheticians, namely Allen Carlson and Yrjö
Sepänmaa. Thanks to the works by these four thinkers, environmental aesthetics now enjoys a robust life. The field today looks
vastly different from the early '80s when I completed my doctoral
dissertation on the aesthetic appreciation of nature.

Hepburn's step toward expanding Western aesthetics' art-centered orientation by re-introducing nature was soon followed by the
inclusion of built environments and cultural landscapes. The primary focus in these explorations was on the spatial dimension,
with particular attention paid to the multisensory bodily engagement in our aesthetic experience. In a series of seminal works,
Arnold Berleant has been arguing for such a participatory model of
aesthetic experience by calling into question the validity of a

spectator model of aesthetic experience that has dominated modern
Western aesthetics.[2] Furthermore, natural environments and some
cultural landscapes lack the human intention that determines their
precise appearance, again challenging the applicability of art-
centered aesthetics concerned, among others, with artists' intention and the conventions of the artworld. Thus, while sharing with
art-centered aesthetics issues such as the appreciation of aesthetic
qualities and the exercise of imagination, environmental aesthetics
widened the scope of inquiry. Environmental aesthetics needed to
carve out its own sphere within the aesthetic discourse in order to
give due attention to those aesthetic issues specific to environment. Otherwise, under art-dominated aesthetics, environment
tends to be treated as a second-rate art or wannabe art because of its
relative paucity of unified formal structure and expressive quality
typical of art.

At the same time, these features characteristic of environment,
such as multisensory engagement and lack of artistic intention,
provided new directions for art practice, creating a fruitful cross-
pollination between art and environment. This is most evident in
the environmental art of recent years, which emulates, appropri-
ates, or sheds light on our typical experience of the environment.
Environmental art helped to open up the Western artworld by challenging the spectator-model of art appreciation, privileging of so-
called higher senses, the practice of art-making with a total control
by the artist, and the static nature of the work.[3]

Further Expansion of Environmental Aesthetics I:
Inclusion of More Elements

I propose that the scope of environmental aesthetics be expanded
further, a process that has already been initiated by many of the
aforementioned pioneers. My first suggestion is to move the inquiry
beyond spatial environments to include various ingredients that
make up these environments, namely individual objects, activities,
and human relationships. We are yet to develop an aesthetic discourse regarding artifacts such as utensils, furniture, and other
objects with which we interact in everyday environment and activities that we undertake with them, such as cleaning, cooking, and
socializing with others. I believe that it is important to attend to the
aesthetics of these objects and activities beyond simply for the sake
of "the more the merrier."

I have three reasons for this proposed expansion. First, these ingredients share with spatial environments a number of aesthetic characteristics which are considered irrelevant or detrimental to aesthetic values by modern Western art-centered aesthetics. For example, many objects that make up our environment are primarily created and appreciated for their practical values. This contrasts with typical modern Western art, the primary function of which is to generate an aesthetic experience. According to traditional aesthetic attitude theory, when aesthetically appreciating a tool or a utensil, we need to suspend considerations of its functionality. However, as Glenn Parsons and Allen Carlson argue in their recent book, consideration of an object's function does not only *not* take anything away from its aesthetic value but is necessary in determining its functional beauty.[4] Furthermore, with art, its more-or-less stable identity is expected, reflected in the museum practice of conservation and restoration, as well as in the general prohibition of modification out of respect for the integrity of the art object and the artist's authorial right. In comparison, when it comes to those objects with which we interact in our daily lives, we expect that they go through changes, whether through aging, repeated use, accidental damage, or modification we make. Our attitudes toward their changing nature is rather complex, sometimes motivating us to repair the damage, while other times guiding us to appreciate the broken-in appearance.[5] Including artifacts of our everyday environment in the aesthetic discourse thus widens its scope by addressing issues such as functional beauty and the aesthetic values associated with transience and transformation.

In addition, our environment is constituted not only by objects but also by various activities we undertake. Sometimes they are pragmatically oriented, such as cooking and cleaning, while other times they are our social interactions. These activities themselves involve important aesthetic dimensions. For example, besides producing an object for multisensory aesthetic appreciation, cooking as an activity is also aesthetically appreciable. The kinesthetic sensation of cutting a vegetable with a sharp knife on a cutting board is accompanied by a series of staccato sounds, and these sounds can, in turn, enhance the comfort and security of the domestic environment. A substantial part of domestic chores is devoted to cleaning: dishes, interior space, yard, exterior and interior of a car, and clothes and linen. Although performed primarily for practical purposes like hygiene, the activity of cleaning is also guided by aesthetic considerations which help create a certain environment, such as a well-maintained yard and a spotless kitchen.[6]

We also create a certain atmosphere for the environment, such as tense, relaxed, harmonious, or alienating, through our interactions with others. Furthermore, as Ronald Hepburn points out, the character of personal space has an aesthetic dimension, often determined by human interactions.[7] Philosophical issues related to human relationships and social interactions are usually regarded as ethical matters. However, Arnold Berleant has been pioneering the discourse on "social aesthetics," guided by the insight that "social aesthetics may . . . *be* a kind of environmental aesthetics, for it is both needless and false to restrict environment to its physical aspects."[8] He argues that the civilized and humane human interactions share with aesthetic experience certain desiderata, such as acceptance of the other on its own terms, willingness to participate and reciprocate, and respecting the uniqueness of the other.[9] Barbara Sandrisser's long-standing exploration of the aesthetic dimension of etiquette, particularly embodied in the Japanese cultural tradition, also illuminates the way in which the quality of human interactions is determined not only by moral considerations but also through their aesthetic manifestations.[10]

Thus, the constituents of environment go beyond the spatial dimension to encompass objects and activities that exist in it, as well as the social interactions that determine its atmospheric character. Including all of them in environmental aesthetics will enrich the discourse by providing a useful comparison with, and sometimes departure from, the art-centered aesthetics. Furthermore, it is important to pay attention to these objects and activities because they have a considerable impact on the quality of life and the state of the world due to their pervasiveness and our frequent engagement with them. Their all-too-familiar presence in our lives tends to make their aesthetic impact invisible on the radar that has been calibrated to capture standout experiences.[11] Despite Dewey's insight that "an experience" is possible with our everyday activities, we still tend to think of art as typically providing such a break from the humdrum flow of life.[12] However, in reverse proportion to their invisibility, the aesthetic dimensions of these objects and activities play a significant role in directing our thoughts and actions, whether we are aware or not. I call this efficacy of the aesthetic "the power of the aesthetic," and it underlies the second reason for expanding the scope of environmental aesthetics.

Let me give three examples of how aesthetics plays a significant role in determining the quality of life and the state of the world. First, as Yrjö Sepänmaa argues, aesthetic matters are not "high cultural icing"; they have serious implications constituting what he calls "aesthetic welfare," a term he quotes from Monroe Beardsley. Aesthetic welfare is an ingredient necessary for a good society, along with justice, equality, freedom, and social welfare.[13] If we are surrounded with aesthetically poor artifacts and environments, what we miss is not simply prettier spaces and more beautiful artifacts. Such objects and spaces indirectly communicate to us an attitude of indifference and disrespect by the providers of these objects— whether designers, creators, or government—who did not care enough about our experience. In contrast, aesthetically appealing environments and objects express care and thoughtfulness, and provide both tangible evidence that the experience of citizens does matter and the material conditions upon which other social and political ideals can flourish.[14] Thoughtfully created objects and humane environments tend to encourage and inspire us to "pay it forward," as it were. Aesthetics can thus be characterized as a crucial gauge in determining what is/is not working in our society and world, and it helps steer us toward better world-making.

Second, political propaganda through the use of arts is rather well known, but equally effective is utilizing the aesthetics of everyday environment and objects. For example, in addition to the frighteningly brilliant use of films and music, Nazi Germany worked to create an everyday environment worthy of the Aryan race by eradicating alien species of plants.[15] The Japanese military also took advantage of their long-held tradition of the aesthetics of falling cherry blossoms to glorify Kamikaze pilots' missions. The potency of this aesthetic symbol as a national emblem can also be seen in the "Japanization" of the foreign soils that Japan invaded, namely Korea and Manchuria, through planting cherry trees. Even before the military's conscious appropriation of this potent aesthetics, there were a number of influential writings celebrating Japanese landscapes and everyday environments, and they helped promote nationalistic sentiment and citizens' resolve to protect their beauty from foreign power.[16] Alan Tansman's analysis of several Japanese literary pieces popular before World War II is instructive in this regard. Though none were intended as political propaganda, their praise for everyday things, such as bridges, was instrumental in uniting Japanese citizens under nationalism. He observes that fascism finds a solution to presumed societal problems "not in a radical change of economic systems but in policies and rhetoric ostensibly meant to beautify work, the workplace, and everyday life," and this "diffuse yet thorough 'administration of aesthetics'" was "insidious and effective . . . to the extent they worked atmospherically."[17]

Although without the dire political consequences like in the cases of Nazi Germany and Japan during World War II, the American wilderness aesthetics that developed during the nineteenth century was also motivated by the relatively young nation's attempt to formulate its own nature aesthetics as a way of promoting national identity and pride.[18] Its influence is far-reaching, both positive and negative, ranging from the formation of the national park system and the resultant protection of the wilderness to the displacement of the indigenous Native American population and suppression of forest fire. Allen Carlson acknowledges that this culturally—and historically—situated nature aesthetics "has been extremely influential in a number of landmark decisions concerning the preservation of some of North America's most magnificent environments."[19] These historical precedents suggest that the cultural tradition of a landscape aesthetic often helps determine the course of history. That is, it leads to the creation of a desired landscape, such as a forest devoid of alien plant species, an invaded foreign soil filled with newly planted cherry trees, and a seemingly wild area of nature achieved by forcibly removing its native inhabitants. Furthermore, it contributes to enhancing a nationalistic sentiment, sometimes with problematic consequences.

The third way in which our aesthetics regarding everyday environment and objects and activities within affects the quality of life and the state of the world is its ecological ramifications.[20] Our aesthetic attraction to scenic landscapes and awesome-looking or cute and cuddly creatures leaves unattractive parts of nature, such as wetlands and insects, vulnerable to destruction because of our indifference toward their fate. Dramatic aesthetic effects of environmental disasters, such as smoke stacks belching black smoke and oil spill, garner our attention, eclipsing the equally serious environmental harm resulting from the invisible effect of our daily activities.

Aesthetics also plays a significant role in consumers' purchasing decisions and their attitudes toward their possessions. At least in the United States today, more often than not the aesthetic interests work against ecological concerns. A prime example is the throwaway mentality manipulated by the industry practice of planned obsolescence regarding not only the function but also the style and fashionableness of products.[21] Our penchant for rare wood such as mahogany, smooth paper with no imperfections, and bright white laundered shirts is responsible for unsustainable resource extraction and the use of harmful chemicals. The cultivation and maintenance of a green lawn is one of the quintessential American domestic practices, even today after its environmental cost of using water, fertilizer, and pesticide became well publicized. Although mingled with a culturally—and historically—specific notion of work ethic and civic duty, the primary motivation behind "keeping up with the Joneses" is aesthetic—the lawn has to be green, not brown, of uniform appearance and height without any weeds, and it has to be velvety smooth. While the green lawn exemplifies an aesthetically desirable but ecologically questionable phenomenon, the opposite case exists as well. One such example regards wind turbines, best illustrated by the vociferous objection to the Capewind project, the largest off-shore wind farm in the world proposed for the Nantucket Sound, Massachusetts. The primary reason against this project is its eyesore-like effect that, it is argued, will spoil the beauty of the pristine seascape.[22] A similar aesthetic objection is raised against outdoor laundry-hanging, leading roughly 300,000 homeowners' associations in American suburban communities to prohibit it, affecting 60 million people, despite its undisputed environmental benefit.[23]

These examples illustrate that the quality of life and the state of the world are profoundly affected by the aesthetics of environments and the objects and activities within. In light of this, environmental aesthetics should take on an educational role to reveal this power of the aesthetic, both in its intentional utilization for a certain purpose, such as a political agenda, and in the unintended and sometimes unforeseen consequences of our collective and cumulative aesthetic decisions. If the responsibility of a citizen, whether on the local or global level, includes engaging in the communal project of better world-making, we need to cultivate aesthetic literacy and to promote vigilance regarding the ramifications of our aesthetic responses.

Further Expansion of Environmental Aesthetics II: Normative Discourse

The need to cultivate aesthetic literacy and vigilance suggests another way in which environmental aesthetics should be expanded:

developing a normative discourse. The examples in the last section indicated that the perceived aesthetic value of an environment or an object has the power to move us toward a certain direction. Why then not utilize this power for contributing positively to the project of world-making? For example, it can help promote greener aesthetic sensibility or cultivate civility and respect through thoughtfully designed environments and objects. As Friedrich Schiller argued in his vision of the aesthetic education of man, we are affected by and operate on the sensible as well as on the rational realm, and what really moves us to action is that which appeals to the sensible part. In discussing the aesthetics' role in nationalism, Tansman points out that, despite "the dangerous alignment of aesthetics and politics" in the past fascist regimes, "the aestheticization of politics has a more positive lineage as well—an aesthetically grounded ethics that can evoke sympathy for one's fellows and ground freedom in the experience of beauty."[24] Similarly, those who have been promoting a sustainable future also recognize the potential of aesthetics to serve this cause and argue for its utilization. To cite one example, David Orr holds that "we are moved to act more often, more consistently, and more profoundly by *the experience of beauty* in all of its forms than by intellectual arguments, abstract appeals to duty or even by fear." Therefore, he continues, "we must be inspired to act by examples that we can see, touch, and experience," toward which we can develop an "emotional attachment" and a "deep affection."[25]

I believe this power of the aesthetic is recognized by psychologists, educators, propagandists, and advertizing agents but curiously not sufficiently by aestheticians. I thus suggest that environmental aesthetics include not only an analysis of what "is" the case with our aesthetic response but also venture into exploring the possibility of an "aesthetic ought," as suggested by Marcia Eaton.[26]

Now, some thinkers are leery of the aesthetic discourse's foray into the normative realm. One reason is that the stipulation of an "aesthetic ought" is thought to compromise the special freedom that we enjoy in the aesthetic realm with the exercise of imagination, in comparison with factual and moral discourses. The "aesthetic ought" may indeed sound dogmatic and inflexible, but I don't think the normative dimension is unique to environmental aesthetics. In the case of art, it is true that there is no *one* way that a work of art "ought" to be interpreted, making disagreements all too common. However, within such disagreements, we distinguish between an appropriate and inappropriate appreciation of art, the latter derived from highly idiosyncratic personal associations or not based upon sufficient correct information. Except for diehard relativists who believe anything goes, we do seem to have some minimum requirements for interpreting, appreciating, and evaluating a work of art, without thereby compromising the freedom of exercising one's imagination and creativity. Why can't we recognize the same importance of cultivating a more informed appreciation of the environment?

With environmental aesthetics, instead of cultural-historical context, an artist's intention, technique of production, and the like, we have other factual matters to consider, such as scientific facts, social significance, and ecological ramifications. The notion of "appropriate" aesthetic appreciation of nature and environment has been one of the most contentious issues in environmental aesthetics. Allen Carlson has been vigorously arguing for this notion in the form of scientifically based cognitivism. The ensuing debate on this issue can be characterized by the varying degrees to which each thinker agrees or disagrees with Carlson's view.[27] However, the debate specifically concerns whether scientifically based appreciation has an *exclusive* claim to appropriateness over other cognitively or imaginatively based appreciations, but *not* whether there should be some distinction between better or worse appreciations.

For example, Ronald Hepburn challenges the claim which states "one perspective, one view, one set of resulted perceived qualities takes precedence over another, and so can discredit or undermine another or even all the others."[28] However, his disagreement with Carlson's scientific cognitivism is directed toward rejecting the kind of scientific information that gets us away from the sensuous surface, such as the molecular account of a rock, as well as including the aesthetic experience that deepens an existential self-reflection on one's relationship to nature. He does distinguish between "superficial" or "trivial" and "truer" or "serious" appreciations of nature by recognizing that "appreciation can be more, or less superficial, more or less serious."[29] Superficial appreciations include a fortuitous resemblance between a cloud and a laundry basket or the stalagmite in a limestone cave and the Virgin Mary, insofar as "it distorts, ignores, suppresses truth about its objects, feels and thinks about them in ways that falsify how nature really is."[30] Equally problematic is to limit appreciation of natural objects and environments to "their immediately given perceptual qualities, the sensuous surface," which reduces the falling autumn leaf to "a small, fluttering, reddish-brown material object."[31]

Emily Brady's emphasis on the role of imagination in the aesthetic appreciation of nature can be interpreted in a similar manner. She argues against "making scientific knowledge a condition of appropriate aesthetic appreciation" because such a "necessary condition is too limiting on the aesthetic response" and "scientific knowledge can impede attention to these [perceptual] qualities, thus diverting aesthetic attention."[32] However, like Hepburn, she also makes a distinction between imagining well and trivial or irrelevant imagining where "imagination let loose can lead to the manipulation of the aesthetic object for one's own pleasure-seeking ends."[33] Thus, despite the controversy over whether science is the only or the best foundation on which to base our nature aesthetics, some degree of normativity can be found in the views held by even those who emphasize the importance of imagination and freedom.

Furthermore, just as various cognitive considerations cannot *dictate* the meaning and aesthetic value of a work of art, scientific, environmental, social, and other facts about the environments cannot *determine* their aesthetic properties or values, either. For both art and environment, the proof is in the pudding, though its taste must be experienced in light of these various facts. It would be irresponsible of us to ignore everything we find about the harmful effects of a perfect green lawn, although it does not mean that this knowledge nullifies its gorgeous appearance. What "ought to" happen is that the appearance becomes transformed in some way, for example from innocently beautiful to morbidly gorgeous or somewhat garish.[34] Or we may begin to attend to the contrast between the beautiful appearance and the unnerving and invisible toxicity behind the appearance, similar to the way in which Edward Bullough describes a boat passenger's aesthetic experience of a thick fog as consisting in the "uncanny mingling of repose and terror" and the sensuous qualities of the water and fog which are "hypocritically denying as it were any suggestion of danger."[35]

Similarly, the environmental benefit of laundry hanging may soften the eyesore-like appearance in some cases, but not in other cases such as an unabashed parade of one's underwear. Furthermore, some ways of hanging laundry are more aesthetically pleasing than others, particularly when arranged according to the size, color, or kind of items. Indeed it is interesting to note that those who are engaged in this work, almost exclusively women, quite consciously consider the aesthetic effect of their labor.[36]

The same judgment applies to the aesthetics of the wind farm. Although its environmental benefit should count positively toward modifying its supposed aesthetic disvalue, the overall aesthetic impact has to be determined on a case-by-case basis by considering the particular landscape that will be altered and the specific design and placement of the turbines. The decisions have to carefully negotiate between knee-jerk objections to any machines in the garden and indiscriminate exhortation of the environmental and aesthetic virtues of wind turbines. Some landscapes or seascapes "ruined" or "spoiled" by the construction of turbines may be more scenic or historically and culturally significant than others, and such individual contexts should be considered in formulating the aesthetic evaluation of each project.[37]

Some thinkers are skeptical of the possibility of the cognitive affecting the sensuous, such as the green lawn looking gaudy after incorporating the knowledge of its environmental harm. For example, David E. Cooper asks: "Can the look of a lawn really change according to ecological savvy? Or wind farms begin to look beautiful when their benefits are explained at a consultation meeting?"[38] He further questions "how the way that aesthetic responses are supposed to track moral considerations differs from the 'environmental determinism'" that I argue against in my book. The relationship between the cognitive and the sensuous is indeed another contentious issue in environmental aesthetics, referred to as the problem of "translation" or "fusion." However, again, the issue is not unique to environmental aesthetics. In art-centered aesthetics, this is a perennial topic of discussion, generating various positions regarding how to determine the expressive properties of works of art and the aesthetic status of forgery. In those debates, the strict formalist view that rejects relevance of any cognitive considerations has been largely discredited. It seems to me that cognitively informed environmental aesthetics is not that different from art aesthetics that anchors the aesthetic value of a work of art in some cognitive considerations. The only difference is that in environmental aesthetics, the relevant cognitive content is primarily science, environmental ramifications, and social/cultural/historical significance. I admit that the precise way in which the cognitive affects the sensuous needs to be explored; however, such an explanation is needed not only for the appearance of a green lawn but also for the appearance of things like a perfect forgery and the expressive qualities of perceptually indistinguishable works of art with different origins, most famously discussed by Arthur Danto.[39]

Another reason often cited against developing a normative dimension of environmental aesthetics is that using the power of the aesthetic for non-aesthetic purposes, such as sustainable future or cultivation of civility, no matter how praiseworthy, is to relegate the aesthetic to something else, thus compromising its autonomy and independence. Cooper expresses this concern regarding what he calls "the unashamedly 'instrumentalist' approach" or "'pragmatic' instrumentalism" that "threatens to obliterate all traces of aesthetic autonomy."[40] I don't deny feeling a bit uneasy about advocating a kind of social engineering through utilizing the power of the aesthetic, particularly in light of the aforementioned precedents where this power was utilized effectively for problematic cause.

However, I have two responses to this objection. First, if we protect autonomy of the aesthetic by severing its tie with a sustainable future, virtuous life, and a better society, in a way we are adopting a laissez faire attitude toward the use of the power of the aesthetic and tacitly allowing it to be utilized for any purposes or agenda. However, such a laissez faire approach has already been co-opted by those who seek to "nudge" or even legally coerce our aesthetic lives toward a certain "aesthetic ought." As Richard Thaler and Cass Sunstein point out in their recent discussion of "nudge," "there is . . . no way of avoiding nudging in some direction, and whether intended or not, these nudges will affect what people choose."[41] We have already looked at examples of this type of nudge or coercion, such as the prohibition against laundry hanging and the pressure to keep up with the Jones' green grass. If we do not promote an alternative "aesthetic ought," we are in effect supporting these existing "aesthetic oughts" by default.

The instrumentalist utilization of the aesthetics' persuasive power ultimately leads to the question regarding the end for which it is supposed to serve. There is no consensus as to what constitutes a good life and good society. Is it better to be a dissatisfied Socrates than a satisfied pig? Should an ideal state operate on unbridled capitalism or socialism with tight state control? Aesthetics cannot be expected to solve these perennial debates. However, on the other hand, I think it is safe to assume that some basic facts and values can be accepted as common to humanity's success: health, a sustainable future, a humane and civil society, and comfortable, stable, and welcoming environment, among others. Mobilizing aesthetic sensibility and strategy to serve these goals, Arnold Berleant points out, is "not a call for a rigid plan or a prescriptive order" because "humane environments require time to develop and they must reflect local needs, conditions, and traditions."[42] He further states that "utopian thought . . . has a strong aesthetic component. Utopianism is pervaded by moral values of social and environmental harmony and fulfillment. Its goal of facilitating living that is deeply satisfying through the fruitful exercise of human capacities is as aesthetic as it is moral."[43] If aesthetics can be a powerful ally in enhancing these basic amenities for human flourishing, I cannot think of any good reason against utilizing its powerful influence. At the same time, if aesthetics can be a formidable enemy, as some of the aforementioned examples have shown, then I believe that it is our collective responsibility to expose its role and oppose it. Aesthetics' significance, as Berleant declares, "lies not only in the ability . . . to serve as a critical tool for probing social practice but as a beacon for illuminating the direction of social betterment."[44]

My second response to the criticism of instrumental use of aesthetics is based upon my observation that the concern over aesthetics' loss of independence is specific to the historical context in which contemporary Western aesthetics is situated. The history of modern Western aesthetics since the eighteenth century can be characterized as a series of attempts to declare and maintain the independence of aesthetics from cognitive, practical, and moral realms. However, while aesthetics may have gained some stature by these attempts, it may have also paid a price. For example, the theory of aesthetic disinterestedness and distancing, as well as aesthetic formalism, encouraged the aesthetic realm to be disconnected from the rest of life, and it is only recently that we are trying to recover the important connection between the aesthetic and the rest of life. One could argue that the worry over reconnecting aesthetics with the rest of life's concerns is a response specific to the way in which modern Western aesthetics developed. Indeed, when we go beyond the confines of Western aesthetics, we realize that the concern for securing aesthetics' autonomy is not universally shared. This leads to my third proposal for expanding the scope of environmental aesthetics: to go beyond the Western aesthetic tradition.

Further Expansion of Environmental Aesthetics III:
Beyond Western Tradition

In many cultural traditions, the aesthetic appreciation of nature and environment has long been inseparable from their general world-view. One such example is Taoism. In addition to its process ontology, its praise for the attitude of "yielding" and "bending" has important implications for environmental aesthetics. Tao being nature in the sense of "self-so," human actions should be guided by working "with," rather than "against" or "irrespective of," Tao, whether in ruling a country or working on the land. Lao-Tzu advises in *Tao Te Ching*: "Achieve results, but not through violence" because "the stiff and unbending is the disciple of death," "an army without flexibility never wins a battle" and "a tree that is unbending is easily broken." Instead, "yielding" and "bending" with "flexibility" will be more successful because "the gentle and yielding is the disciple of life."[45]

This yielding and bending attitude is further reinforced by *wu wei*, translated as "no action." Different from "inaction" where we literally do nothing, *wu wei* is rather engaging in an action in such a way as not to contradict *Tao* by observing and working with the native virtue of objects or people. Baird Callicott argues that the *wu wei* method of irrigation is to acknowledge, respect, and take advantage of the native disposition of the hills, upland trees, and streams.[46] Indeed, Sim van der Ryn and Stuart Cowan, both architects and early advocates of ecological design, explain that Taoist water engineers "were content to observe flows of water over the landscape and design accordingly" and believed that "water should meander over the landscape, following its inherent tendencies," in contrast to Confucian engineers who "saw the need to discipline water" and "favored strict control of water flow," a design strategy typically adopted by American Army Corps of Engineers.[47] Realizing the problematic consequences of this latter method, we are now engaging in projects such as de-damming and re-meandering of rivers in order to restore, honor, and work with the native disposition of water.

Another tradition in which aesthetics and the rest of life concerns are inseparable is Japanese aesthetics. Although the precise character continues to be debated, the Japanese cultural tradition is characterized by many centuries of aesthetic appreciation of nature.[48] Supported by the spiritual worldview of its indigenous Shintoism and further enhanced by Buddhism imported from India by way of

China, one of the distinguishing features of Japanese aesthetics is its celebration of transience, giving rise to the culturally shared sensibility toward the ephemeral beauty of nature and the aging effect on material objects. While the aesthetics of falling cherry blossoms had problematic consequences as mentioned before, the ontology, metaphysics, and resultant aesthetics based upon "becoming" provide an alternative to the Western preference for "being." So does the Japanese cultural heritage that emphasizes the relational identity of both humans and nonhumans, in comparison with the primacy placed over discrete and independent existence of "being" in Western philosophy.

The Japanese cultural tradition also values the Buddhist concept of "emptiness" or "nothingness." Originally referring to the denial of substance, hence no-thing-ness, this notion developed into the moral virtue of transcending one's self and eventually permeated many aspects of people's lives: moral, social, and aesthetic. Its artistic expression includes the strategic absence of color, sound, and action in painting, music, and theater performance. In addition, one must "empty" and transcend oneself when trying to cultivate artistic excellence. This artistic virtue is also a moral virtue that should underlie human relationships that are marked by other-regarding virtues such as civility, courtesy, respect, and thoughtfulness. The tea ceremony is perhaps the best artistic expression of the way in which such moral virtues are practiced and expressed aesthetically. The host's thoughtfulness and care are communicated and gratefully acknowledged by the guests through aesthetic means: flower arrangement, choice and arrangement of implements, preparation of tea and snack, and the bodily movement of making, serving, and drinking tea, to name only a few. One could describe the Japanese tea ceremony, established as an art form in the sixteenth century, as an early model for social aesthetics.[49]

Finally, in addition to providing artistic strategies and social aesthetics, this notion of "emptiness" also guides today's cutting-edge design practices, contributing to creating certain environments. For example, in discussing the relationship between emptiness and the color white, Kenya Hara, a contemporary designer well known as the director of MUJI design group, relates his thoughts on emptiness:

> "Emptiness" (*utsu*) and "completely hollow" (*karappo*) are among the terms I pondered while trying to grasp the nature of communication. When people share their thoughts, they

commonly listen to each other's opinions rather than throwing
information at each other. In other words, successful communication depends on how well we listen, rather than how well
we push our opinions on the person seated before us. People
have therefore conceptualized communication techniques
using terms like "empty vessel" to try to understand each
other better.[50]

A similar point is made by his designer colleague at MUJI, Naoto
Fukasawa, who also claims that "if a designer believes that people
and time have created a form, then they want to *get rid of the ego*
that says, 'I designed this object.'"[51] If I am correct in thinking that
one of the necessary ingredients of a good society is well-considered
environments and artifacts, both Taoist *wu-wei* and the Buddhist
emptiness offer rich food for thought. Here it would be difficult to
carve out the autonomous realm of aesthetics separated from the
rest of life concerns and deny the legitimacy of using aesthetic
means for a worthwhile goal.[52]

The project of world-making is not a sole responsibility of professional world-makers, such as architects, designers, and manufactur-
ers. The rest of us are not merely passive recipients of the
environment created by these professionals; rather, we are all impli-
cated in the project of world-making through the choices and decisions we make in our daily life. And to a surprising degree, our
actions are motivated by aesthetic interests. The aesthetic dimension of our life thus affects the state of the world and the quality of
life profoundly, for better or worse. In light of this serious ramifica-
tion of our aesthetic engagement with the environment, I propose
that environmental aesthetics includes a strategy of utilizing aesthetics to assist in the humanity's ongoing world-making project.
Gathering wisdom from various cultural traditions should provide
one such strategy. We can only gain by mining the fertile fields of
diverse cultural traditions.[53]

CHAPTER

3

On Universalism and Cultural Historicism in Environmental Aesthetics

Jonathan Maskit

Introduction

While the history of environmental aesthetics has yet to be written, this history, it seems, should be divided into three periods. The first of these occurred during the eighteenth century and constituted what we might term "the heyday of environmental aesthetics." To call it "the heyday," however, is somewhat misleading, as at this time there was no such thing as environmental aesthetics at all. Instead, there was only philosophical aesthetics, which was far more concerned with questions about aesthetic judgment and the responses of human subjects to aesthetic experience than it was with the ontology of aesthetic objects, and thus drew no distinction between the aesthetics of nature and the aesthetics of art. As a result, early aestheticians often treated works of art and natural objects as equally provocative, even if they were importantly different in their genesis. The second period in this history might be termed "the dark ages" or "the years of forgetting." During these years, roughly from the beginning of the nineteenth century to the latter half of the twentieth, nature and its objects became far less important for aestheticians to the point of their being ignored altogether. Over the course of the last four decades or so, there has been a great increase in interest in nature amongst aestheticians, as well as an increase in interest in nature's aesthetic characteristics among environmental philosophers. While one might be tempted to call this third period "the renaissance of environmental aesthetics," indicating by this term the rediscovery of nature's aesthetic value that had already been recognized in the eighteenth century, I prefer to think of this period as its inauguration or debut as a full-fledged area of philosophical inquiry. These terms ("inauguration" and "debut") are intended to make clear what "renaissance" hides: This is not a rebirth of eighteenth-century environmental aesthetics, since, as indicated earlier, there was no such thing.

The appearance of environmental aesthetics has made difficult the easy convention by which the terms "philosophy of the arts" and "aesthetics" functioned as synonyms (even if for many they continue to function as synonyms to this day). One important outcome of this history is that those inaugurating contemporary environmental aestheticians found themselves outfitted with the tools of a discipline that had been developed for other purposes and were often ill-suited to the tasks to which environmental aestheticians wished to put them. While eighteenth-century aestheticians moved easily between art and nature, and had developed, as a result, a great ease and fluidity in distinguishing between them and what was needed to discuss them philosophically, the ensuing 150-odd years of the philosophy of art meant a great deal of work had to be done even to figure out what sort of aesthetic objects nature and natural objects are. Given the emphasis often put on artistic intention or expression or on communication in the philosophy of art, environmental aestheticians often found themselves needing to search about for newly crafted tools or, less radically, needing to beat the swords of the philosophy of art into the plowshares of environmental aesthetics in order to be able to work this new field.

One problem with the previously sketched history is that it focuses almost entirely on environmental aesthetics *in* English. Were one to consider work done in other languages, the history would be more complicated. For one, there are several figures working in German during the middle period for whom nature is important aesthetically. These include Arthur Schopenhauer, Friedrich Nietzsche, and Martin Heidegger, yet other than Schopenhauer, these names are rarely if ever mentioned in the English-language literature. The other complication is that while environmental aesthetics was developing in the English-speaking world in the 1960s and after, there were parallel, yet unacknowledged, developments going on elsewhere. Most importantly, Theodor Adorno, one of the twentieth century's greatest aestheticians, devoted significant time to nature in both his *Aesthetic Theory* and other texts, a fact which goes largely unacknowledged in the English-speaking world. (To be fair, today's German-speaking environmental aestheticians, such as Martin Seel and Gernot Böhme, pay no heed to their contemporaries working in English.) Treating these parallel histories is beyond the scope of this chapter, although surely a complete history would need to do so.[1]

While the history sketched previously is, I would hope, not contentious, neither this history nor any other has played a great role in the development of contemporary environmental aesthetics. Instead, the field, at least in the English-speaking world, has developed in a way that has thought history of little import. What this chapter seeks to do is to argue for the importance of history and culture in environmental aesthetics. To make this case, I will give an overview of the current state of the field from a new vantage point. Up until now, environmental aesthetics has been characterized following a more or less agreed upon set of divisions. I will argue that there is an important, alternative distinction that can be used in looking at work in the field that will carve things up differently and, I hope, help us to see things more clearly. I first present what I call the "standard view," rehearsing the distinctions between cognitivists and noncognitivists, proponents of science versus proponents of imagination, and so forth. I next provide a brief excursus on so-called "continental" and "analytic" approaches to philosophy, arguing that the differences between them have been largely misconstrued and that these differences in approach could be of great benefit for an understanding of where we as environmental aestheticians ought to go from here. I then return to environmental aesthetics, arguing that we can divide the field into a majority strand where work is pursued largely universalistically and individualistically, with little regard for the import of culture and history and a minority strand where a sensitivity to culture and history (the basic insights of the continental approach) is essential (even if most of these authors would not self-identify as continental philosophers). Finally, I argue that this aspect of the minority strand is worth emphasizing as a necessary corrective to the overreaching universalism of the majority strand.

The Standard View

While there is no consensus among environmental aestheticians as to the best approach to the subject matter, there is both a general agreement as to which approaches are nonstarters as well as how best to carve up the positions currently held. First off, I know of no one working in the field today who could be called a formalist. While all environmental aestheticians acknowledge Kant's monumental contribution, and many have built views based upon what we might term neo-Kantian foundations (Ronald Hepburn and Emily Brady, both of whom have argued for the import of imagination, are two), no one embraces the sort of neo-Kantian formalism developed by Clive Bell.[2] Bell's view, developed in the context of philosophy of the arts, holds that what is distinctive of an artwork is its *significant form*, and that this form can be appreciated without any regard to what the artwork portrays or was intended to be. Nor ought one to consider how the work functions socially or politically or even, really, what it is (beyond being a work of art). This view, grounded in the Kantian claim that what counts in aesthetics is the consideration of the object's form with no regard to its purpose (if any), genesis, or context, has been widely rejected by environmental aestheticians because it fails to take account of two crucial facts about natural environments: they are natural (not artificial) and they are environments (not objects). Formalism can only treat non-art objects as if they were art objects, which can, in general, be moved from one location to another while suffering no aesthetic consequences. But it is generally agreed among environmental aestheticians that context matters, as does genesis. Furthermore, there seems to be a marked difference between encountering an environment, which is multisensory and surrounds us, and encountering an object that can often be sensed using only one or two of our senses and which can be regarded at a distance. Indeed, one might be tempted to say that an environment is all context and no object.

Second, and perhaps not surprisingly, I know of no one who endorses either a naïve environmental aesthetic, which holds that one needs simply to experience nature and natural objects to find them appealing, or what we might term an "empirical" or "descriptivist" view, which would hold that one need only observe how actual people judge nature and its objects to know both what is to be judged positively and how we are to do so.

On the contrary, all (so far as I know) practicing environmental aestheticians agree that there are better and worse ways to approach natural environments and that one requires something more than just what meets the senses in order to judge well. That is, they are all normative in their approach. Indeed, it is the hallmark of very much of the work in the field that "better and worse" are not the terms one ought to be using here. Instead, there has been much debate about the right or appropriate way to appreciate an environment, which, of course, means that all other ways must be wrong or inappropriate. Allen Carlson, for example, having begun with the question of "what and how to aesthetically appreciate concerning the natural environment," quickly refines this to be a question about the "appropriate [model] for the appreciation of nature."[3] Yuriko Saito seeks to "develop the notion of the appropriate aesthetic appreciation of nature," while Emily Brady asks, "What guides our aesthetic appreciation of nature?"[4] Thus all (so far as I know) environmental aestheticians agree that *something* more than mere sense perception is needed for the aesthetic appreciation of nature.

Where disagreements begin is with the question: *What* is this something that we need? And it is the various answers to this question that provide the basis for the primary line of demarcation in the standard view of the field. Thus Emily Brady makes clear that the most important division to be found in contemporary environmental aesthetics is that between cognitivists and noncognitivists. In writing the introduction to their *Aesthetics of Natural Environments*, Allen Carlson and Arnold Berleant concur.[5] Ronald Moore puts things this way:

> The core of the controversy lies in the fact that, although we are reasonably confident of the critical and analytical framework appropriate to intelligent appreciation of artworks, we are less confident of the corresponding framework of ideas appropriate to intelligent appreciation of natural objects. We are generally prepared to believe that our aesthetic response to natural objects is, despite any conceptual deficit, not naïve, not unsuited to its objects, and fulsome. But, if the appreciation of natural objects is not supported by *some* kind of cognitive apparatus, something like—even remotely like—that which supports our judgments in the artworld, how can it be anything but shallow, subjective, and inaccessible to critical assessment? At present, philosophers are generally inclined to respond to this question in one of two ways.[6]

Moore prefers to call the two camps "conceptualists" and "nonconceptualists," but the result is the same.

The cognitivists, such as Carlson, Holmes Rolston III, Glenn Parsons, Marcia Eaton, and, to a lesser degree, Saito, hold that what is needed to judge natural environments properly are *concepts*, and, furthermore, a particular sort of concepts: those provided by the natural sciences.[7] Thus when we are unsure how to judge some part of nature, we should ask for guidance from biologists, ecologists, geoscientists, and so forth, just as we seek guidance from curators, critics, art historians, and so on when we are unsure how best to approach a work of art. For the cognitivists, aesthetic judgment is primarily an intellectual affair which, at least in principle, ought to approach toward something like objectivity.

On the other side is a more disparate group: the noncognitivists. Here we find thinkers such as Noël Carroll and Mark Sagoff who emphasize the importance of emotion; Brady who stresses the role of imagination; and figures such as Berleant and Arto Haapala who take what we might call a phenomenological approach. What unites these views is their rejection of the idea that science and scientific concepts are the *sine qua non* of environmental aesthetics. In addition, someone like Berleant holds that we make a mistake when we treat environmental aesthetics as distinct from the aesthetics of art and that we would do well to provide a holistic aesthetic theory.

I do not take issue with this characterization of the field insofar as it goes. What I will argue later is that there are other ways we could carve things up, which might yield more interesting results. In other words, rather than simply seeing us proceed skirmishing along this time-worn battle front, I will argue that an alternative characterization of the field might make possible new and fruitful work going forward. Before offering this new characterization, I would like briefly to revisit the so-called continental-analytic distinction in philosophy more broadly, as I think it is instructive here.

Excursus: Continental and Analytic Philosophy

If my interest is in helping a debate in one area of philosophy move beyond entrenched positions, invoking another set of entrenched views seems like a strange tactic to choose. Nevertheless, I do think there is something of import to be learned by pursuing this strategy. Let me be clear at the outset that I have no interest in re-igniting the generally fruitless set of misunderstandings that characterized many parts of philosophy in the closing decades of the last millennium, and I want to be clear that I am painting here with a very wide brush.

That having been said, it seems to me that the debates between continental and analytic approaches to philosophy were never so much settled as set aside. Let me propose that what was really at issue in these debates was not so much differences in rigor or geographical location, but a dispute about the role and import of culture and history for our understanding of ourselves and the world we inhabit. Let me propose thus some new terms, so that, if nothing else, I might help to resettle the hackles that so quickly rise when one hears about continental and analytic philosophy. It seems to me that much of philosophy in the nineteenth and twentieth centuries was characterized by a dispute between what I will call universalists and cultural historicists.

For the universalists, it is clear that when we speak about human beings or nature we are talking about stable concepts. While we clearly have much to learn about what a human being or nature is, it seems, to the universalist, to be clear that what we mean by "human being" or "nature" is continuous with what our philosophical forebears meant. Thus it is perfectly reasonable to read Plato, Aristotle, Aquinas, Descartes, and Russell all together as posing what are fundamentally the same questions about the same domain of enquiry.

For the cultural historicists, to the contrary, it is clear that terms such as "human being" or "nature" are far more fluid and doubly so. First, there is a historical fluidity to these terms, which, depending upon one's outlook, may or may not be developmental. Thus when we in the twenty-first century say "nature," it is not at all clear that we mean anything like what the ancient Greeks meant by *phusis* or the medievals meant by *natura* any more than it is clear that when we say "human being" we mean anything like what our predecessors meant by *anthropos* or *homo*. For some cultural historicists, a developmental story, at the very least, can be traced, so that even if "human being" and "anthropos" are not synonyms, we can at least see how we got from the latter to the former. For others, there is no necessary development or progress, but only change. For these cultural historicists, we are hard-pressed to argue that our notion of "human being" is better, in large part because the cultural contexts are so radically different.

The second type of fluidity is cultural. However different we modern Europeans and Euro-Americans are from our European ancestors, we at least can reconstruct a historical connection (although perhaps not a developmental one). This is not nearly so clear if we look at our relationship with many of the world's other cultural traditions. While there has clearly been an unprecedented degree of cross-cultural exchange in recent decades, it remains the case that cultures such as Japan's, India's, or Morocco's, to name only three, are markedly different in their understandings of many of the terms the universalist takes to be universal. (It is worth adding here that each of these cultures has its own history, meaning that when we speak of *the* Japanese or *the* Indian understanding of a concept we distort no less than when we seek to efface the differences between one culture and another.) Cultural difference from this perspective is not to be explained away as the consequence of one or both sides being mistaken. Rather, it is to be accepted and confronted as a part of the human condition that requires understanding and perhaps negotiation.

Because of this difference in philosophical outlook, there is a greater tendency toward both monism and individualism among universalists, while cultural historicists are more inclined to be pluralists. Why this is so is clear from even a cursory history of continental philosophy.

Immanuel Kant, who was either the first continental philosopher or the last pre-continental philosopher (or both), argued quite strenuously in the *Critique of Pure Reason* that there is no way for us to encounter the world other than through concepts, which means always through *our* concepts.[8] He divided these concepts into two types: the pure concepts of the understanding (the categories) and empirical concepts. While he argued that the categories (most importantly substance and cause) were universal, in other words, there could be no experience whatsoever without them, he was far more open (and far vaguer) about empirical concepts. These can never have the certainty about them that the pure concepts do and would seem to require a historical, genetic account to be explained. Whether there could be cultural variability in such concepts, Kant does not, so far as I am aware, address. Nevertheless, Kant is clear in his universalist commitments in all aspects of his philosophy. This is to say, despite his great respect for empirical concepts as part of our scientific and cognitive attempts to understand the world, the true basis for science, morality, *and* aesthetics (albeit in three very different ways) are the universally valid categories and their analogues (the moral law, conceptuality in general, the ideas of reason, etc.). Given this universal character of human reason, it is no surprise that Kant, in line with his modernist forebears, embraces the philosophy of the subject and sees truth, morality, and aesthetic judgment as all fundamentally individualistic enterprises, even if he recognizes the need for a like-minded community (of investigators, of ends, of participants in the *sensus communis*) in order for any of them fully to be successful.

The most important successor to Kant is the man who took the historical genesis of concepts absolutely seriously: Georg W. F. Hegel. While Kant had taken only empirical concepts to have a historical character, for Hegel *all* of our concepts are historically developed, which is to say that there are no transcendental concepts for him. Despite this historical character, which we might think would make these concepts thoroughly contingent, Hegel argues that they are no less binding upon us than if they were transcendentally grounded. Furthermore, while there may appear to be a necessity to this development, this is a necessity that only appears to us retrospectively. That is, that certain concepts develop when and how they do *does* have a certain contingency to it. The concepts so developed, however, are not themselves contingent (once having been developed). Nevertheless, for Hegel there is but one world history, meaning that while our concepts may be historical in their genesis, there can be no meaningful talk of cultural difference.

There is another aspect to Hegel's thought that is relevant here. For Kant, concepts are almost always described as mental, which is to say that they are to be found in individual minds. Kant is, of course, aware that concepts are deployed socially: Scientists build off of each other's work and must submit their conceptual (theoretical) advances to the crucible of investigation by others. Nevertheless, what it means for a concept to be universal is that *my* concept is the same as *your* concept. That is, concepts are, at bottom, held individually, even if their validity is public. For Hegel, concepts are first and foremost communal and only secondarily individual. Thus even if new concepts always begin with individuals, what is most important is not their genesis but their validity, which can only be determined socially. This commitment to the sociality of concepts means, among other things, that aesthetics becomes far more a question of community or culture and far less about individuals and their judgments. These Hegelian insights see further development in the work of Martin Heidegger.

While the early Heidegger (in *Being and Time*) seems to be broadly Hegelian in his approach, emphasizing the historical development of concepts, in his later years Heidegger became more and more interested in problems of cultural difference. In particular, this came out with his discussions of translation, which presented itself to him not merely as a problem between ancient and modern European languages but between German and (in his example) Japanese. He wondered whether there was always something lost in translation, so that the experience of being Japanese and having what we term "aesthetic experience," might just not be fully graspable by someone outside the culture.[9] In addition, like Hegel, Heidegger is committed to the view that concepts are first and foremost social and only secondarily individual.

What we can see in this all-too-brief history is the development of a philosophical standpoint that sees concepts in general, and thus the world to which they give us access, as being both historically and culturally developed. Such a view, not surprisingly, will tend to be pluralist in its philosophical outlook, hermeneutic in its method (since interpretation is now ineliminable), and deeply committed to the importance of community (as the necessary "site" for the development of concepts).

I am aware, of course, that simply invoking the names and basic positions of Kant, Hegel, and Heidegger (or anyone else, for that matter) does nothing to convince anyone of the value or rightness of their positions, nor should it. Much more careful philosophical argumentation would be required to do so. I seek merely to suggest that there have been important philosophers, philosophers whose influence extends far beyond the world of "continental philosophy," who have argued in various ways that the universalist position is far from self-evident. To proceed as if these arguments simply hadn't been made or are obviously mistaken seems to me no more credible than proceeding as if cultural historicism were obviously true. My goal is not to displace the universalist position but to call it to account, to make its premises clear and in need of justification. I return now to environmental aesthetics to see whether this way of thinking might profitably be applied there.

A New Way to Look at Environmental Aesthetics

It should come as no surprise, given the story contemporary environmental aestheticians tell of the discipline's origin—a story about a small and growing band of malcontents among analytic aestheticians—that most contemporary practitioners are universalists with tendencies toward both monism and individualism. While

Carlson, Brady, Berleant, and others disagree quite strenuously as to what the correct way to appreciate an environment aesthetically is, they agree that there *is* a correct way and that if we could just figure out what that way is then we could set this particular philosophical problem in the sparsely populated box labeled "solved." They further agree that the appreciation that takes place is one that is largely individual in character. While there may be possibilities for discourse and learning from one another, at bottom aesthetic experience is a solitary affair, taking place between one subject and some object or set of objects or an environment.

Nevertheless, there do seem to be some environmental aestheticians whose approach is more cultural historicist, even though some of these authors would shrink back at the mere suggestion that they were somehow "continental" in their approach. Interestingly, these authors often are concerned not so much with what we might term "pure nature," but rather with nature and culture in their interactions. Given the import that the cultural historicist approach gives to culture, we should not be surprised to find that such aestheticians are committed to the idea that nature itself is a cultural concept, in other words, one that can vary in its meaning and import. The point could be put differently and perhaps more provocatively. While some of the authors I name in the following discussion have been consistently cultural historicist in their approach, others, such as Saito, seem to be less firmly either cultural historicist or universalist.

First among the authors who have been consistently cultural historicist is a pair of Finnish aestheticians: Arto Haapala and Pauline von Bonsdorff. Haapala, in trying to make clear the idea of "spirit of a place" (*genius loci*), draws upon the culture and history of the place whose spirit he is trying to elucidate.[10] To understand a place, one needs to understand the people who live there (or have lived there) as well as their cultural practices. To do so requires a certain degree of cultural bridging—a hermeneutic practice. Haapala contrasts the aesthetic judgments of those for whom a place is strange or foreign with the judgments of those familiar with the place, writing "our perceptions and judgments [as foreigners] are not any more objective than the judgments of those who see the environment as familiar."[11] This is not to say that judgments are subjective, but that the relevant rubric for evaluation must be worked out in relationship to culture. To feel at home someplace requires working out connections with the place, which is a very different enterprise from trying to understand the place using the resources of science, whether natural or social.

While it's true that Haapala is writing here about a built environment, we can imagine extending his argument to natural environments as well, since many of these, too, have historically been inhabited in various ways. Haapala's position requires setting aside the idea enshrined in the United States' Wilderness Act that in nature, human beings are only "visitors who [do] not remain." On the contrary, an environment, as Heidegger argued, simply is the world around us, the world that we inhabit through our cultural practices. Of course, we can appeal to science as *one* sort of cultural practice for interacting with an environment, but there are many others, too: hunting, camping, subsistence agricultural, and so forth.

Von Bonsdorff, again in the context of discussing built environments, argues that our approach to such environments cannot be purely contemplative, but must be practical as well.[12] She argues that a successful built environment fulfills four sorts of characteristics: affordance, enticement, generosity, and recognizability. "Affordances," a term von Bonsdorff borrows from James Gibson, are environmental characteristics that allow certain actions or activities: they offer possibilities. Gentle slopes afford walking, steeper ones hiking, steeper still climbing. One can no more walk up a cliff than one can climb a beach; they just don't afford those activities. Enticements are "environmental promise[s]."[13] An environment may not only afford our doing what we planned on doing, it can entice us into doing something we hadn't planned on. Benches entice us to sit, even if we had been planning on walking or cycling. Paths, conversely, entice us to walk, particularly if they turn in such a way that we cannot see where they lead. Generosity is a sign of care on the part of inhabitants. Well-cared-for environments are more welcoming than run-down ones. Finally, recognizability is what allows us to find our way in an environment—to see it for what it is and what it affords. We must recognize it as the particular *sort* of place that it is if we are to recognize its affordances, enticements, and generosity. Built environments that embody these characteristics are the ones that welcome their inhabitants as well as visitors.

While we might think that these characteristics are irrelevant to the non-built environment—that would be a mistake. For, following Heidegger, von Bonsdorff argues that our primary relationship to the environment is one of building. Although what we build and how we do so varies from place to place and culture to culture, it is a characteristic of being human that we transform where we are. Indeed, even the activities we engage in while in wild nature are often forms of building: cutting trails, putting up climbing routes, digging latrines, and so on. For Heidegger, even naming is a form of domestication (from *domus*—house), for it brings that which is not human into our sphere. In a certain way, even not doing anything— letting a place be—is a conscious decision *not* to build. Thus we name places as parks or wildernesses, erecting borders around them, and then forbid building in them. But mostly we don't just leave places be: We change them in various ways, which means that we ought to do so with sensitivity not only to the ecology of the place, but also to the culture and the history of those whose place it is.[14] There can be no *one* right way to build, because building well depends first of all upon the available materials and the demands of the climate: Straw huts work well in Micronesia but not so well in Lapland. Additionally, building well demands an understanding of the culture and history of where one is building. Even if we choose *not* to build in order to preserve a place, we often do so not because of its scientifically demonstrated virtues, but because of its cultural or historical significance, which surely affect how we experience the place.

Two Americans, Barbara Sandrisser and Yuriko Saito (the latter of whom was born and raised in Japan), also seem to me to exhibit this sort of cultural sensitivity, in both cases, with particular regard for the culture of Japan. Sandrisser, in her thoughtful meditations on the building practices, emplacement, and temporality of traditional Japanese culture offers us not a prescription for how all of us ought to relate to our environments, but a model of how one culture has done so.[15] Sandrisser's point is not that the Japanese got it right and we need simply to do what they did, but rather that they figured out a way that worked for them—a set of building and cultural practices that allowed nature to show itself to them not as an enemy to be conquered but as a home to be inhabited. We cannot import Japanese practices and beliefs, at least not without changing them significantly, but we can see what we might learn from them and how we might look at our history and practices and change them. To do so, however, requires careful and respectful work as well as the acceptance that we may not fully grasp how everything works or how it all fits together given our external perspective. It is worth mentioning here, although Sandrisser does not do so, that, whatever may be said for traditional forms of Japanese architecture as well as some modern Japanese architects (Sandrisser is particularly enamored of the work of Tadao Ando), the problem of how to build in a way that "works" with nature is one that the contemporary Japanese have as well. One worry with work such as Sandrisser's is that it can tend toward a romantic Orientalism with all of its attendant problems.[16] While Sandrisser is careful in this regard, it is worth remembering the import of the sort of hermeneutic sensitivity Heidegger demonstrates when trying to understand another culture. Cultures seen from the outside are never the same as when seen from the inside. An awareness of how our presuppositions can shape our encounter with another culture and how that culture can then shape our presuppositions for the next encounter can only help.

Saito, too, seems far more open to cultural pluralism than many. While she agrees with Carlson that we need to begin with science, she argues that we cannot end there, if our goal is to approach nature, as she puts it, "on its own terms."[17] Saito is more aware than many scientific cognitivists of the shortcomings of science. She pays heed to social constructivist arguments (even if she rejects them in the end), but also to science's Cartesian/Baconian heritage and its legacy of control and manipulation. She suggests that science inevitably uses *our* language and *our* concepts, even if it is nevertheless *trying* to tell nature's story. That is, science can only tell nature's story in human words, that is, using human concepts. Furthermore, through her openness to additional frameworks for approaching nature, whether Jim Cheney's bioregional narratives or the sorts of stories traditional cultures tell, Saito leaves open the possibility of an aesthetic encounter with what we might term "enchanted nature." More importantly, she recognizes the role that culture and tradition play in our aesthetic appreciation of nature as well as the possibility of nonmonological aesthetic experience.

My final examples are Martin Seel and Gernot Böhme, Germany's foremost environmental aestheticians, whose (as yet) largely untranslated work deserves to be better known in the English-speaking world.[18] Seel argues that the three key questions we have to answer when discussing the "aesthetic and moral recognition [*Anerkennung*] of nature" are these:

1. *Whose* recognition do we mean, when we speak about a "recognition of nature?"
2. *As what* will nature be recognized when we do the recognizing?
3. *Why* is our acting in a way that recognizes nature to be recommended or required?[19]

Seel argues that an answer to these questions can be framed in four key sentences, the first two of which constitute answers to the first two questions, while the latter two answer the third question:

I. The aesthetics of nature should be an *aesthetics*.
II. The aesthetics of nature should be an aesthetics of *nature*.
III. The aesthetics of nature should be part of an *ethics of the good life*.
IV. The individual ethical—and entirely anthropocentric—aesthetic of nature should be part of a pathocentric *ethics of recognition*.[20]

I focus here primarily on the first two sentences, as they are particularly germane to my purposes. By aesthetics, Seel understands the possibility in human perception to encounter things in a way that we describe with some sort of aesthetic characteristic, often, but not always, beauty or sublimity. Like Kant, Seel is clear that beauty is only a characteristic *for us*: "There is no such thing as beauty 'in itself.'"[21] Thus the answer to the first question must be something like "human beings in general." Interestingly, Seel leaves open the question of whether this is a theory of individual or collective encounter. Given that he is concerned to locate this aesthetics of nature within an "ethics of the good life," it must be possible, insofar as ethics has to do with our relationships with others, for it to be communally experienced. Like Carlson, Seel argues that what makes an aesthetic encounter with nature different from other sorts of aesthetic encounters must lie in the characteristics of that encounter as an encounter *with nature*—thus his second key sentence. From here, however, the differences with a view such as Carlson's (or even Saito's) become stark. While Carlson insists that the key to an aesthetics of nature is to encounter nature using scientific concepts, Seel writes "[t]hat nature from which everything comes, is affected in its existence, and in which everything perishes is no aesthetic object to be compared to other sorts of aesthetic objects. An [aesthetic] encounter [*Betrachtung*] that is devoted to the particularities of natural, as opposed to artistic objects [*Gebilden*], has no opportunity to make this concept of nature its basic principle." What Seel is insisting upon here is that the nature revealed to us through scientific thinking—a nature that is entirely general and in no way particular—cannot be the nature that we encounter aesthetically. Rather, the aesthetics of nature concerns "much more that relationship to nature in which we encounter a nature that we can, first, *individuate* into animals, plants, stones, or landscapes and, second, that we can apprehend as more or less *free* nature, in contrast to human artifacts." Seel's position can be further differentiated from Carlson's by his insistence that "the nature dealt with in an aesthetics of nature, is a threatened region *within* the human world [*die menschliche Wirklichkeit*]."[22] For Seel, because the nature encountered in aesthetics is a nature that only exists in the aesthetic relationship, there is no sense in discussing nature on its own terms or nature independent of us, at least not in this domain. That said, Seel's view does not go so far as some others; he has certain universalist tendencies of his own, even if they are voiced in more nuanced language.

Like Seel, Böhme insists that the nature we encounter is never entirely other from us and that to use modern science as the paradigm of how we are to encounter nature *aesthetically* is highly problematic. The nature we encounter aesthetically is for Böhme a "socially constituted nature," which is as much the product of industrialization as of philosophy and science.[23] Since that nature is partially constituted by science, to turn to science as a guiding light for aesthetics constitutes a serious error. For Böhme, modern science and aesthetics share an origin in modern philosophy's constitutive division between subject and object. That is, the nature investigated by science is already shaped by processes of alienation. To use this nature as the guidepost for aesthetics means using a nature that has already been radically transformed. What is needed, argues Böhme, is not the valorization of this alienation, but its overcoming. "The situation in which aesthetics today finds itself is comparable to that of the romantics, who demanded that aesthetics reconcile subject and object."[24] The nature with which we seek a reconciliation presents itself, however, in two different aspects. While both natures are external to the subject, one is closer at hand. The first external nature is what we usually think of as nature: the nonhuman aspects of the world. But the second external nature is the human body itself. Böhme reminds us that modern philosophy begins in Descartes with a cleavage between the human subject and "its" body. While Böhme is not the first to notice or attempt to overcome this cleavage, his method is novel.[25] The goal of an ecological aesthetics of nature thus becomes, for Böhme, the project of reconciling not just subject and object but mind and body.

The point can be put even more strongly. We need not merely a reconciliation of mind and body, but an overcoming (in Hegel's sense) of the very distinction. We must first grapple with the nature that we are before we can approach external nature. The goal of this reconciliation is a reconceptualization of what we mean by sensibility, which is, after all, the beginning of aesthetics. To this end, Böhme returns to Baumgarten, who he sees as a figure with a far more embodied understanding of sensibility and perception than what we find elsewhere in the seventeenth and eighteenth centuries. This new understanding of sensibility is one that leads us to see perception as fundamentally characterized by the presence of the human body in the world. We might even say it requires us to think of the human body as a site of interchange with the world.

Thus, when we do come to external nature, for Böhme, we must do so in a way that recognizes the fundamentally hermeneutic character of this encounter (although he does not use the term hermeneutic). If we understand "sensibility as bodily presence, then from the very beginning there will be a two-sidedness [to the encounter with nature]: our surroundings will become sensible in our state [*Befinden*] *and* we diffuse an atmosphere in our surroundings."[26] This concept of the atmosphere is central not only to Böhme's ecological aesthetics of nature, but to his aesthetics in general.[27]

Böhme's project strikes me as both exceedingly interesting and promising. I worry, though, that in his insistence on shifting the focus to the body and atmosphere, external nature ends up having to wait, meaning that we end up with an aesthetics of nature that is, albeit in a very different way, much more about us than it is about nature.

A New Way Forward

What ought we do with the previously offered observations? My suggestion is this: If we look at the literature on environmental aesthetics with new lenses, we may find echoes of debates that have already surfaced elsewhere in environmental philosophy as well as in philosophy more generally. In particular, we find echoes of the debates about the social construction of nature and the nature of wilderness.[28] Those debates died down relatively quickly, not because the universalists won through argument but because they greatly outnumbered the cultural historicists. Even if one does not wish to go down the cultural historicist path, it seems to me simply untenable after Kant and his successors to maintain that we can ever have unmediated access to nature. I would rather see the universalists take more seriously the difficulties in their own position, which can only happen if one first takes seriously both the alternatives as well as the import of the sort of distinction I have here argued for.

For the cultural historicist, reifying nature as a noncultural category is simply untenable. Just what would it mean to encounter nature *directly*? And once we admit that we can't encounter nature directly, *of course*, it is human beings who encounter nature and of course we do so using *our* senses, *our* language, and *our* concepts, it's not far to the recognition that those concepts and languages themselves have histories and that they vary from one time and place to another. And it's only one small step further to the realization that our senses, too, are culturally shaped; aesthetics teaches us this quite clearly. One has to learn to look, to listen, and to taste, and one can learn to like and enjoy many things that one would not have thought would be appreciable. Even the cognitivists admit that some cultural institutions can play an important role in shaping our aesthetic judgments. Their mistake is in insisting that there is only one such cultural institution (science) and it holds universally.

The history of both environmental aesthetics and environmental ethics (not to mention of philosophical aesthetics and ethics more generally) ought to teach us that we would do well to give up the search for the one, true way. It seems to me that some of us already have.[29]

PART

II

Rethinking Relationships

The Cultural Aesthetics
of Environment

Arnold Berleant

Introduction

Considering environment aesthetically is a comparatively recent development. The focus on the aesthetic dimension of environment began in the 1970s and gained increasing prominence. Appearing sporadically at first, interest in environmental aesthetics developed during subsequent decades in the United Kingdom, Canada, and the United States, and more insistently and intensively in Finland. Beginning in the 1990s, the aesthetics of environment gained wide attention in China. Environmental aesthetics can now be considered an established domain of inquiry that is international in scope and that draws on and influences several disciplines. It appears most prominently in philosophical aesthetics, environmental psychology, and landscape design, and it is a recognized focus in the visual arts, literature, and the environmental sciences.

Interest in environmental aesthetics has indeed become a global phenomenon, cutting across philosophical styles as well as cultural traditions. Much remains to be gained by continuing this momentum. Yet while we all face similar environmental problems, ways of thinking about environment vary. Different cultural traditions, different philosophical cultures, and different conditions of life influence the way we understand environment, aesthetics, ecology, and their place in life experience. There are obvious reasons for this variety. At the same time, environmental issues are no longer only regional but involve changes whose effects spread without limit atmospherically as well as geographically. There are compelling reasons, therefore, to consider whether there is any commonality on which these differences can converge.

Common problems invite coordinated solutions. It would greatly assist cooperative action on environmental issues if we shared a similar understanding of the ideas that are central to this situation. Encouraging as the global interest in environment may be, it is nonetheless the case that research on the aesthetics of environment displays significant differences in the meaning of its central ideas. It may therefore help reduce the inconsistencies and confusion in what is meant by the key concepts by clarifying their meanings. In such a spirit, I should like to offer some reflections on how we might bring together the sometimes disjointed thinking on the underlying issues.

It seems obvious that any inquiry should begin with a clear understanding of the basic concepts involved. This may seem obvious but it is not easy to do for, as is well known, our concepts are so embedded in historical uses and cultural matrices that ideas that seem intuitively simple and unambiguous may well embody confusion and even contradiction. As an interest in environmental aesthetics has grown beyond the attention of a few widely scattered scholars to enter into national and international discussion, problems with clarity and difficulties in communication have become increasingly troublesome. A comprehensive analysis of terminology would be a worthwhile undertaking, but it is not possible in a brief chapter to offer more than one perspective on this. For the purposes of the present discussion, let me present approximations of our foundational concepts that may provide a common place of reference if not a common ground.

Words About Environment

Let me begin with the observation that no concept in philosophy is self-evident, simple, or self-contained. Every basic idea is unavoidably caught in a network of theoretical assumptions and implications. Any apparent obviousness belies these hidden debts and allegiances. Culture and theory thus combine to oblige us to begin with complexity. There are no simples in philosophy. This is clearly the case with the three basic ideas that inform our discussion: environment, aesthetics, and ecology.

Environment

It might seem obvious to consider *environment* the foundational idea of this inquiry. Surely it is the overall focus of our concern. It is commonplace to speak these days of an environmental crisis, and this is not only a manner of speaking. People across the globe are increasingly distressed by erratic and unseemly weather events: disrupted seasonal changes, freak wind storms, record floods, and tidal waves, not to mention more anticipated if not welcomed environmental disturbances like hurricanes, volcanic eruptions, and earthquakes. Added to these so-called natural disasters are those caused by human action and error. I am inclined to think, however, that rather than beginning with an understanding of environment, the discussion might better terminate in an enlarged sense of environment. That is, our confrontation with environmental issues, such as weather and climate change, is a result of the consequences of people's attitudes and practices and not because of any conceptual order. As one of the leading ideas, environment invites a larger, more inclusive understanding than climatological changes and crises.

Yet the very breadth of environmental concerns makes a clear focus difficult. Environment embraces many regions and perspectives: preservation, conservation, resource protection and use, land use and planning, public policy, recreation, and enjoyment, to name some of the most obvious. All are relevant and all are important, but the concern here is with a clearer understanding of environment and its issues. Perhaps it would serve to focus on an *aesthetic* interest in environment as fundamental. In some sense, it *is* fundamental because our *sensory* engagement with environment precedes and underlies every other interest. I say this because sensory perception lies at the heart of the meaning of aesthetics and is central in aesthetic experience, and the sensible experience of environment stands at the center of every other environmental interest and use.

Aesthetics

It might seem, then, that since our concern here is with aesthetics, that is, environmental aesthetics, *aesthetics* should be our point of departure. Whether we take aesthetics here in a fairly narrow sense to mean the beauty of environment or consider it broadly as sensible experience in general, that is, as the range of sensory perception, aesthetics is necessarily a central point at which environmental concerns intersect human experience and activity. We might even claim that the aesthetic should not only be our starting point but is also our ultimate end as the fundamental understanding of direct perceptual experience.

These two ideas, environment and aesthetics, are clearly at the heart of this inquiry. But there is a third: *ecology*. This may seem like a late addition to the discussion; and as I noted earlier, ecology has only more recently assumed an important place in our understanding of environment. Indeed, as a region of scientific theory and investigation, ecology emerged only in the late nineteenth century. And while it began as a biological theory about the interdependence of organisms in particular environments considered as ecosystems, its basic concept has spread throughout the social as well as natural sciences.

Ecology

Ecology may seem to be derivative, a way of thinking about environment that has only secondary interest here, and until recently ecological concerns have not had a prominent place in environmental aesthetics. Indeed, ecology figures most prominently in discussions of environmental aesthetics by Chinese researchers. Is this a cultural difference or does it entail a theoretical divergence?

Reviewing the theoretical underpinning of an aesthetics of environment, one may conclude that ecology can make a significant, indeed a determinative, contribution. By starting with an ecological orientation, we gain an illuminating perspective on this inquiry, for an ecological outlook transfigures our understanding of both environment and aesthetics. In fact, ecological aesthetics can serve as the leading idea here, an idea whose meaning decides all that follows. Let us see how that is.

An ecological perspective considers environment as a system of interacting, interdependent participating factors. Environment then becomes a complex whole. Because of this interdependence, an ecosystem is not the sum of independent parts or organisms. Rather it is an unstable complex in precarious balance striving to sustain its coherence. I use the word "complex" rather than "whole" because the coherence of an ecosystem is the outcome of a dynamic process involving a multitude of organisms, objects, factors, and conditions. It may achieve balance but that is as a complex, never a unity. We can think of an ecosystem, then, as a context rather than a thing or an object.[1]

Considering environment from an ecological perspective transforms our understanding. It leads to discarding the common meaning of environment as surroundings in favor of re-envisioning it as an all-inclusive whole, embracing humans, when present, together with other living organisms and the physical conditions with which they live, including geographical features and climate. Because ecology envisions these as interconnected, it is necessary to think of the constituents of environment as all-inclusive and continuous. In this sense, environment is holistic: nothing outside, nothing apart. It is clear from the conception of ecology that there are ethical as well as aesthetic implications: An ecological aesthetics is inseparable from an ecological ethics.[2]

Humans, then, should be understood as participating parts of their context, understood and experienced from within. From the human standpoint, in relation to people's lives, environment becomes experience. Thinking ecologically, environment must be understood as *contextual* experience. Aesthetics fastens on the sensible aspects of that experience, and so environment, considered aesthetically, is perceptual. Thus the language of environmental aesthetics brings us to the idea of *experience*, for our understanding of experience is fundamental to everything we say about environment.

The Matrix of Experience

Experience has been an important idea in the history of philosophic thought, beginning with the pre-Socratics and extending to the very present. Generally considered synecdochically as sense experience, its transitoriness and ephemerality have troubled philosophers in their search for coherence, regularity, and stability. Thus a dialectic developed around change in favor of permanence, denigrating change as unworthy and destructive of human good in comparison with the ideal of absolute permanence, of things *sub specie aeternitatis*. Experience has a history that runs the length of philosophic time, yet, oddly enough, the history of experience remains to be written. In our present discussion, understanding experience is basic to understanding environment.

Starting with experience may seem a strange way to pursue a discussion of environment. Environment, of course, is usually thought of in a scientific or quasi-scientific, objective sense as *the* environment, a definable subject-matter, something to be studied by various branches of physical science, such as physical geography, climatology, and ecology. These identify environment objectively, as an object, but it is an object that becomes more personal when we ponder the effects of global warming, since all living creatures,

humans included, are affected by climate change and its consequences. These affect the habitability of various regions of the
earth's surface, they influence agriculture and food production, and
they force us to cope with the effects of changing temperature gradi-
ents and new and more extreme weather patterns. It is convenient
when considering global climate change to externalize environment,
to speak of *the* environment as if environment were something apart
from ourselves about which we are concerned.

But this, I think, offers only a partial and misleading understanding. It is partial because it fragments environment by circumscribing
and objectifying environmental experience, abstracting it into
separate parts, and treating problems as isolated events requiring
specific, local solutions. It is misleading because, by regarding these
abstractions as if they were real and objective, it takes a derivative
understanding as if it were the basic one. The lesson of ecology is
that, in relation to human needs and human uses, there is no environment out there apart from and distinct from us.[3] This leads us to
recognize that the fundamental meaning of environment is its
human meaning, more pointedly, its meaning in experience. And
environment is not experienced objectively but always here with us,
where we are. By beginning with experience, then, we begin with
ourselves, with the human world of which we are an integral part.
And when we come to speak of environment, then, it only falsifies
things to think that we can objectify environment and consider it
independently of human place, participation, and use.

The intent here has been to offer an orderly progression of the
leading ideas of environmental aesthetics. Oddly enough, what has
emerged is actually two orders. We began with environment, turned
next to discuss aesthetics, and followed with ecology. And we concluded by interpreting all within the matrix of experience. This is a
logical order: with environment as the broadest concept, which we
then combine with aesthetics, and arrive at a special sense of environmental aesthetics as ecological.

The Logical Order of Environmental Aesthetics

environment
    aesthetics
        environmental aesthetics
          ecological aesthetics

There is another order, however, one that is truer to experience. Indeed, when we cast our ideas in the language of experience, the order becomes inverted. For starting with experience, all experience is actually contextual and so can be understood ecologically. And as experience is primarily perceptual, it is always aesthetic. Finally, taken most broadly, we come to understand the idea of environment as ecological aesthetics. From this line of reasoning, then, the aesthetics of environment is ecological.

The Experiential Order of Environmental Aesthetics

ecology
    aesthetics as sensibility (perception)
      environment as ecological aesthetics

Our choice is the language of experience, beginning with a commitment to the largest perceptual context, one that the concept of ecology reflects most adequately. This, as we have seen, is not the biological setting alone nor the physical conditions of environment only. Since our reference is to experience, the human perceiver is central, and the condition that binds together all aspects of the context is perceptual experience. When central, such experience is thus aesthetic, and the aesthetic becomes the primary mode of experience. For these reasons, then, environmental aesthetics can be considered ecological aesthetics, and this implies a cultural ecology.

Environmental aesthetics thus translates ecology into experience; it is the human meaning of ecology. This is another way of saying that the concept of ecology is of an environment understood as a complex of interdependent objects and factors. The scope of such an environment is defined by the activity and intensity of such interdependence. As its force begins to fade and other factors become prominent, a different ecosystem begins to emerge. Such boundaries are rarely sharp, but distinctions are nonetheless possible as, for example, between an urban ecosystem and a suburban one or between the city and the countryside. Mountains and valleys are distinguishable even though their precise boundaries cannot be plotted.

The aesthetic experience of environment is thus the perceptual counterpart of ecology. Environmental aesthetics embodies the ecological meaning of environment. It has profound implications for environmental understanding and design and thus for ecological aesthetics.[4] Ecology in this sense requires constant reference to aesthetic experience as a guide and a criterion in environmental design. The work of many environmental artists is important in pointing up the experiential aspect of environments, that is, the awareness that environments do not consist of objects but of experiential relationships. Pioneer work is being done in integrating an aesthetic dimension in ecologically oriented environmental design, and such work is significant for both environmental and ecological aesthetics.[5]

Ecology and Culture

The interplay of humans within the natural world is experienced and understood in sharply different ways in Western and Eastern cultures. An observation such as this would seem to force us into broad and overpowering generalities, and this is invariably misleading when joined with a commitment to the diversity and particularity of experience. Still, recognizing the dangers should not prevent us from recognizing common patterns, despite differences that exist among the many writers and movements that reflect them. And these patterns are revealing.

A full historical analysis would undoubtedly display a richly varied tapestry describing the human world. And a nuanced commentary would reflect their intermingling and divergent strands. But at the same time, and for our purposes here, it is important that this variety and complexity not obscure the broad patterns that emerge. It is these that stand as a potent illustration of the cultural influences on experience. In its bold outline, the characteristic patterns by which experience is understood in Western cultures display a sense of separation of humans from the natural world. Eastern cultures, in contrast, reflect an understanding of the harmonious integration of nature and humans.

Both opposing views have ancient origins. The Western understanding is embodied in early texts that have had a powerful influence. The two most influential intellectual sources are works written down at approximately the same time, i.e. the fourth century B.C.E., and largely middle Eastern in origin. One justifies taking possession of the natural world for human purposes; the other denigrates sensory experience. The first is the Hebrew *Bible*, which establishes a justification for humans appropriating the creatures, objects, and resources of nature for their own interests and uses.[6]

The other is Platonic philosophy that ascribes to natural objects a lowly status in the order of things and posits a higher reality that is the refuge of truth and reality itself, an understanding found throughout Plato's dialogues and most famously in *The Republic*.[7] Whitehead's comment that Western civilization is a footnote to Plato testifies to its effect.

These influences have combined to shape the Western view of the natural environment. "Environment" is an idea we have devised to identify our material matrix, commonly defined as "surroundings" in Western languages, giving linguistic credibility to a way of thinking endemic in Western culture.[8] It reflects a tradition that we can trace to the religious beliefs and practices of ancient Greek Orphism that separated the physical world from what is distinctively human.[9] It was an understanding that appeared in various forms during the Golden Age of classic Greek philosophy and continued in religious and philosophical formulations to emerge in the Enlightenment in Descartes' dualistic objectification of the physical world as the full rational reconstruction of human experience.

This historico-cultural development of Western civilization led to understanding the world as an objective condition separate from and independent of humans, and it turned environment into an object for humans to control and manipulate. Thus we speak easily about the relation of person and environment, as if they were two distinct things that can be causally connected. Such a conception fits easily with the growth of early modern science and the technological revolution it generated. This was a development that quickly altered the human environment and led, among much else, to the environment-transforming practices that have reached a crisis level in our time.

In their rapid industrialization, Eastern countries—such as China, Japan, and India—have compressed Western development into a few short generations, resulting in many of the same environmental problems that the West is confronting. At the same time, the cultural historical influences in Eastern cultures provide the basis for a very different conception of environment that is struggling to assert itself against short-term economic and political interests. Common to the many different strains of Daoism is an understanding grounded in the view of living in harmony with nature. Eastern culture here offers a remarkable parallel with recent Western ecological thought, for it is a way of thinking that we can describe as ecological in character. Of course, the first is a religio-cultural understanding and the other a scientific one. But what is relevant here is not their differing sources but their similar understanding. While originating as a biological theory, ecology offers a compelling theoretical framework that has not only shown its value in the social sciences but has special relevance for the environmental sciences and for environmental philosophy.

What ecology offers is an understanding of environment as an integral whole. Environment thus does not consist of a relation between humans and their environment as distinct and separate entities. Environment rather *includes* the human as an interdependent and engaged constituent. One of the most important lessons we can draw from ecology is that there is no environment apart from and distinct from humans.[10] Humans and environment need to be understood as interdependent constituents of a complex whole that has identifiable contributing factors but not separate parts. This is a way of thinking about the world, and it may help explain the attraction of ecological aesthetics for Chinese environmental aestheticians.[11]

It is interesting to consider whether this cultural matrix is simply an alternative world view. That would imply a cultural relativism in which the differences are essentially arbitrary. However, there are more or less accurate ways of representing environment, and we can claim that an ecological model better reflects our present knowledge of environment, whether understood in a physicalistic, scientific sense, in an experiential one, or philosophically. This does not imply an "objective," absolute truth but rather a less assumptive understanding that shares the compelling, evidentiary claims of science. The conception of environment as ecological affirms its meaning as a human meaning, its meaning as experienced. As experienced, environment does not stand apart but is always related to humans, to the human world of interest, activity, and use. That is the human meaning of ecology.

On the subject of experience, we encounter a great body of thought. From the physical and social sciences to the literary arts and philosophy, one can consider human experience the most inclusive subject of inquiry. This discussion of environmental aesthetics offers but an endnote to that research. Perhaps, rather than an endnote, it is more of a searchlight that may be directed over the range of scientific and scholarly commentary, since it centers on understanding that experience on which all other inquiry rests.

At the risk of affirming the obvious, it will be useful to call attention to some characteristics of experience that are easily overlooked.

The categories into which we pour the molten intangibilities of experience are so engrained in habitual thinking that we are likely to assume them as ontological rather than customary: categories such as emotions, sensations, thoughts, memories, ideas, feelings, imagination, consciousness, cognition, perception, and more. The challenge is how to make the ephemeral tangible, and these categories have long served as convenient receptacles. But like the proverbial emperor's new clothes, though we persist in thinking we see those categories as something (i.e., as ontological), there is nothing there. Moreover, taken alone, whatever meaning content such categories have is informed and constrained by the habits of so-called "common sense," heavily clouded by the multitude of influences that give them conceptual shape and content. Think of the many meanings given to "perception" and of the severely limited vocabulary with which we identify emotions, as well as the metaphors with which we attempt to grasp consciousness, from James's "stream" to Locke's atomistic theory of substance and his corpuscular theory of mind.

Thus there are multiple "overlays" through which we discern and interpret experience. One obvious overlay is cultural, expressed through our natal language, traditional practices, prevalent beliefs, and systems of belief, all infused with regional geographical and climatological conditions as their context of reference. To this cultural overlay must be added a historical one. Our understanding is subtly and not so subtly influenced by our historical circumstances: the notable events and conditions of the time, in addition to their influence on the cultural climate. We can identify still other overlays of differing scope, such as professional, avocational, social, and educational, along with the more transitory influences of taste, style, fads, and fashionable ideologies. All of these, moreover, are themselves categories through which we isolate and identify dimensions and perspectives of experience. These observations on the multiple matrices of experience are not intended to obfuscate our attempts at illuminating it. Rather they begin to make more explicit the multidimensional landscape of experience and lead us to recognize the conditions under which we attempt to grasp the human world.

What, one might ask, do these general comments have to do with the aesthetics of environment and how we think and talk about it? In one respect, merely to ask the question is to answer it, for environment is a fundamental category of experience through which we organize our understanding and identify the issues. It is important, however, to make these observations more definite by identifying basic cultural differences in understanding environment, recognizing all the while that large trends mask many variations. These differences, deeply historical and cultural, characterize differing relations of nature and humans that are fundamental in Western and Eastern thought.

Whether a resolution of this divergence is possible is a difficult question. The answer will not lie in a choice between simple alternatives but requires determinations that are circumstantial and may be complex. Satisfactory resolutions must be decided in relation to the specific context and to the particular points of balance between the options that are available. These will vary with scientific, poetic, and political environments and will reflect the order of values chosen, itself a cultural determination. Is it possible to attain equipoise between the technological capabilities of Western cultures and the cosmic proportionality of the Eastern? The answer to this rests with whether the social and political development of human civilization has attained the capacity for such a resolution.

Conclusion

This rich array of ideas does not allow for a simple summary. We have tried to reshape the issues so that the relationships between conceptual understanding (ecological aesthetics) and perceptual experience (environmental aesthetics) become clearer. It is important to realize that the former must be seen in the light of the latter. When we recognize that ideas originate in perception and should be translated back into experience, we can then proceed to reshape our world in ways that better meet our interests and fulfill our needs. The possibilities are there, often hidden in a miasma of false constructions and misty assumptions. The question remains whether we will be able to find our way through them clearly enough to survive and prosper.

CHAPTER

5

Toward an Aesthetics of Respect

Kant's Contribution to Environmental Aesthetics

Denis Dumas

Kantian aesthetics represents the culmination of eighteenth-century nature aesthetics. I will attempt to show that it can be fruitfully deployed in the field of contemporary environmental ethics. First, I will present the general context of this meditation, which is an environmental philosophy founded on humanist or post-metaphysical anthropocentrism. Next, I will analyze the concept of respect in Kant's ethics. Finally, I will show that beginning from Kant's aesthetics, it is possible to construct a concept of respect for the aesthetic value of nature.

Ethics Based on Post-metaphysical Anthropocentrism

A distinction should be made between two types of anthropocentrism, which I call *classical anthropocentrism* and *humanist*, or *post-metaphysical anthropocentrism*, respectively. The essential components of classical anthropocentrism confirm the *ontological primacy* of humanity over the rest of the natural world by the application of religious or metaphysical worldviews.[1] On this basis, one deduces the *ethical primacy* of human beings over other beings. In other words, only human beings have moral and legal standing due to their objective superiority in the natural and cosmological order. In this context, the criticism directed by Lynn White toward the Judeo-Christian foundations of western society, for example, is worth recalling.

Humanist (or post-metaphysical) anthropocentrism, on the other hand, rejects the ontological primacy of humanity over all other

73

natural beings. Thus it is perfectly compatible with the ecological tenets we have developed over the past century in which humanity is seen as part of the natural world and understood in the context of our constant interaction and interdependence with nature. This relation is organized along the lines of a symbiotic model, not a parasitic one.

Humanistic anthropocentrism maintains the ethical primacy of humanity in the form of the person's moral and legal status based on the freedom which, at least partially, conditions human agency. In other words, only human beings qualify as ends-in-themselves or, in what amounts to the same thing, possess an intrinsic value, which deserves respect in and of itself. Though unable to justify it here for reasons of scope, in what follows I will adopt this version of anthropocentrism as my own. Suffice it here to indicate that non-anthropocentrism is untenable on the theoretical level and counter-productive on practical grounds.

In my view, most philosophers opt for an extensionist environmental ethic because their approach to the ontological decentring of the human being is not sufficiently nuanced. On the basis of this descriptive ontological premise, with which I am in agreement, they draw the normative conclusion that the human being should hold no ethical priority with respect to other natural beings. But this conclusion does not follow. It rests on an additional, intermediary normative principle, namely the a priori attribution of intrinsic value to certain nonhuman entities. The question of grounding or locating such value, which has motivated countless debates during the last thirty years, underlines the problem of the theoretical justification of ethical extensionism.

We find a perfect example of this line of reasoning in the keystone text by Arne Naess titled "The Shallow and the Deep, Long-Range Ecology Movement."[2] The first principle of deep ecology is presented as follows: "Rejection of the man-in-environment image in favour of *the relational, total-field image.*" Here we can clearly see the descriptive premise corresponding to what I have called the ontological decentring of the human being. From this derives the second principle: "*Biospherical egalitarianism*—in principle" and further on: "*the equal right to live and blossom,*" in which is affirmed the ethical decentring of the human being, to the advantage of extensionism. Naess justified this second principle by recourse to self-evidence ("an intuitively clear and obvious value axiom"); extensionist philosophers have since attempted to improve upon this justification without having produced satisfactory results. I will add one final, brief remark on this subject: To the extent that extensionism is untenable in theory, it is also counterproductive on practical grounds, since it is impossible to seriously apply the principle of biospherical egalitarianism. It is necessary to constantly restrict its scope, for reasons that are admittedly humanistic. Naess himself appeared to be aware of this, as evidenced by his qualification: "in principle." Rather than adopt an extensionist ethic which must be applied so conservatively in practice, it seems preferable to me to take as our point of departure a humanist ethic and to push its application as far as possible to ensure sustainable development, protection and preservation of natural environments, and, finally, the survival of future generations.

Now, we must ask ourselves whether an environmental ethic follows from humanistic anthropocentrism. In fact, the affirmation of human ethical primacy entails that we recognize the threat of negative effects on the environment as well as an implied moral obligation to ensure the maintenance of favorable conditions for the survival of humanity's future generations. As a result, post-metaphysical anthropocentrism necessarily implies the obligation to organize the long-term survival of humankind under progressive conditions based on solidarity as well as principles of both international and intergenerational justice. This approach aptly justifies what I will call the *imperative of prudence*, which is advanced not only to diminish the immediate effects of natural resource exploitation but also to maintain, insofar as possible, ecosystem integrity, biodiversity, and genetic heritage. Humanism in this sense is practically compatible with certain legitimate claims of non-anthropocentrism while extending considerably beyond what Naess refers to as the principles of Shallow Ecology.[3]

My argument to this point has briefly suggested that humanism allows us to derive an environmental ethics which, without directly identifying a moral value in specific terms of individual natural beings or systems, nevertheless provides an injunction for their protection by virtue of the long-term interests of humanity. However, the imperative of prudence is inadequate in one significant respect: As strong as the arguments for its development are, they remain essentially pragmatic. In fact, if we reject an ethical extension by which non-anthropocentrism establishes a more reciprocal relationship between nature and humankind, we will be forced to use pragmatic arguments to justify the necessity of environmental protection.

Now, one of the undeniable strengths of non-anthropocentrism is its ability to elicit moral respect for nature and, at times, a comparable spiritual dimension of experience which inspires the expression of humility and awe in the face of the natural world. Humanism does not rely on moral reciprocity with nature, raised to the level of a subject or entity endowed with intrinsic dignity. Instead, it can use our aesthetic experience of the world to enhance the pragmatic argument for a recognition of the value of nature: An *aesthetic of respect* can thereby round out a humanist environmental ethics.

It is in this spirit that I will reconstruct the Kantian concept of respect. It is necessary to begin in the ethical sphere, where the concept has its source, in order to show that an aesthetic of respect can be constructed beginning from Kant's philosophy.

The Concept of Respect in Kant's Ethics

Following the critique of metaphysics elaborated in the *Critique of Pure Reason*, Kant grounds his ethics in the freedom of the will. The latter is defined as the faculty of acting in accordance with principles, which is to say in accordance with the representation of laws. The sole determining ground of the free will is the moral law.[4] But human beings are not purely rational; they are also sensible beings. Thus they have equal need of incentives (*Triebfeder*) both logically posterior to the moral law and capable of generating interest in conforming to moral duty. This interest is itself an incentive of the will; it makes possible the transition between reason and experience. The incentive which pushes us to want to act morally is the *feeling of respect* (*Achtung*) that we show when faced with the moral law.[5]

The moral law therefore excites in us a feeling, that of respect, by virtue of which we have an interest in realizing our moral duty in experience. In the *Groundwork of the Metaphysics of Morals*, despite the well-known differences between the latter and the *Critique of Practical Reason*, Kant formulates the same thesis: Respect is defined as a feeling produced by reason itself, or as the immediate effect of the moral law on the subject, and morality *interests* us because we manifest a *satisfaction* (*Wohlgefallen*) at the accomplishment of moral duty.[6] Respect for the moral law is also, as Kant says in both texts, the representation of a value at odds with self-love in its empirical dimension.

Here we see emerge a first, highly important characteristic of the Kantian concept of respect: Strictly speaking, it is only the *moral law* which can be the object of respect, and never human beings.[7] But Kant makes an *extended usage* of this concept, which permits him to claim that morality compels us to respect other humans; *through them, it is the moral law that we are respecting.*[8] For precisely this reason, it is humans and humans alone which both can and should be made the objects of this "extended respect":

> *Respect* is always directed only to persons, never to things. The latter can awaken in us *inclination* and even *love* if they are animals (e.g., horses, dogs, and so forth), or also *fear*, like the sea, a volcano, a beast of prey, but never *respect*. Something that comes nearer to this feeling is *admiration*, and this as an affect, amazement, can be directed to things also, for example, lofty mountains, the magnitude, number, and distance of the heavenly bodies, the strength and swiftness of many animals, and so forth. But none of this is respect. A human being can also be an object of my love, fear, or admiration even to amazement and yet not be an object of respect.[9]

It is therefore comprehensible why respect for the human other is a moral commandment for Kant. We see this very well from that formulation of the categorical imperative which, without explicitly invoking the concept of respect for the other, commands nonetheless a respect for the dignity of humans, which are the sole exemplars of an end in itself (*Zweck an sich*) in nature: "*So act that you use humanity, whether in your own person or in the person of any other, always at the same time as an end, never merely as a means.*"[10]

In *Metaphysical First Principles of the Doctrine of Virtue*, which constitutes a part of the *Metaphysics of Morals*, Kant explicates his conception of the moral duty of respect. This is an aspect of his theory that I will simply mention, since it adds nothing essentially new to what I've explained so far. Respect toward oneself as well as respect toward the other (which cannot be conceived, strictly speaking, as a duty) are discussed and distinguished from other forms of the relation to self and other.[11]

The Aesthetic Experience

Let us now consider Kant's aesthetics and the *Critique of the Power of Judgment*.[12] Here we will examine another extension of the concept of respect—one which will prove particularly interesting for our purposes. I will limit my analysis to two aspects which seem to me to be the most important: namely, the near total absence of the concept of respect in the experience of the beautiful and, subsequently, its appearance in the experience of the sublime.[13]

Kant's *Critique of the Power of Judgment* is devoted to the study of the finality of nature and, in particular, to the formal finality we encounter in the exercise of reflective aesthetic judgment, which we subordinate to our experience of beauty and the sublime.[14] Reflective judgment, in contrast to determinate judgment, does not concern knowledge of the objective world. The judgment of taste (in, for example, the statement "This rose is beautiful") does not describe properties of things. It is simply subjective. In contrast to other kinds of states generated by sense experience, like states of pleasure, we realize our experience of beauty and the sublime as *both subjective and universal*.[15] This means that it evokes in us the desire to communicate our opinion to others because we are certain that they would be able to share it with us, even if there are no criteria or universal concepts that justify these judgments. This is why Kant applies the term "formal finality" or "finality without end" to that which produces the feeling of aesthetic satisfaction in us. It remains impossible to demonstrate judgments of this kind objectively. As an a priori principle, the finality of nature resides within us and not within the objective natural world. It is demonstrated on the basis of our feelings of pleasure or displeasure elicited by the diversity of experiences we create on the basis of the convergence of our faculties; for example, imagination and understanding in the case of beauty, or imagination and reason in the case of the sublime.

Natural Beauty. I will now sum up what is at stake, for our purposes, in the "Analytic of the Beautiful": The concept of respect is totally absent from it, which signifies that the satisfaction which manifests itself in the experience of natural beauty is accompanied by a positive pleasure. The latter is altogether different from the negative feeling called respect, by virtue of which I demonstrate in experience the superiority of reason over my sensible inclinations.

There exists nonetheless a link of primary importance between the aesthetic experience of beauty and Kant's ethics: We find it in the famous declaration of §59 according to which beauty is a symbol of morality.[16] Let us remark once more that for Kant, the stakes are to explain how concepts may be presented in experience, and it is under the title of hypotyposis that he classifies the different possibilities of this sensible presentation. The doctrine of schematism illustrates, in theoretical philosophy, the way in which pure concepts of the understanding can serve the determining power of judgment in its work of subsuming the particular under the universal. By analogy with the schematic procedure permitting the categories to apply to empirical cases, the theory of symbolism in the third *Critique* accounts for the link between concepts of reason and sensible intuition: Symbols contain an indirect presentation of the concept. Put differently, our experience of natural beauty and the satisfaction it procures us reveal indirectly the moral calling of the rational beings that we are.

As I have already mentioned, neither the "Analytic of the Beautiful" nor the theory of symbolism make room for the concept of respect. We must therefore conclude that for Kant, in the absence of an essential link between our experience of beauty and our moral calling, *beautiful objects and beautiful natural scenes do not evoke in us the feeling of respect*. I will return (at the end of the section "An Aesthetic Respect for Nature?") to this difficulty which Kant's theory presents to the concept of an aesthetics of respect.

Sublime and Subreption. Let us now turn to the experience of the sublime, where things are presented differently. This experience, according to Kant, puts the imagination and reason into relation via the reflecting power of judgment. Concepts of reason are presented indirectly in sensible experience: This presentation takes the form of the sublime feeling, which is a negative pleasure felt in face of the infinitely large (the mathematical sublime) or the terrifying power of nature (the dynamical sublime).[17]

The concept of respect appears in the analysis of the mathematical sublime. It is here a matter of an experience through which we feel displeasure when faced with the infinitely large—for example, a natural scene, which seems to extend to infinity. The displeasure stems from the fact that the imagination fails to present, in experience, the idea of infinity forged by reason. This displeasure produces, in turn, a second-order negative pleasure: We are, in a manner of speaking, brought back to ourselves, which is to say the superiority of our reason and our moral vocation. In contemplating nature, the human being experiences the sublime feeling, which reveals her to herself as a moral being. It is at this moment that a feeling of *respect* becomes manifest:

> The feeling of inadequacy of our capacity for the attainment of an idea *that is a law for us is respect.* . . . But our imagination, even in its greatest effort with regard to the comprehension of a given object in a whole of intuition (hence for the presentation of the idea of reason) that is demanded of it, demonstrates its limits and inadequacy, but at the same time its vocation, which we show to an object in nature through a certain subreption (substitution of a respect for the object instead of for the idea of humanity in our subject), which as it were makes intuitable the superiority of the rational vocation of our cognitive faculty over the greatest faculty of sensibility.[18]

The sublime feeling thereby elicits from us a respect for ourselves *qua* rational beings. This is exactly the same result that we noted earlier. Kantian ethics explains how a respect for the human being is possible by extension, beginning from its sole object, which is the moral law. What is more, the existence of an extension to the second degree is clear in the citation that we have just read: In effect, the phenomenon of subreption is such that *we project onto the natural object the respect that we owe to ourselves.*

An Aesthetic Respect for Nature?

We must now ask whether, for Kant, we have a duty to respect nature.

Strictly speaking, this is not possible from the moral point of view, for reasons we have already seen and which rest on the ethical primacy of the human being *qua* reasonable being. The human is the only being which constitutes an end in itself or—what amounts to the same thing—possesses an intrinsic value.

This said, a respect for nature stemming from its aesthetic value is explicitly analyzed by Kant (though he mentions it but once in the entire *Critique of the Power of Judgment*): By *subreption*, we respect the infinite grandeur of the natural scene which unfolds before us.

On the other hand, even if no aesthetic respect flows directly from the experience of natural beauty, Kant adds that *we can have an interest in that of beauty which exists in nature* in general. Above and beyond the disinterested character of the judgment of taste applied to the beauty of singular objects, the subject who loves the existence of beauty in the natural world displays, indirectly, a moral preoccupation or, at the very least, a predisposition to morality (§42):

> But since it also interests reason that the ideas (for which it produces an immediate interest in the moral feeling) also have objective reality, i.e., that nature should at least show some trace or give a sign that it contains in itself some sort of ground for assuming a lawful correspondence of its products with our satisfaction that is independent of all interest (which we recognize *a priori* as a law valid for everyone, without being able to ground this on proofs), reason must take an interest in every manifestation in nature of a correspondence similar to this; consequently the mind cannot reflect on the beauty of *nature* without finding itself at the same time to be interested in it. Because of this affinity, however, this interest is moral, and he who takes such an interest in the beautiful in nature can do so only insofar as he has already firmly established his interest in the morally good. We thus have cause at least to suspect a predisposition to a good moral disposition in one who is immediately interested in the beauty of nature.[19]

I will mention in passing that it is otherwise with artistic beauty, given Kant's privileging of natural over artistic beauty. But we can retain from these observations the fact that the disinterested experience of natural beauty, for Kant, does not culminate in a purely aestheticizing attitude, detached from all practice toward the human being, but also the world itself.

Let us return now to the general question of whether, for Kant, it is possible to respect nature. Kantian thought bases itself clearly upon an anthropocentric conception of our relationship to nature: Human beings occupy a privileged position. They are the only beings capable of being *ends in themselves*, as no other natural object can ever attain the status of a moral subject. Any attempt to extend the ethical domain to other natural beings would be incompatible with this thought.

Nonetheless, it seems to me that starting from Kant, a sort of *aesthetic respect for nature* can be plausibly envisioned. We could discuss the well-established justification for limiting this feeling to the experience of the mathematical sublime, but I cannot address this here. What is above all important is that I signal this possibility that seems to me to be promising and starting from which we could, beyond a Kantian orthodoxy that nothing imposes on us, sketch the contours of an *anthropocentric theory of our relation to nature capable of including a relation of respect towards its aesthetic value*.

Insofar as it avoids the theoretical and practical pitfalls of a philosophy recommending direct ethical respect for nature, we can consider *respect for the aesthetic value of natural environments* to be a more promising avenue.

Other passages pulled from Kant's texts support the idea that I have attempted to explicate here. I will cite two. First, Kant affirms in §67 the *Critique of the Power of Judgment*:

> We may consider it as a favor that nature has done for us that in addition to usefulness it has so richly distributed beauty and charms, and we can love it on that account, just as we regard it with respect because of its immeasurability, and we can feel ourselves to be ennobled in this contemplation—just as if nature had erected and decorated its magnificent stage precisely with this intention.[20]

It is interesting to note here that Kant mentions respect for nature in general rather than for particular natural objects, as appeared to be the case in his analysis of the sublime. Moreover, he associates this respect with the feeling of love for nature and thereby joins it to common sense. A highly interesting passage from the *Metaphysics of Morals* (§17) suggests as much:

> A propensity to wanton destruction of what is *beautiful* in inanimate nature (*spiritus destructionis*) is opposed to a human being's duty to himself; for it weakens or uproots that feeling in him which, though not of itself moral, is still a disposition of sensibility that greatly promotes morality or at least prepares the way for it: the disposition, namely, to love something (e.g., beautiful crystal formations, the indescribable beauty of plants) even apart from any intention to use it.[21]

We can see from this last text that Kant considers the natural object to command love by virtue of its aesthetic value, and independently of its instrumental value. Saying as much means that the aesthetic value of the object imposes upon us an indirect duty with respect to it, *as though it possessed an intrinsic value.*

In sum, we find elements in Kant which render plausible the notion of an aesthetic respect for nature: the disinterested judgment of taste vis-à-vis natural beauty, beauty as a symbol of morality, the substitution of respect for the natural object by respect for humanity (subreption), interest in the existence of natural beauty, love of beautiful nature, and the moral duty not to destroy such beauty. [22]

As mentioned previously, the following problem remains to be considered: If we wish to draw upon Kantian philosophy to conceptualize the link between aesthetics and an anthropocentric environmental ethic, like I am doing here, it seems that the concept of respect applies solely to the experience of the sublime, and not to that of the beautiful. Is not the concept of an *aesthetics of respect* therefore too narrow? If we stick within strictly Kantian parameters, we must answer in the affirmative. Thus the idea of thinking a respect for the aesthetic value of the (natural and built) environment implies the necessity of enlarging the scope of the concept of respect, such that it can also apply to our experience of beauty. Such a transformation can be justified if we consider the broad sense of the concept of respect, being that of an incentive—which is to say, a sentiment that pushes us to act morally. Recall that in the strict sense there is respect for the moral law alone—but that indirectly, the human being can respect the law in respecting herself. Further, the concept of subreption in the experience of the sublime permitted us to suppose that respect for the human being, for her part, can likewise be experienced indirectly via respect for nature and sublime human constructions. This is precisely what I had in mind earlier when speaking of an extension, to the second degree, of respect. The integration of beauty into the aesthetics of respect becomes plausible if we take into account the numerous links, described earlier, which unite the sentiment of the beautiful and of morality, in the sense of an indirect self-respect via the interest we have in natural beauty and the duty not to destroy it—both of which are translatable into our moral obligation to respect the beauty of environments. As underlined at the outset, this aesthetic of respect rounds out a humanist environmental ethic which enjoins us to protect the environment so as to ensure the existence of future generations. It might be objected here that love of nature, rather than respect for its aesthetic value, constitutes a more appropriate foundation for linking aesthetics to ethics. It seems to me, nonetheless, that respect

should be privileged; it possesses a greater force than love, norma-
tively speaking.

A Critical Look at Kantian Aesthetics

The aesthetics of respect could see its relevance expanded considerably if we applied it not only to natural environments but also to
environments transformed or entirely constructed by humans.[23]
This would imply going beyond the framework of Kantian thought.
This perspective is promising because it permits recognition of the
aesthetic value of buildings, monuments, and urban environments,
deducing from these a duty of respect. As in the case of aesthetic
respect for nature, the same essential idea is affirmed: In respecting
the environment, the human being respects herself.

Another limitation inherent to Kantian theory must be sur-
mounted. I refer here to the picturesque paradigm typical of the
nature aesthetics elaborated in the eighteenth century. The works of
Arnold Berleant and his model of the aesthetics of engagement could
help to surmount this limit of Kantian aesthetics.[24] The non-
orthodox reading of Kant that I have presented here could be compatible with Berleant's idea of engagement, on the condition that it
conserves the concept of disinterestedness, which is problematic for
him. On this subject, I will offer the following three remarks.

First, it is perfectly possible to adapt the Kantian paradigm to
"engaged" aesthetic experience (i.e., the active and multisensorial
experience of a subject who is part of the environment). The experience of beauty is quite compatible here, whether we are concerned
with natural or urban environments. As for the experience of the
sublime, types of experiences presupposing menacing natural environments do not lend themselves to the subject's engagement. This
said, an element of the sublime experience is compatible with active
engagement, as much in natural as in urban contexts.

Second, the disinterested character of the experience of beauty and
the sublime does not necessarily imply that these latter be restricted
to the picturesque paradigm. Engagement, in my view, can be quite
compatible with disinterestedness—the latter being taken in the
sense of a non-instrumental and purely aesthetic rapport with the
environment (be it natural or urban). Consequently, it is not necessary to eliminate disinterestedness from aesthetic theory and it is
even preferable to keep it, insofar as it captures an essential component of aesthetic experience. Moreover, the idea of disinterestedness

should not cause us to lose sight of the fact that there is, for Kant, an interest of the second order toward the existence of natural beauty. Aesthetic disinterestedness should not be confused with a neutral attitude (i.e. indifference to nature).[25]

Third, the picturesque paradigm should be retained because it, too, reflects an essential dimension of our experience; the best approach would consist in considering it to be one of the possibilities of aesthetic appreciation, while giving engaged experience its due.

The conception that I present here proposes to put aesthetic experience at the service of ethics. It is not, however, a matter of instrumentalizing aesthetics and depriving it of its autonomy but of underscoring the value of *one of its dimensions*. It is necessary, in my view, that the discipline of environmental aesthetics continue to study for itself our aesthetic relationships to various environments, since this province of human experience possesses a distinct value which is irreducible to that of ethics. This is what Kant wanted to emphasize by insisting on the disinterested character of judgments of taste.[26] I therefore argue in favor of the relative autonomy of environmental ethics and aesthetics; neither could found nor be subordinated to the other.[27] This autonomy is nonetheless relative because ethics and aesthetics should be mutually enriching. The concept of cross-fertilization proposed by Emily Brady seems to me to express this relationship quite well.[28]

Conclusion

I have attempted to show that an environmental philosophy that is both anthropocentric and humanist or post-metaphysical needs to include: (1) an ethics founded upon our moral obligations toward future generations, which permits formulation of the pragmatic imperative of prudence; and (2) an aesthetics of respect for the aesthetic value of natural and fabricated environments.

This conception presents the advantage of escaping certain theoretical and practical problems posed by non-anthropocentrism. It equally permits us, as it seems to me, to derive normative results placing humans under the obligation to protect as far as possible the environment as though it possessed an intrinsic value.[29]

I will conclude by presenting a last argument in favor of the integration of aesthetic respect and environmental ethics. It is that my thesis fits easily with the sometimes confusing yet often insightful perceptions of common sense. In fact, the idea of establishing an essential link between self-respect, respect for the environment, and respect for those who will follow us has, in my view, an incontestable intuitive force of conviction. This immediacy is often seen in the tenacity with which groups demonstrate for the protection or improvement of their natural and urban environments in the interests not only of their practical needs but also of their aesthetic values.[30]

CHAPTER

6

From Theoretical to Applied Environmental Aesthetics

Academic Aesthetics Meets Real-World Demands

Yrjö Sepänmaa

Introduction

At the XXII World Congress of Philosophy in Seoul (August 5, 2008), Professor Ken-ichi Sasaki recalled our first meeting in Nottingham in 1988. He said that he thought at that time, twenty years ago, environmental aesthetics was a strange field, but now he regarded it as being in vogue, and important. In his concluding speech at the 15th International Congress of Aesthetics in Tokyo in 2001, Sasaki, the president of the event, raised the environment as one of the points of emphasis in aesthetics and one of its most promising lines of development.[1]

The authority of environmental aesthetics has continued to grow and its visibility has increased. In less than half a century, the field has established its position in the totality of aesthetics. This can be seen from anthologies, publishers' lists of new titles, congress programmes, university teaching and research programmes—and even from the fact that my own academic position is that of a professor of environmental aesthetics. New researchers have entered the field, some of whom have already created a prominent career (Emily Brady, Glenn Parsons); those who have envisaged it and worked in it for a long time are still active (Arnold Berleant, Allen Carlson, Holmes Rolston III, Yuriko Saito, Barbara Sandrisser); and work in this area has increased—especially in Asia (China, Korea, and Japan).

The spread of interest and ideas outside academic circles is also noteworthy. Questions of aesthetic and other values relating to the environment have become part of cultural discourse—and from there the term itself has moved to general use. A lively cultural discourse on environmental values, in which researchers, too, participate, has arisen alongside the academic tradition. In Europe, the discussion has been initiated particularly by the Green movement.

Spreading Rings

I regard the development of environmental aesthetics that has led to its present form as having begun in the 1960s; the point of departure was Ronald W. Hepburn's defining article "Contemporary Aesthetics and the Neglect of Natural Beauty."[2] The return from art philosophy to the philosophy of beauty proclaimed by Hepburn, and from there to the consideration of nature and its beauty, was the start and manifesto of a modern ecologically weighted environmental aesthetics that maintained links to cultural and environmental sciences. It did not signify a rejection of art philosophy but rather a reconquest by new means of a ceded subarea.

The natural core area and growth base of research into environmental aesthetics is nature in a natural state and the relation of humankind to it. This has been important for the understanding of the bases of and justification for nature protection. Expansion began from wild nature—at a stage when this was vanishing. The arts that use and adapt the environment form a common ground with the philosophy of art. This expansion has meant seeing in the same frame of reference such subjects of art philosophy as building art, garden and park art, town art, and, of course, present-day environmental art. Environmental aesthetics gathered these subjects and the cultural environment outside art into a single entity. A common feature of these fields is that our real world is the object of artistic design, the material of works of art, and the location of their realization.

The specific quality and richness of the cultural environment is nowadays a subject of general interest; 2010 was the year of a cultural environment campaign in Finland, which included many events with the theme *Everyone's Own Environment*. Recognition and value will now be given to the fact that people make a space for living, as well as the objects in it—everything that is not waiting ready in nature. Therefore justification, or at least understanding, will be given to the achievements of culture, even though the implementation may have taken place at the expense of a state of nature or a previous cultural environment. Environmental culture is the human footprint in nature.

Thus, from the consideration of a state of nature—without forgetting wild nature—we have progressed to cultural environments and towns, from there to interior spaces, from there to virtual environments and a parallel world (*Second Life*), and finally to such areas of social life (the environment) as human relations and the work atmosphere. One can wonder how much further it is sensible, or even possible, to expand the field; of course, the points of emphasis change.

Glenn Parsons, who recently published the systematic general presentation *Aesthetics and Nature*, sees the appearance of overall presentations and anthologies as a sign of the field maturing.[3] With the future in mind, particular research programmes have been prepared and implemented. Thus, a move has been made toward more detailed, specific studies while nevertheless retaining a philosophical approach. At the same time, the links to environmental aesthetics as a whole and to the field of aesthetics more generally must be retained.

The increase in academic interest is accompanied by an awareness of independent aesthetic thought that is expressed in practice. Such hidden aesthetics are detected and recognized. Practical and everyday aesthetics are put on display and regarded seriously; this has mainly been an area of sociological studies of taste. Interaction is being achieved between the investigative academic and the practical everyday aspects. The demand of strict philosophicality is loosened when others besides a few academic professionals—representatives of other scientific fields, specialists in environmental fields, and ordinary people—discuss aesthetics.

Three Traditions—and a Fourth, Environmental Aesthetics

The three traditions of academic aesthetics—the philosophy of art, the philosophy of beauty, and metacriticism—are all alive today, and each one incorporates environmental aesthetics. Together with its common areas and links, the field forms its own totality. It no longer operates in the margins of others but has its own identity.

The philosophy of beauty has returned to its position precisely through the means of environmental culture, extending to all aesthetic culture. Of course, the traditional emphasis on beauty as harmony is still strong in terms of relating to the environment, though contemporary art has expanded and reinterpreted aesthetic values. Indeed, it remains an open question as to what anti-art and negative aesthetic values, along with all that is associated with them, signify for environmental attitudes. A camp-spirited interest in kitsch inspired by Susan Sontag as well as interest in negative aesthetic values is expanding in the direction of industrial land-scapes, for example. The art critic Alexandra Koroxenidis writes about the second biennial in Athens (summer 2009), which had the theme of *Heaven*: "[I]n the end visitors leave wondering why beauty, in the more classical sense, is taboo for contemporary art. Does art always have to appear so alternative or obscure?"[4]

I will take another example, Lars von Trier's film *Antichrist* (2009), which is a combination of images that are astoundingly beau-tiful on the surface and the suffering and brutality of people and animals toward each other—deer, wolves, ravens.[5] The film's milieu contrasts sharply with the more pleasant nature documentaries of television, such as *Vast Nature*, though that, too, like other nature programs, has become more action-packed and violent.

The criticized emphasis on negative aesthetic values—which appears, for example, in present-day photography and films—may give the management of the environment an undesirable model, as then a contradiction easily arises with ethical and ecological values.

From Theory to Practice

Our ability to affect the environment has increased—but it has produced more problems than it has solved. This has become a challenge to aesthetics, too; since, of course, even damaged envi-ronment can be a subject for study. Research seeking practical applications of aesthetics has increasingly emerged from theoreti-cal studies.[6] This new kind of approach is typified by concreteness: the use of examples and case studies. The landscape effects of wind farms, noise barriers, and power lines are considered on a general and individual level. The same transition toward applicability found in ethics is taking place in aesthetics, though somewhat more slowly. Applied ethics functions as a pioneer and example for applied aesthetics. The aim is to link theory with practice, and the movement is two-way, so that practice also affects and tests theory.

However, according to its philosophical nature, aesthetics deals with *general* questions of depiction, interpretation, and evaluation—how does one move from them to individual cases while retaining philosophicality? How far is specialization in the name of aesthetics possible? Here we have an internal boundary-drawing problem in applied aesthetics. Of course, in terms of actual matters it is of no importance within the frame of reference of which field one acts; in practice the differences arise from differences in the intellectual and school-of-thought background and frame of reference of those involved.

The recognition of the activities and contribution of environmental aesthetics increases the demand for research, teaching, and consultation, creating very concrete expectations. While this is flattering, it is also necessary to resist the pressure when necessary. It is important for both the client and the implementer to know what is appropriate and reasonable to expect from aesthetics. Aesthetics by itself cannot answer questions requiring multidisciplinary competence and expertise. It also does not provide absolute rules of beauty of a kind that could be programmed into computer-aided design programs. While the limits of a style can be stated and deviation from the style prevented, no single style (e.g., functionalism) has a monopoly.

A Profession Based in Competence

Theoretical research creates a foundation. Science for science's sake is needed, but so is science for practice, and applied philosophy is needed as an extension of theoretical philosophy. There is a social opportunity for the skills and competence of the aesthetician, and responding to it means a demand and work for a representative of the field. The task of academic research and teaching is—besides ensuring its own continuation—to train experts for the needs of working life. Thus, it is naturally linked to society.

In the field of philosophy, private consultation, course activity, reviews, and lecturing have developed, as MAs and PhDs who having qualified in the field have taken up the professional practice of philosophy. I am not referring so much to university and research institute project researchers as to independent entrepreneurs. Like a physician or psychiatrist, they have private practices where they deal with questions that trouble customers. Joint discussion seeks solutions, which start from the particularization of the questions and the development of alternative answers. This kind of discussion is not a cure of an illness because the worry need not be a fault in the questioner. The philosopher may also have a column in a newspaper and answer readers' questions, the best known of these being *The New York Times'* Sunday magazine's *The Ethicist*. A similar expert service is provided especially for businesses, government, and municipal organizations. Universities are expected to meet their social responsibility by seeking to meet the social opportunity with teaching and research programs.

Aestheticians act as experts in aesthetic culture, relying on their own value expertise. Understood broadly, this expertise is the expert consideration of beauty and the experiences and feelings it arouses. If beauty is not only the protection and care of the environment, but also the goal of new architecture and development, and if it is even required in law, there must be means to detect its presence and show not only its effects but also the possibilities for its creation.

One's own individual, private experience is not sufficient for an expert, who must be able to justify the existence of beauty to others, especially to decision-makers. An expert must be able to use and create the necessary language and set of criteria. It is often held to be self-evident that beauty is more difficult to justify than ethical and financial values. The scale of variation is wider in questions of taste—and aesthetic differences more tolerable from the community's view—than with moral concepts. While art criticism has specialized in setting forth aesthetically significant quality and value differences in art, environmental criticism does the same for the environment.

Sensitivity, for which accurate senses are one precondition, is the primary requirement. As has been discussed by many philosophers in the history of aesthetics, a sense of beauty and a highly developed taste, which is open to alternatives, are also, arguably, required. Further support may also be sought from scientific expertise and practical experience.

Mastery of the language needed to articulate and express experience is essential. It is usual to speak of and write about the subject itself in a coolly neutral manner, and to deal with the experience and its relationship to its origin, its cause, more warmly and personally, using emotional language. Precision of argumentation and ease of understanding are always the ideal for putting across one's message, especially when communicating with non-philosophers. Effectiveness is increased by rhetorical means, which appear in a more refined form in essayistic nature-writing.

Ecocriticism and Its Metacriticism

Being a philosophy of values, environmental aesthetics either describes value concepts (descriptive) or directs them (prescriptive, normative). The task of metacriticism, which has developed from a basis in Wittgensteinian analytical and linguistic philosophy, is retained as the core of aesthetics. Knowledge of prevailing valuations produces empirical research, which deals with the concepts of experts and the public. Applied aesthetics signifies a step in opening up the field and taking a step toward normativity.

Environmental aesthetics acts as metacriticism of ecocriticism. The most obvious ecocriticism is nature literature, though it also appears in travel literature and belles lettres; nature photographs and films are also ecocriticism. The experts in, and masters of, depiction act as communal pioneers in experience. These environmental critics can consider both the subject and themselves; it is a question of a relationship and an interaction. The model they provide is a recommendation or proposal to see the subject in a certain way; in a deeper sense, it is an expression of the depicter's way of thinking and acting, which is suggested for adoption and critical following.

A depicter writing in the first person is "I," whose place can be taken by the reader to see through the writer's eyes, to speak with their tongue, and to adopt—at least experimentally—their way of thought. The reader of a description or the viewer of an image follows the depicter. The reader learns from a representative, a prereader, the art of observation, develops discernment and sensibility, and adopts a language, by means of which observations and experiences can be articulated and expressed to others. If a sufficient number accept the model to be good, general opinion will change; this will, in turn, cause a change in attitudes and business culture, education, upbringing, and, even, for example, legislation.

Art criticism is one model of speaking when depicting, interpreting, and evaluating the environment. Environmental criticism has developed something similar by itself and from the specific nature of its subject. The classics of nature depiction are people like John Muir or Aldo Leopold, Ansel Adams in photography, and Jacques-Yves Cousteau in deep-sea nature films. The emphasis in our culture has moved to the side of visuality, to photography, to television's nature documentaries and travel programs (see, for example, *National Geographic*). At least in principle, depicters have an acquaintance with nature or culture, which has been acquired partly through theoretical studies, partly in practical work. The attitude of friends of nature is marked by an emotional attachment, by the personal. The landscape is seen *face-to-face, eye-to-eye*.

Metacritical aestheticians also operate in relation to environmental protection. Various organizations regulating and supervising the treatment of the environment provide guidelines written anonymously by committees. Advisory organizations for forestry, renovation and new building, and landscape care provide a great deal of material for the public, too, in which aesthetically flavored procedural guidelines are given. It is the task of the aestheticians to critically examine this material; feedback is given to the authors and users of the material, thus creating influence. The aestheticians need not provide their own advice for the public, the "consumer," but instead examine the internal logic of advice, instructions, and education.

The critics need not resolve how matters should be; instead they bring out the deficiencies and erroneous conclusions of the attempted resolutions—while, of course, drawing equal attention to the merits. The aim that the author had in mind remains known only to the author; the critics start from how they see the aim as an outsider and how far the implementation corresponds to it.

The Knowledge and Skill of the Aesthetician

A desire and readiness to deal with concrete questions creates a base for cooperation between researchers in environmental fields, practical workers, and enlightened laypersons. Emily Brady set for the aesthetician the duty "to bring expertise to a wider audience, other disciplines, decision and policy-makers . . . expertise from other disciplines."[7]

One must be conscious of the limits of one's competence and of one's role: When is one acting as an expert in one's own field, and when as an enlightened citizen? An aesthetician becomes effective through the agency of experts acting in managerial tasks and the media but also through direct connections to the field. Different methods and means reach different audiences—thus demanding many different forms of action, as well as language appropriate to the situation. A researcher, an essayist, and an artist each have a different audience. The language and type of style divide, but the goal unites.

The basic philosophical question of how to move from facts to norms, which is seen as being unsolvable, still remains open—the clients, who are external entities, expect it to be possible to solve. One kind of compromise, though one that is open to counterarguments, is the development of a justified normative aesthetics. In any event, far-reaching decisions and solutions concerning the environment are made all the time; everything starts from the idea that these solutions could be better justified than at present, if the basis was a culture of diverse and open discussion, acquaintance with concepts of taste, and powerful expertise as background scientific support.

Testing Cooperation: A Series of International Conferences on Environmental Aesthetics

A general solution to the problem was tried and tested in a seven-part series of international conferences on environmental aesthetics. This took place in Finland from 1994 to 2009 under my direction, through the efforts of the University of Joensuu and various partners. The series began with a general consideration of landscape, followed by the central forms of landscape—forest, bog, water, field, stone, and sky.

The examination was concentrated and focused on the beauty of the environment. It was hoped that everyone would approach this theme by exploiting their own knowledge, work experience, and expertise. As definers of the approach, the aestheticians had a home-field advantage; they were theoretically prepared for it, even when the type of landscape was unknown to them and had not been studied in aesthetic circles. For professionals in environmental fields, the aesthetic viewpoint was less well known as a theoretical question, though the actual subject was otherwise more familiar. The challenge was how to deal with matters together, where to find a common language, how to create a link to players who were not so accustomed to use language to articulate their thoughts and actions.

The first conference, *The Landscape as a Meeting Place*, arranged at Koli in June 1994, involved meeting and living together for four days in the same milieu. The most significant aspect was the intellectual encounter. There were already challenges for the organizers in finding how to get the various entities moving. The main challenge was a simple question of gain—why would it be worth participating, and how could each person benefit professionally? On a deeper level, the challenges were how to become sufficiently detached from one's own way of thinking and speaking that intellectual encounter and interaction would become possible.

The task and aim was to promote an understanding of aesthetic values, the protection of notable objects, and the creation of new values. The aesthetic values were to be integrated in action and cooperation to be developed between the entities responsible.

The project differed from traditional meetings of a single interest group in that the group that was assembled at any one time was a diverse and randomly selected group of those who had responded to the open invitation. They were researchers and artists from various fields, as well as environmental professionals from business life, public administration, the media, and the world of education; in addition, active laypeople came along. The core was formed of internationally distinguished aestheticians, who were invited as the main lecturers, along with experts in each type of landscape.

Another unique aspect of the project was that an integrated academic-experiential totality was created from the academic lecture, art, and field-trip parts of the meeting. The academic part comprised invited and submitted sessions; the art was mostly performance and environmental art; and on the field trips, we acquainted ourselves with the landscape form being dealt with at the time. In fact, each conference formed a total work like a work of art, as well as being one part of a seven-part series.

Contact with the media helped in spreading the important results. A wide audience was reached by gaining exposure through newspapers, radio, and television. The book series based on the conference and individual articles published by the lecturers will have a longer-term effect. Particular attention is paid to the illustration and appearance of the series. All of the seven books have now been completed in Finnish. In these, the presentations have been broadened and more highly finished. The most impressive part of the photographic illustration of the publications is a visual essay running through them, which is supplemented by factual images relating directly to the articles. The aim was for a book, which emphasizes the importance of aesthetics, to be in itself a beautiful object of book art.

Problems also appeared (and I do not mean the search for funding). It is difficult for researchers to speak understandably across boundaries of their own fields and to come sufficiently close to everyday working life; practical workers, for their part, are naturally not as practiced in presenting the theoretical and philosophical dimensions of their work. In addition, aesthetics may, even as a field and how it frames questions, be foreign to them. At times, reference was even made to aesthetics without differentiating between it in the sense of the academic field, or the system of taste and way of life of a person or group.

Results were achieved: The representatives of aesthetics had their ideas broadcast; those outside, for their part, began to see more clearly the aesthetic significance of their work and the responsibility brought by having an influence. A contact network expanded over scientific, regional, and professional boundaries. Engagement proved possible, common interests were found, networking was stimulated, and a start was made on developing future projects between groups.

When speaking across the boundaries of scientific fields and professions, one is forced to pay attention to expression and more generally to manner of delivery. Difficulties arose from a lack of a common terminology, manner of delivery, and language, but above all by the diversity of conceptions of science. The conference series did not aim at popularization—at least in a conventional sense; the aim was to create innovative thought by bringing together people with different knowledge, skills, and experience backgrounds. The boundary wall between the two cultures—humanist and natural scientific—demonstrated already half a century ago by C. P. Snow, has in that half century become lower and has even broken down in places, but has not disappeared.[8] At least ignorance of the other side is no longer a matter of pride. Openings and border crossings have been made in both directions. Conferences of this kind do not replace meetings within interest groups, but they are irreplaceable for exchanging information and ideas across boundaries.

In Finland, much has recently been said about the country's image. I believe that these conferences renewed the "country image" of aesthetics as a discipline—and in doing so also renewed Finland's image.

Conclusion

In his old age, the well-known English aesthetician Harold Osborne made an opening for general aesthetics comparable to Hepburn's manifesto of the 1960s. He did so in a paper titled "An Intellectual Crisis in Aesthetics," which he presented at the conference *A Crisis in Aesthetics?*, organized by Professor Maria Golaszewska in 1979 in Cracow, Poland.[9] In it, Osborne demanded a move from an *outsider* attitude to an *insider* approach. He regarded avoidance of this move as a dereliction of responsibility.

Osborne's message is that a move must be made away from cool observation and its related passive approach to an active, "warm," participatory, and engaged one; a descent must be made from the position of a divine observer to that of a player, a responsible participant. This represented a radical change in direction from the researcher who demanded metacriticism quite as programmatically in the early 1960s. Nevertheless, a link can be seen between the young Osborne and the old Osborne: In the future, too, the aestheticians will continue to serve above all by means of their skill in argumentation, using a metacritical approach.

Participation is not always concrete group work. It is also preparation for publishing and publishing one's own work written alone or in one's immediate circle. A condition for the relevance of the field is taking needs and expectations into account and responding to them, as well as the ability to use manners of presentation that open to the recipient—the listener or reader, viewer or author.

The aesthetician has and retains two roles. The first is to make the aesthetic practices of different areas of life visible by collecting them and writing about them, to analyze and evaluate them, to demonstrate and correct errors in logic. The second is to act as an expert in beauty, to work as an active party, to cooperate with and to contact individuals and institutions from a base and foundation of knowledge of and experience in art and beauty and of speaking about them.

The same person is not always able to, and need not, perform the tasks of both analyst and guide, but the field in its entirety can do this; the social opportunity exists. A response can be made to the challenge by cooperation and a division of work. An unbroken refrigerated chain is needed in foodstuffs logistics; I would now like to suggest a hot line from academic aesthetics to the grassroots level, and back again.[10]

Nature, Art, and the Power of Imagination

CHAPTER

7

Environmental Art and Ecological Citizenship

Jason B. Simus

Introduction

Environmental art has received a lot of attention recently.[1] Most of the attention has been focused on evaluating the ethical and aesthetic qualities of the art object—how such works might constitute aesthetic affronts to nature, for example.[2] Issues just as important, such as the social, cultural, and ecological contributions artists, critics, and audiences make in creating, evaluating, and appreciating environmental art, have been largely neglected. This is unfortunate because the ethical and aesthetic qualities of environmental artworks are to some extent a function of the broader social, cultural, and ecological contexts they inhabit. Artists, critics, and audiences, of course, also inhabit these contexts, and understanding their contributions will not only figure into our evaluation of environmental artworks but may also provide us with a better understanding of the nature of ecological citizenship. In what follows, I explore the relationship between environmental art and ecological citizenship. I start with defending environmental artworks against the aesthetic affront charge by arguing that aesthetic qualities of artworks are to some extent a function of other sorts of qualities, such as moral, social, and ecological qualities. Next, I show that by appealing to a new ecological paradigm, we can characterize environmental artworks as anthropogenic disturbances and evaluate them accordingly. Then I look to Andrew Light's model of ecological citizenship (opposed to what he calls "ecological identity"), which emphasizes public participation in ecological restoration projects, as these projects are very similar to (and sometimes identical with) environmental artworks. Finally, I argue that participation in the creation, appreciation, and criticism of environmental art can count as a form of ecological citizenship when these practices provoke public deliberation about environmental and other community-regarding values.[3]

Why Environmental Art Is Not an Aesthetic Affront to Nature

In "Nature and Art: Some Dialectical Relationships," Donald Crawford notes that critics of artworks like Christo's *Running Fence* (a twenty-four-mile nylon "fence" installed across northern California) call it "an *aesthetic* affront to nature that goes deeper than the scientific assessment of environmental implications," and that these works "forcibly assert their artifactuality over against nature."[4] Allen Carlson holds that some (if not most) environmental artworks are *aesthetic* affronts in that they offend independently of their "social, moral, ecological, or other such qualities"; and these works are aesthetic affronts to *nature*, not human appreciators, even though human appreciators are those who recognize the insult.[5] Carlson makes these remarks in a chapter of his 2000 book *Aesthetics and the Environment*, "Is Environmental Art an Aesthetic Affront to Nature?"

Critics label environmental artworks *aesthetic* affronts for two reasons. First, by stating that an aesthetic affront goes "deeper than the scientific assessment of environmental implications," they imply that the aesthetic qualities of environmental artworks are both independent of, and more basic than, their ecological impacts.[6] By "deeper," I take it, these critics mean more emotionally resonant than the cold hard facts science gives in environmental impact assessments. Thus recognizing an aesthetic affront requires an emotional sensitivity to the dignity of nature that transcends scientific knowledge of any actual harm (or lack thereof) that the work inflicts on nature. I generally rely upon knowledge, rather than emotion, when appreciating both art and nature, so my disagreement with these critics will end here because it seems we do not share the same assumptions concerning the ground of aesthetic judgments.[7]

Carlson and I, on the other hand, do share a common standard for aesthetic evaluation. He and I defend cognitivism in aesthetics, the view that appropriate aesthetic appreciation should be informed by relevant knowledge about what is being appreciated. Yet when it comes to environmental art, Carlson's version of cognitivism appears to differ very much from mine. For example, he says that an aesthetic affront "is generated by the aesthetic qualities of an object, rather than by, for example, its social, moral, ecological, or other such qualities," as if knowledge of these other qualities were irrelevant in evaluating the object.[8] Citing Peter Humphrey's example, the hypothetical *Asian Floodwork*, which is meant to "show Third-World agriculture under water," Carlson says that while this work may have "unacceptable moral and ecological qualities, it would not constitute an aesthetic affront to nature (or to the Third World) on these grounds. Whether or not it would constitute such an affront would depend upon its aesthetic qualities, whatever they might be."[9] On this point, I agree with Carlson, whether something constitutes an affront depends upon its aesthetic qualities. But I disagree that it depends *only* upon its aesthetic qualities apart from any relationship to its other qualities. In my view, the aesthetic qualities of a work should not be divorced from other social, moral, or ecological qualities when the question is whether the work constitutes an affront. In the case of *Asian Floodwork*, there certainly is an aesthetic affront being committed, but it is an affront with respect to the work's socially, morally, and ecologically offensive qualities, as these qualities count toward (but do not strictly entail) it being aesthetically offensive. In other words, because an artwork can be morally, socially, or ecologically offensive, we should look at all the qualities that figure into an object's evaluation in order to determine whether it is aesthetically offensive, all things considered.[10] Determining whether a work is an affront is a matter of overall aesthetic *evaluation* in which the relationships between aesthetic and other sorts of qualities play an important role. It seems to me that affronts have more to do with comprehensive aesthetic values than aesthetic qualities alone.

For example, in my view, if I know a particular work is ecologically destructive, then that would count toward it being an aesthetic affront. But the very same work would not be an aesthetic affront insofar as it is elegant, or expressive, or, for example, promotes environmental values (I will return to this point later). Its elegance, expressiveness, or ability to promote environmental values would then count against it being an aesthetic affront. In other words, that a particular work is morally, socially, or ecologically reprehensible does not strictly entail but only counts toward it being an aesthetic affront, and a particular work is an aesthetic affront only insofar as it is morally, socially, or ecologically reprehensible. An artwork's morally, socially, or ecologically reprehensible qualities, then, are neither necessary nor sufficient conditions for it being an aesthetic affront. In my view, whether a particular work is an aesthetic affront should be determined by weighing the aesthetic and other relevant qualities to arrive at a comprehensive evaluation that takes all the work's qualities into consideration.[11] Now I return to the question of what constitutes an aesthetic affront to *nature*.

According to Carlson, environmental artworks can be aesthetic affronts to *nature*, not only to human appreciators. Of course, nature itself cannot recognize an aesthetic affront—that would require an appreciator. Nevertheless, Carlson admits that while "this seems peculiar," one could, by analogy, insult Jones even though Jones may not, or may not even be able to, recognize the insult.[12] Thus, according to Carlson, environmental artworks may insult nature even though nature is not able to recognize the insult. There are two points I want to make here.

First, I don't think the analogy between Jones and nature holds. There may be certain conditions in which Jones finds himself where he cannot recognize that he is being insulted, but most human beings under standard conditions are at least capable of recognizing an insult, whether they actually do or not. Nature itself has no agency and is thus incapable of recognizing an insult, much less an aesthetic affront. Therefore it is impossible for nature to be aesthetically affronted because nature is altogether indifferent and without agency. I understand the intuition, however, of *attributing* aesthetic affronts to nature, and this brings me to my second point.

I think what's at play here is that the *idea* of nature is being aesthetically affronted. But whose idea of nature? Perhaps not the one currently prevailing in the relevant sciences of nature. There are no aesthetic affronts to nature itself, but some environmental artworks certainly do aesthetically insult the idea of nature as "primordially innocent" in which nature is paradigmatically pristine.[13] Consider Michael Heizer's *Double Negative*, a 50 foot by 30 foot by 1500 foot double cut in the Nevada Virgin River Mesa. Heizer's piece surely offends the idea of nature as paradigmatically pristine. But the idea of nature as primordially innocent or paradigmatically pristine may no longer be an accurate characterization of the natural world.[14] Contemporary ecology now tells us that natural systems are better characterized as being in a dynamic state of flux, where disturbances are the norm and humans play an integral role in eco-system structure and function.[15] Nature, or our idea of nature, then, is anything but primordially innocent and paradigmatically pristine according to current science. In this view, environmental artworks are not aesthetic affronts to nature, and this can be illustrated by drawing an analogy with avant-garde art. Carlson explains that in the same way Marcel Duchamp's *L.H.O.O.Q.* (a dada artwork in which a reprint of Leonardo's *Mona Lisa* is given a mustache and goatee) is an aesthetic affront to art, some environmental artworks are aesthetic affronts to nature. Note, however, that Duchamp's *L.H.O.O.Q.* is only considered an aesthetic affront under a theory of art that takes the classic beauty of Leonardo's *Mona Lisa* as its paradigm example. Just as Duchamp's works force us to question our assumptions about art, many environmental artworks force us to question our assumptions about nature. And just as beauty is no longer the paradigm of artistic achievement, neither is primordial innocence the paradigm characteristic of the natural world.

In this sense, avant-garde and environmental artworks are similar in their ability to push the boundaries of what we consider standards of artistic achievement and aesthetic appreciation, and this is typically marked by talk of aesthetic affronts when, for some, the boundaries get pushed too far. Letting go of the deeply ingrained idea that nature's beauty is dependent upon it being undisturbed and pristine is difficult and may throw into question the thesis known as positive aesthetics. Positive aesthetics, according to Carlson, is the view that "all the natural world is beautiful . . . insofar as it is untouched by humans," and this view, along with talk of aesthetic affronts, is indicative of the old eco-logical paradigm (though both views can be updated).[16] In fact, it seems talk of aesthetic affronts appears most often when such a paradigm shift is imminent, and this illustrates the theory-dependent nature of aesthetic appreciation. There are no permanent aesthetic affronts, only new standards of interpretation, and theories come and go. From all of this it should be obvious that I think environ-mental art has tremendous potential, and I would hope that talk of aesthetic affronts could be replaced by a more fruitful and timely discussion regarding sustainability and the role of public art in a given community, which I will address in the last section. Now I want to return to what kinds of ecological and ethical conditions environmental artworks must satisfy under our new ecological theory.

Evaluating Environmental Artworks under a New Ecological Paradigm

As stated earlier, an artwork's morally, socially, or ecologically reprehensible qualities are neither necessary nor sufficient conditions for it being an aesthetic affront. Whether a particular work is an aesthetic affront can be only be determined by weighing the aesthetic and other relevant qualities to arrive at a comprehensive evaluation that takes the relationships between all a work's qualities into consideration. For the cognitivist, having the knowledge that an artwork is ecologically destructive counts toward—but does not strictly entail—it being an aesthetic affront (i.e., it is an aesthetic affront insofar as I know it is ecologically destructive). So, what constitutes ecological destruction under the new theory? It seems overly strict to deem artworks as aesthetic affronts if they cause *any* ecological destruction; in that case, no artworks, environmental or otherwise, would be ethically sound. Thus identifying the appropriate degree to which a work makes an impact on its environment is necessary to make the creation and appreciation of ethically sound environmental art possible.

The notion of *scale* is central to current theory in ecology that characterizes nature as a dynamic series of fluctuating disturbances (e.g., droughts, floods, fires, species invasions, and extirpations, etc., both naturally and anthropogenically caused), so we might think of environmental artworks as anthropogenic disturbances that are either temporary or relatively permanent. The scale or degree to which these kinds of anthropogenic disturbances, in comparison to naturally occurring non-anthropogenic disturbances, can provide the appropriate ethical constraint we seek in evaluating environmental artworks. For example, J. Baird Callicott amends Aldo Leopold's land ethic according to the new ecological paradigm as follows: "A thing is right when it tends to disturb the biotic community only at normal spatial and temporal scales. It is wrong when it tends otherwise."[17]

We can apply this ethic to temporarily installed environmental artworks in order to avoid them causing excessive harm to the environment. In the case of more permanent works, a similar approach could be taken in which the works should not significantly impact biodiversity and ecosystem functions beyond the typical flux of local invasion and extirpation. In both cases, the ethical constraints are set by determining the appropriate scale or degree to which the works disturb the ecological system they inhabit in comparison to regularly occurring non-anthropogenic disturbances in the same locale.

Along these lines, Carlson objects that

[i]f we take the comparison between environmental works and natural occurrences such as earthquakes completely seriously, it becomes difficult to see any point or purpose in environmental art . . . One cannot consistently hold that these works have the point of improving upon nature and that they yet have the natural purposelessness of earthquakes and volcanic eruptions.[18]

Here I want to address two points. First, note that I am not comparing environmental artworks to catastrophic events such as earthquakes and volcanic eruptions. The effects of those kinds of events far exceed the normal spatial and temporal scales I referred to earlier. Natural disturbances are ongoing processes such as droughts, floods, fires, species invasions, and extirpations that occur with some degree of regularity. Second, I agree with Carlson that natural processes or disturbances may have no purpose or *telos*. However, because natural and anthropogenic disturbances play no teleological role, this does not mean they are without significance. Natural disturbances may have no purpose, but they certainly have the *potential* to effect changes in the integrity of the system in which they occur, and often those changes actually do occur. So if the comparison between environmental artworks and natural disturbances holds, these artworks have the *potential* to effect changes in the local ecosystem in ways comparable to how droughts, floods, and fires do. These works also have the potential to effect *cultural* change when they promote public deliberation about environmental issues, whether those changes actually come about or not. Sustainable artworks maximize that potential by being more ecologically and culturally integrated than the kind of works that, for example, come with a promissory note for economic compensation after excessive damage has been done.[19] By integrating the cultural and the ecological, sustainable artworks are examples of what is possible in achieving artistic excellence within the constraints of what is ethically and environmentally sound.

Interpreting environmental artworks as anthropogenic disturbances is very similar if not identical to how ecological restoration projects have been characterized according to the new paradigm in ecology described earlier.[20] One of the more interesting social aspects of ecological restoration is the public's participation in these kinds of projects, such as removing invasive species and replanting native ones in a given locale. Andrew Light has described this sort of public participation in ecological restoration projects as a form of ecological citizenship.[21] In the last section, I turn to the question of whether public participation in the creation, appreciation, and criticism of environmental art counts as a form of ecological citizenship in a way similar to how more "hands-on" practices do for ecological restoration. But first we need a working definition of ecological citizenship.

Ecological Citizenship

In general, to be a citizen is to be a member of a community who possesses certain legal rights and assumes their corresponding political responsibilities. Where the liberal conception of citizenship emphasizes rights, the republican emphasizes responsibilities. These two conceptions of citizenship are typically divided by the liberal focus on the individual's *private* legal status and the republican focus on *public* political agency. An essential characteristic of citizenship shared by both the liberal and republican conceptions, however, is the sense of identity that comes with membership in a community, and the communities that members identify themselves with are sovereign, territorial nation-states, traditionally speaking.[22]

While the traditional distinction between the liberal emphasis on private legal rights and the republican emphasis on public political agency remains largely intact, the sense of identity that comes with community membership is no longer necessarily tied to the traditional nation-state in the age of multiculturalism, globalization, and pluralism. The communities that members identify themselves with now need not be sovereign, territorial nation-states. Membership in a plurality of other kinds of communities, then, comes with a plurality of corresponding rights and responsibilities.

One of the more sustained articulations of *ecological* citizenship is given by Andrew Light in a series of articles on the democratic potential of public participation in ecological restoration projects.[23] Light defines ecological citizenship as

> the description of some set of moral and political rights and responsibilities of agents in a democratic community, defined in terms of their obligations to other humans taking into account those forms of human engagement and interaction that best preserve the long-term sustainability of nature.[24]

According to Light, voluntary public participation in the practice of restoring ecosystems that have been damaged "is as much about restoring the human relationship with nature as it is about restoring natural processes themselves."[25] Participation in restoration projects, he argues, will not necessarily make better ecological citizens, but the democratic potential of this sort of participation is inherent. He writes,

> Participation in restorations should count as at least one practice that can help promote attempts at achieving long-term sustainability within a context that assumes that such sustainability will best be achieved by appeal to human interests as they evolve in democratic processes.[26]

Taking cues from William Jordan, a founder of the ecological restoration movement, Light draws an analogy between participation in natural processes and democratic processes when he writes, "our activity with nature is analogous to our activity with each other in a democratic society."[27] The link in this analogy is that both of these processes are ongoing and subject to change and fluctuation to which we must adapt. Jordan claims that "what is involved [in ecological restoration] is a continual dialogue rather than a program, paralleling in our dealings with the biotic community the dialogue that sustains a democratic society and makes it adaptable to change."[28] For both Jordan and Light, participation in restoration projects strengthens human-nature relationships among members of the biotic community and strengthens relations between members of a social and political community in a democratic and egalitarian framework, where each member plays a role in the planning and execution of the project. Thus the public's participation in an ecological restoration counts toward it being evaluated as a good restoration, as opposed to one privately, professionally, or involuntarily executed.[29]

Light contrasts ecological citizenship with what he calls "eco-logical identity," which is similar to what I have described here. "An ecological identity," he says,

> conceives of the right relationship between agent and nature as more a matter of one where nature shapes the subjectivity of the agent, which in turn creates a political framework whereby agents feel that they have individual and collective duties to nature and to those humans who share that same subjectivity. Ecological identity would count as a form of identity politics, usually defined in terms of those forms of politics at the heart of the new social movements emerging since the 1960s: feminism, race-based politics, the politics of sexual identity, and so on.[30]

While I share Light's worry that environmentalism as a form of identity politics will be less effective than a full-blown ecological citizenship, I do so for different reasons. First, I see no problem with nature shaping one's subjectivity. As long as the concerns of other communities are not excluded, and as long as one's perspective toward nature and other communities is relatively consistent, that is consistent with ecological citizenship. In fact, intersubjective discourse across communities (about values, not preferences) seems necessary for ecological citizenship to be viable in a pluralistic context. Nature may only shape our subjectivity, whereas social practice gives it content.

Second, the sense of identity conferred upon members of a community is an essential characteristic of most theories of citizenship, but it is also one of the most problematic. When members of a community identify with a set of values, rights, and responsibilities that are particular to one community and not another, they may also identify themselves as individuals in these terms. Such identification brings with it two problems. First, the concerns of communities other than the ones members identify with, and the associated rights and responsibilities therein, are considered less important. Second, the members of other communities themselves, because they identify with other values and concerns as members of other communities, are given less attention at best and discriminated against at worst. So identification of this sort seems inherently exclusionary.

The first problem with identification, however, may be minor. Ideally, we would like to give equal consideration to all of the concerns we have as members of all the communities we belong to. So as long as we do not exclude other issues from consideration, identifying with a particular set of concerns held by a particular community seems relatively innocuous.

On the other hand, to identify oneself *by* rather than merely *with* a particular set of concerns is to see oneself as separate from the community. This second problem is related to the first because the boundary between identifying oneself with a set of concerns and identifying oneself by those concerns is quite vague. The result is a form of identity politics, where one not only makes pronouncements about one's beliefs (e.g., "*I* care about rainforests") but also about who they are in virtue of what they believe (e.g., "*I'm* an environmentalist"). Notice the use of first person singular in both of these examples. In neither case are the rights of members of a community or the responsibilities that come with membership mentioned at all.

In this case, "environmentalists" set themselves apart from other equally important issues such as race, gender, class, and so forth, by defining themselves in terms of their stance on a single issue. In doing so, environmentalists limit their political agency to issues that are purely ecological, such as preservation of wilderness areas. For example, Dave Foreman, the founder of radical environmentalist group Earth First!, once wrote that "the preservation of wildness and native diversity is *the* most important issue. Issues directly affecting only humans pale in comparison."[31] In "The Trouble with Wilderness," William Cronon responds by saying:

> This would seem to exclude from the radical environmentalist agenda problems of occupational health and safety in industrial settings, problems of toxic waste exposure on "unnatural" urban and agricultural sites, problems of famine and poverty and human suffering in the "overpopulated" places of the earth—problems, in short, of environmental justice.[32]

Foreman's environmentalism as a form of identity politics neglects the relationships that hold between ecological concerns and broader social concerns. By identifying with an exclusive set of environmental issues, the environmentalist sets himself apart from members of other communities as well, which results in a kind of alienation on the part of those excluded. This alienation is apparent in contemporary society. Many citizens are concerned about environmental issues, and some are even aware that they have certain responsibilities that come with their membership in the biotic community. But few are willing to identify themselves as "environmentalists" because they realize that the environment is only one of many interrelated social and cultural concerns that need to be addressed collectively. Thus we may need more ecological citizens than environmentalists.

Restoring Citizenship through Environmental Art

Environmental artist Robert Smithson once said in an interview that "as an artist it is sort of interesting to take on the persona of a geologic agent where man actually becomes part of that process rather than overcoming it."[33] Smithson created the most widely recognized example of environmental art, *Spiral Jetty* (1970), a fifteen-hundred-foot-long curl of black basalt, limestone rocks, and earth on the northeastern shore of the Great Salt Lake in Utah. *Spiral Jetty* is today mostly underwater, yet the effects of erosion and fluctuating tides of the Great Salt Lake are still essential to appreciating the work as Smithson intended. Most environmental artworks like *Spiral Jetty* are works that, by design, are more in a state of process than they are static physical objects, and this ephemeral characteristic of many environmental artworks is shared with ecological restorations.

Recall that my earlier interpretation of environmental artworks as anthropogenic disturbances was grounded in an ecological paradigm that characterizes ecosystems as a series of fluctuating processes punctuated by natural and anthropogenic disturbances. Under this same ecological paradigm, ecological restoration projects are seen as anthropogenic disturbances designed to facilitate natural processes, and in this way share much in common with environmental artworks.[34] In fact, many environmental works are explicitly designed to serve double duty as ecological restoration projects, thereby highlighting their intertwined cultural and natural aspects.[35] I will not address these kinds of environmental artworks, however. It is the works that are primarily intended as making a contribution to the artworld—such as the works of Smithson, Heizer, and Christo—that I want to focus on because they are so provocative and challenging to our cultural and environmental sensibilities. That these works are ongoing processes rather than static physical objects is the most significant element shared by environmental artworks and ecological restorations which links them to the new ecological paradigm. Otherwise, environmental artworks are subject to the charge of "faking nature."[36] Regarding restoration, my purpose here is not to debate the ethics of these projects but only to investigate whether environmental artworks have the same democratic potential these projects do because they share so much in common. While I have some misgivings about how participation in the logistics and manual labor involved in ecological restoration can do all the work of restoring human-nature relationships, natural and democratic processes, and ecological citizenship, the potential of engaging in these kinds of practices is encouraging. And though participation in the creation, appreciation, and criticism of environmental art may do all of this in a more cognitively and culturally enriching way, I will here only argue that these practices have as much democratic potential as restoration does.

Environmental artworks such as Michael Heizer's *Double Negative*, Christo's *Running Fence*, and Robert Smithson's *Spiral Jetty* are difficult to be indifferent to. Anyone with the slightest amount of aesthetic sensitivity is compelled to respond in some way to these kinds of works just because they are so provocative and challenging. Because these works are large-scale public pieces, they transcend the exclusivity of the gallery space and the commodification of collectible art. They are thus experienced by those normally reluctant to participate in museum exhibitions where art is more often consumed than experienced.[37] In *Economy of the Earth*, Mark Sagoff draws a distinction between being a consumer and citizen. He writes,

> As a *citizen*, I am concerned with the public interest, rather than my own interest; with the good of the community, rather than simply the well-being of my family . . . as a *consumer* . . . I put aside the community-regarding values I take seriously as a citizen, and I look out for Number One instead . . . I may ignore the values that are mine only insofar as I consider myself a member of the community, that is, as *one of us*.[38]

Sagoff's articulation of ecological citizenship hinges on this distinction, which is drawn along private/public, liberal/republican lines. One of the stated objectives of Sagoff's book is to show that not all values, such as ethical and aesthetic values, are economic values, and that these non-economic values are held by and for members within a community as such. Aesthetic values, according to Sagoff, are *community-regarding*, not just individual subjective preferences held by a consumer.[39] Yet aesthetic values are notorious for being dismissed as "in the eye of the beholder" and are therefore often considered as merely subjective, even trivial. And while it is common to hear that "there is no disputing about tastes," aesthetic judgments certainly can and do facilitate critical and evaluative discourse, and in this way can be community-regarding, as Sagoff suggests.

Publicly expressed community-regarding aesthetic judgments then form an atmosphere of criticism and evaluative discourse in which community members play a variety of roles. As Smithson alluded to, the environmental artist plays the role of ecological agent by participating in natural processes, but the artist also acts as a *cultural* agent by creating works that facilitate deliberation about community-regarding environmental and cultural values. For example, a seemingly anti-environmental work like Heizer's *Double Negative* may provoke public deliberation about whether the community values art over sustainability, or to what extent such a work may, in fact, promote sustainability, either directly or indirectly.[40] In these kinds of cases, critics, too, play the role of cultural agent in terms of articulating the community-regarding values these works represent, express, or otherwise facilitate. Over time, audiences bring these values up to scale which forms a canon of cultural, aesthetic, and artistic standards according to which community members can make informed judgments. Artists, critics, and audiences, then, shape the cultural, aesthetic, and environmental communities they are members of by participating in the ongoing critical and evaluative dialogue regarding environmental artworks and the values they instantiate. Art critic and aesthetician Arthur Danto called this atmosphere of theory and critical discourse "the Artworld," in which artworks are defined by their context rather than by their physical characteristics alone.[41]

As Sagoff reminds us, the roles we play as consumers and citizens are as fundamentally distinct as the private/public distinction drawn in most accounts of citizenship. And the roles we privately and publicly play are especially important when considering how discourse regarding our aesthetic judgments is analogous to ongoing democratic dialogue. For example, when confronted with an environmental artwork like Christo's installation *The Gates* in Manhattan's Central Park (a work that generated an enormous amount of public participation in aesthetic discourse), one might offer the response, "I like it." But of course, this is a statement about one's personal preferences, not the value of the work. One could also personally dislike the installation, yet still recognize how it embodies community-regarding values.

When engaging in this sort of evaluative deliberation as citizens, we set aside our private interests and are more concerned with how a given environmental artwork reflects cultural and environmental community-regarding values, even values we may not necessarily identify with privately. And when we make judgments about the community-regarding values environmental artworks reflect, we expect others to agree with us (though not necessarily for the same reasons) because if they don't, we think either we are out of touch with the values held within the community or they are.[42] Deliberation ensues as a kind of corrective, where we check our values against the values of others in a public context. Disagreements regarding our personal preferences may be irreconcilable, but community-regarding values, even aesthetic community-regarding values, should be relatively coherent among the members of such a community, given that the community is somewhat functional. This is not to say that we necessarily *will* agree, but by publicly deliberating about our community-regarding values, we can at least set coherent standards necessary for meaningful disagreement. Contrary to Light's worry about subjectivity and its relation to an ecological identity, the shaping of our subjectivity is only a threat to citizenship if we equate subjectivity with personal preferences or private interests, rather than our community-regarding public values. While the language we use in making aesthetic judgments may be subjective, it is never private.[43] As ecological citizens, then, our seemingly private aesthetic judgments are always subject to public scrutiny.

Here I want to address an important possible objection to what I have argued in this section. The objection is that many environmental artworks such as Heizer's and Smithson's are in locations that are extremely remote, thus the majority of ecological citizens will be unable to participate in appreciating them, and this severely limits their democratic potential to further public deliberation about environmental and other community-regarding values.[44] I have only argued that these works have inherently democratic *potential*, but how their remoteness limits this potential reveals the full force of this objection. I have two responses. First, ironically, that these works are so remote may in fact *increase* their potential to further deliberation. That is, *because* they are so remote more people discuss these works and deliberate about their values than actually visit them. The same is true for most art. Most people haven't been to the Louvre, the Sistine Chapel, or MoMA, but this does not discourage them from discussing and deliberating about the values of the works exhibited within those institutions. Because the artworld is more of an atmosphere of criticism and evaluative discourse than a physical institution, participation does not require us to directly perceive every artwork we value or discuss. If it did, that certainly would be undemocratic. In that case, anyone who had never directly laid eyes on Michelangelo's *David* or Picasso's *Guernica*, for example, could participate in any discussion about the values those works embody and facilitate. The only difference I see between these kinds of works and environmental artworks, in terms of how they might promote citizenship, is that environmental works facilitate discussion about more particular values, such as ecological sustainability, though these more specific values fall under citizenship more generally. Thus, like appreciating museum pieces in distant locations, directly appreciating environmental artworks in remote locations is not necessary for these works to potentially further deliberation about specifically environmental and other more general values. In both cases, geographical distance makes a difference, but it should not be a relevant difference in terms of how these works can facilitate the kind of evaluative discourse that is part of citizenship.

Second, these works are set in remote locations for important aesthetic and environmental reasons, and as ecological citizens, most of us should *not* visit these kinds of works in their remote locations. Like the problem of national parks being overrun by crowds of tourists leaving large ecological footprints, herds of environmental art enthusiasts may end up ruining the very works they travel so far to appreciate, both aesthetically and ecologically. This is one reason why the documentation of these works is so important. Like some conceptual artworks that have only a temporary location, an abstract location, or even no location at all, environmental artworks in extremely remote locations or those that have decayed beyond recognition rely heavily upon their documentation.[45] Perhaps as ecological citizens, we should first get to know these works through their documentation and deliberate about their values accordingly before we make the trek to visit them in numbers that would defeat our purpose.

Conclusion

By now it should be clear that my defense of environmental art is contingent upon these works being recognized as successful, where the measurement of success is how the relations between their aesthetic and other qualities promote public deliberation among community members. Unsuccessful environmental artworks lack an overall coherence of their aesthetic and other qualities, such as moral, social, and ecological qualities. And for this reason, they fail to adequately promote public discourse about community-regarding values of the same type. The sorts of qualities and values these works exhibit and evoke are the same sorts of qualities and values that form the community-regarding interpretive framework I suggest is necessary for ecological citizenship, the interpretive framework provided by current ecological science. Thus the relation of these works' qualities to our community-regarding values sets the standards for meaningful disagreement under a particular interpretation. Like unsuccessful artworks that lack coherence between their aesthetic and other qualities, environmentalism as a form of identity politics lacks coherence between ecological and broader social concerns. Ecological citizens, on the other hand—including environmental artists, audiences, and critics—act as agents in their various communities, thereby contributing to the ongoing cultural, ecological, and democratic processes they are a part of. By publicly creating, appreciating, and critiquing environmental art, artists, audiences, and critics reinforce the constitutive roles they play as ecological citizens and, in turn, set the critical and evaluative standards for their communities. It is this capacity to promote the public communication of our community-regarding values that gives environmental art its inherently democratic potential.[46]

8

Can Only Art Save Us Now?

David Wood

Introduction

In the movie *The Day After Tomorrow*, one of the tipping points of climate change has happened: New York is under water, the Eastern seaboard iced over, and the Hobbesian world of the war of all against all has revealed its true colors.[1]

In the minds of some, there are lingering doubts about the reality and genesis of climate change. For these people, the jury is still out. I do not share these doubts. Despite real uncertainty about what precisely awaits us, they merely block access to the big philosophical and political questions: our responsibility to future generations, the adequacy of our social and political institutions to respond to the challenge, the ambivalence of various religious responses, and so on. It seems that while, as a species, we can respond well to an imminent danger, we are less impressive when it comes to dangers in the distant future. "We'll cross that bridge when we come to it," as the saying goes. But why are we so unwilling to act on what is perspicuously in our long-term interest? One answer is that those interests are somehow not pressing or vividly enough present to us. Philosophers are tempted to think that a good article or book should do the trick, or having the ear of the philosopher-king. But deep down, we know that this is not the answer. Reason has already spoken, and its verdict has fallen on deaf ears. We surely need to activate the imagination, not just reason; we need to be aroused to action through a powerful and vivid anticipation of the future. The trouble with *The Day After Tomorrow* is that while it depicted a frightening future, it was not believable. It seemed like . . . a movie. It lacked . . . art. And yet if the problem is indeed a failure of the imagination, would it not be reasonable to look more broadly to art for the resources we need? It is in this way that we come to ask: Can *art* save the earth? Can art bridge the imagination gap? And how could that happen if, as has been repeatedly claimed, art is dead?

Obviously, we need to ask what might be meant by art, but first we need to be clear about "earth."[2] This is no simple matter. When we think of environmental destruction, what comes to mind are mass species extinction, abrupt changes in temperature, changes in weather patterns, disruption to life-sustaining systems, melting ice caps, rising sea levels, and so on. The earth itself *as a planet* will be eaten by the sun in seven billion years—that is not the concern.[3] Saving the earth is not a matter of preserving a piece of rock or some idyllic snapshot earth—freezing it at some artificially privileged moment. So what does saving the earth mean?

Being True to the Earth

The philosophical tradition has not been silent on this question. When Nietzsche spoke of being true to the earth, it was in the context of warning us to guard against those life-denying moves that would project salvation or the good onto some transcendent realm.[4] This not only generates false solutions, it blinds us to the multilayered complexity and dynamism of "earth." Earth is both our unsentimental material groundedness, and, when we come to understand this, it is an opening onto a different kind of thinking, and responsibility. Husserl's sense of earth as "our original ark" is an attempt to recover phenomenologically a sense of the earth as the unmoving center and condition of our lives, one in which there are still sunsets and sunrises, one which reinstates a pre-Copernican situatedness, even as, in other respects, we cannot doubt the astronomers. With Heidegger, however, things get more complex. Earth is evoked in various places in the context of what he calls the fourfold, a fundamental dimensionality of significance within which human dwelling could be said to be suspended: earth and sky, mortals and gods. And he writes explicitly about "saving the earth" as intimately linked to human dwelling:

> Mortals dwell in that they save the earth . . . Saving does not only snatch something from a danger. To save really means to set something free into its own essence. . . . Saving the earth does not master the earth and does not subjugate it, which is merely one step from boundless spoliation.[5]

Saving the earth means recognizing earth as earth, bearing witness, as one might say, to the way its powers operate beneath and before what we call our subjectivity and consciousness. But what *is* earth? It is no mere planet, rather, as he puts it, it is "the serving bearer, blossoming and fruiting, spreading out in rock and water, rising up into plant and animal," very close to what he elsewhere calls *physis*. Dwelling consists in responding to the fourfold more broadly, acknowledging the shape of the cosmic canvas on which our lives are written, and to earth in particular. Art comes to the fore in "The Origin of the Work of Art." In this essay, Heidegger understands a work of art as animating what he calls the strife between world and earth, setting up a world, and setting forth the earth. A Greek temple, for example, is a site of ritual marking and celebration of significant human events, a world, born up on rock, whose power is at the same time recessive, hidden, background. Architecture, as art, lets the struggle between world and earth appear as such. In this sense, art discloses truth. He writes,

> The world is the self-opening openness of the broad paths of the simple and essential decisions in the destiny of a historical people. The earth is the spontaneous forthcoming of that which is continually self-secluding and to that extent sheltering and concealing. . . . The world grounds itself on the earth, and the earth juts through world.[6]

Initially, it is tempting to go along with at least the broad thrust of Heidegger's understanding of earth. Those concerned that Heidegger excludes nonhumans from having a world may perhaps be relieved to discover that they have at least a place on earth. What I would draw out of this characterization is Heidegger's insistence on earth as a hidden process (compare Heraclitus' claim that nature loves to hide). We should not eschew seeking to dominate it just because it would thereby be damaged materially, but because it should not be thought of as a thing at all, at least in the ordinary way. Central to Heidegger's account of saving the earth here, bringing together "The Origin of the Work of Art" and "Building Dwelling Thinking," is the idea of earth as event or process, and of saving it as letting it be understood *as such*, inhabiting it as such. And here, art—whether as architecture, painting, or poetry—plays a vital role.[7]

We can, of course, argue whether, as it sometimes seems, earth is still being characterized according to some deep humanism, whether the central event here is that of "truth," exclusive to and defining of the human, or whether, as Deleuze and Guattari suggest in the chapter "Geophilosophy," we are talking about pre or posthuman forces.[8]

My version of "the earth worth saving" is one in which the value of the lump of rock, water, and air we live on is intimately connected with the fact that it is the home of living beings, and hence of value as such. What is at stake is at least some version of the earth as a milieu in which life is sustained and evolving. Such an earth is home to creative power, which includes human beings, among other creatures and processes.

How Dead Is Art?

Heidegger's answer as to whether art can save the earth is tempting but it cannot simply be affirmed. He rescues us from Hegel's verdict that "art is a thing of the past," but at the price of reaffirming Hegel's focus on the historical destiny of a people. Is this the language we want to be stuck with? Perhaps we need, as Heidegger would say, to "go to his encounter," to engage with what is fundamentally at stake for him in "saving the earth."

It is clear in "The Origin of the Work of Art," and it becomes quite explicit in his "Postscript," that Heidegger is taking issue with Hegel's famous dictum that "[i]n terms of its highest destiny, art has become, for us, a thing of the past."[9] Hegel's argument is that if freedom and truth are the highest human values, philosophy, science, and religion have superseded art as their proper vehicles. In the modern era, art becomes a matter of pleasure, taste, imagination, and so forth, but not enlightenment, not truth. Heidegger's response is that Hegel's verdict rests on a contestable understanding of truth. If, as he suggests, the kind of truth that Hegel privileges—truth as correctness, correspondence—is derivative from truth as disclosure, allowing things to come into the open, to be seen as such, however obvious this might seem, and if art has a special capacity to bring that about, then art has a continuing vital role to play in our culture.[10]

It might, however, be argued that the fate of art is not so much tied to disputes about the nature of truth as to the way in which the practice of art developed in the twentieth century. If Duchamp's *Fountain* and Warhol's *Brillo Pads* are art, or can be successfully absorbed into what we call the history of art, then Rosalind Krauss's account of sculpture's "expanded field" could be applied more generally to art: anything goes.[11] If embodying meaning, and being *about* something, as Arthur Danto might have said, is enough to qualify an item as art, then something has surely died. And that indeed was at the heart of Danto's renewal of Hegel's claim about the death of art.[12] When anything goes, any distinctive sense to "art" is extinguished. Art is dead.

This conclusion seems premature not because art continues unabashed and unabated. That was true in Hegel's time, too. It is premature because unless you are a rigid essentialist, the fact that there is now no agreed understanding of the essence of art is as much a testimony to its continuing vitality as to its death. If there is no consensus about what love is, that does not mean that love is dead but that its meaning is contested. The end of art claim was ambiguous as to whether there was no longer an uncontested understanding of its cultural significance or whether no one really cared anymore. We now need to ask whether the model of art whose funeral rites are being repeatedly read out, typically one which privileges a certain consensus about "great art," has not become a distraction. Might not art function without consensus, indeed with even greater vitality?

It could be argued, of course, that this discussion of "art" is terribly parochial, focused as it seems to be on the West, and implicitly on the fate of high art or great art in the last two hundred years. I will not discuss this worry at length here. Suffice it to say that exposure to a multiplicity of "artistic" traditions is arguably part of what leads to Danto-type theses about the end of art. And it is no accident that the question about whether art can save the earth is indeed being posed as distinctively pressing at the beginning of the twenty-first century, faced with a future largely consequent on the effects of western lifestyles and modes of production. How we think of "art" may indeed profit from nonwestern considerations, but it cannot but start from the culture that is generating the problem it just might help address. How can we best think of that culture?

Art and Commodification

Despite their antipathy to his thinking, Adorno and Horkheimer's famous work on the culture industry seems to parallel Heidegger's concerns about the power of technology and the age of the *Gestell* (framing, construct).[13] The reduction of art to an exchangeable commodity would seem to make it part of the problem, rather than part of the solution. When Heidegger says that only a god can still save us, reflecting less optimistically in his later years, he is alluding to the absence of Hölderlin's gods, to vanishing possibilities and hopes outside our human imaginings—what Derrida would call the impossible.[14] These gods are proposed and sustained by a poetry that seems far removed from commodification. But Heidegger holds out little hope for modern art: "I do not think modern art points out a path."[15] At best, thinking and poetry (perhaps art) can prepare the way for the return of the gods. These are clearly, in part, reflections tempered by having his fingers burnt over his own abortive political engagement.

We may well suppose that the commodification of art is an especially intractable problem because art and commodity share a deep complicity in that they each work with and through appearance. That art can become a commodity with what Marx called a fetish value looks like a substitute for the aura whose waning Benjamin noted. Art is complicit with advertising that creates, promotes, and markets commodities. If a commodity is something whose conditions of production are hidden from view, we might well conclude that the commodity form is precisely the shape of the illusion that allows the destruction of the earth. Our capacity to externalize costs, to blind ourselves to the finiteness of natural capital, to focus on exchange value rather than true costs (e.g., to the environment) could be said to be an aesthetic illusion, one that in the end is to be held responsible for the damage. The idea that we can throw things "away" is a fantasy. The various forms of estrangement (alienation) entailed by the production of such commodities are precisely the kind of dwelling that inhibits truth, or unconcealment. While commodities may not be reducible to artworks, they provide a paradigm for the ways in which illusion is constructed and effectively deployed from which it is hard for art to distinguish itself or for it to resist. And to the extent that truth, as connectedness, as transparency, as unconcealment, is systematically hidden, it is clearly threatened by the commodification of art.

While we have not yet assigned a unique role or function to art, only a narrow understanding of art as entertainment would allow it to actually embrace the commodity form wholeheartedly. Any sense that art might enlighten would then require that enlightenment itself become a commodity. (It could be said that this is precisely the path taken by Andy Warhol or Damien Hirst.) Of course, in some sense that is Heidegger's indictment of philosophy and why he wants to replace it with "thinking." But things are not so simple.

Benjamin's analysis of film is apposite here.[16] Film (and photography and the mass reproduction of images generally) frees us from the aura of the original, from servitude to tradition and ritual. It opens up the possibility of a critical response on the part of an audience so freed. And yet it replaces the process of thought with compelling sequences of moving images, to which it is all too easy to respond passively. No one can pretend there is some sort of balanced struggle between Hollywood and *avant-garde* attempts to encourage a reflective response to film. But the logic of Benjamin's analysis is correct—that whatever the complicity between the commodity form and the art scene, there is also a space of transformative possibility. It is this that I now want to explore.

Earth Art: Outside the Gallery

I will look next at the earth art that flourished in the late '60s and early '70s, and is perhaps being reborn today, where the possibility of art saving the earth could be said to be taken literally and directly. But I will subsequently argue for a much broader role for art in transforming the shape of our dwelling.

In her book *Overlay: Contemporary Art and the Art of Prehistory*, Lucy Lippard writes about various ways in which then recent art (earthworks, body art, sculpture, renewals of ritual) draw on prehistoric megaliths, hill drawings, and burial mounds in a kind of renewal of our situatedness in space and time.[17] The work of people like Robert Smithson (*Spiral Jetty*), Walter De Maria (*Lightning Field*), James Turrell (*Roden Crater*), Michael Heizer (*Double Negative*), and Christo (*Running Fence*) deliberately cut against the whole gallery system, establishing itself often in desert landscapes far from the art scene, far from the city. And this was a self-conscious choice. These works could not be bought or sold, and they seemed to fly in the face of what mechanical reproduction now made possible. They often explicitly staged a renewal of the arc of connectedness between earth and sky in the form of formal cosmic resonance (spiral), electricity (lightning), or light (Turrell's crater). This all looks like an attempt to renew aura, and ritual—and theatre, in the sense that Michael Fried decried.[18]

Of course, from the very beginning this move away from the gallery/market scene was riddled with contradictions. All of these projects required huge investments of capital, usually from private foundations that were offshoots of successful corporations (like Dia) or had wealthy private patrons. Christo's insistence on artistic integrity and independence, refusing all forms of outside sponsorship, rests on him selling advance models and drawings to galleries and collectors for large sums. And the whole show got off the road with the Earthworks exhibition at the Dwan Gallery in NYC (October 1968). Soon Smithson's nonsite installations made gallery exhibitions integral to the work itself. Books and photographs of these works were very much part of the picture. Indeed the remoteness, inaccessibility, and (in the case of *Spiral Jetty*) transience of these works made them essentially dependent on photographic representation. *Spiral Jetty* became iconic as an image, indeed as a set of stunningly beautiful images, even when invisibly submerged in the Great Salt Lake.

One could treat these contradictory relations to the gallery system and the art market as explaining why earth art itself seemed to fade away in the last two decades. But it is more plausible that they made it possible in the first place, gave it a place in art history, and prompted its reemergence (Land/Art New Mexico).[19] In my view, we misunderstand the "art market" and/or the commodification of art if we think it is fatal to the power of art to challenge its very material conditions of possibility. Even if enlightenment is made into a commodity, its power is not wholly extinguished or exhausted by that condition. Conversely, while we may sympathize with Benjamin's analysis of the benefits of the shedding of aura and ritual by modern art, that does not mean that aura and ritual cannot be deployed "progressively." Consider, for example, the work of Richard Long, who maps, records, and photographs his walks both in England and in remote, often scenic, parts of the world.[20] This is an attempt to ritually resurrect a sense of place, both particular local places and the earth as such, and to recommend, and celebrate a mode of dwelling in it or on it, one very close to what Heidegger is calling for. A light touch: Leave nothing but footprints. The politics of walking, and of the multilayered historical sedimentation of pathways in England, and their ritual annual navigation, for example, seem wholly democratic and progressive, rather than nostalgic and reinforcing of authority. In this respect, Richard Long's work lines up with writers like Gary Snyder, Wendell Berry, and David Abram who similarly attempt to promote a renewed sense of place, a theme taken up philosophically to great effect by philosopher Ed Casey.[21] Now we know that the value of place *can* be deployed for reactionary ends. The same goes for community, identity, and home.[22] They can be vehicles for intolerance, racism, exclusion of the Other, and so forth. But we repudiate these values at our peril. The sense of homelessness evinced by the advocates of space colonization suggests a pathology of place, or terrestrial dwelling, that desperately needs attention.

If we follow provisionally Heidegger's sense that art can stage the strife between earth and world, can disclose truth, making available to us "The earth [as] the spontaneous forthcoming of that which is continually self-secluding and to that extent sheltering and concealing," then we can have lost sight of that dwelling on and with earth. And there seem to be two kinds of answers: the first historical and the second metaphysical.

The first answer would rest on some story about the modern age, technology, the commodity form, and so on. It could be aligned with theses about the end of art, which could be dated and motivated in various ways, as we have seen with Hegel and Danto. On this argument, the problem of terrestrial alienation is historical. It might be traced to changes in the material conditions of life, such as the movement from the land to the city or the rise of consumerism.

The second kind of answer, however, would focus on the more universal condition that Heidegger describes in *Being and Time*.[23] Here the story would roughly be that daily existence, even as it represents its own kind of openness, requires a certain dulling of the disclosedness of truth. We need habits—linguistic, material, social, physiological—just to survive. We need lots of auto-pilot settings, even if they blind us to the truth. This is true whether or not those settings are relatively benign or toxic and whether or not we adopt, for example, a sustainable lifestyle. According to this model, thinking and art (or poetry) could offer temporary events of disclosedness that just might open into different modes of dwelling.

Each of these models would prescribe for art the role of reopening, perhaps recalibrating, ways of being in the world that allow us to cope, whether with specific historical conditions or with existence as such. The first would tend toward revolutionary transformation, the second toward an ongoing process of healing, opening access to dimensions of existence that have to take a backseat in everyday life. If we take seriously the need for global changes in human dwelling, it may not be possible to maintain the bifurcation suggested by these two options. We will need dramatic change in our actual patterns of life, not just our attitudes. And while we will need new habits, these will need to include the habit of creative reassessment.

From our brief discussion of earth art, its most direct impact was perhaps on the parameters of human dwelling that Heidegger called the fourfold, reminding us of the deep conditions of our mortal terrestrial existence, with an indirect healing power.

Habit and Trauma

I described earth art as offering a literal example of how art might begin to save the earth. Exploring art's saving power of dehabituation will open up a much broader palette. But first we need to understand more clearly the various sources of habit.

There is, at least, an analogical relation between our everyday habituations and our responses to trauma, whether in the form of dramatic personal events or of the experience of arriving on the scene as an infant, confronting the real. Surprisingly, we have investments in ignorance, in blindness, and in illusion, as Nietzsche so eloquently describes in his essay on truth and lies.[24] This is the case whether we are consumers of simulacra, adrift from the material conditions of our pleasure, or Van Gogh's peasant who has just taken off her boots after a long day's work in the field. If I read Heidegger aright, art is needed not just for us viewers of art to grasp the truth of the peasant's world and relation to the earth but even for the peasant herself, who may be too close to the scene for *that* "as such" to have room to breathe. The point of the analogy with trauma is that what results from trauma are patterns of behavior which may indeed have allowed us to cope with the event or situation, patterns which are deeply embedded and not easily reversed, but which often lock us into suboptimal ways of living. If Heidegger is right, these ways typically involve inappropriate attempts at domination and control.[25] Saving the earth would involve rolling back this project of subjugation, as a hyperbolic exaggeration of a normally much more limited need for order and predictability.

Habits are patterns of repetition that supply, as it were, a domesticated space of intimate meaning in the face of a potentially threatening world. In particular, this would encompass the various ways in which we organize our bodily comportment, our ways of being embodied in the world—home, architecture, travel, work space, community space, urban design, and so on. I will take such bodily comportment as a prime example of a site of habituation.

Habit is both enabling and disabling. It enables by creating layers of the taken-for-granted on which other possibilities can be built.

It disables by hiding the field it concretely occupies, and may well interfere with other modes of bodily habitation if it takes on a hegemonic form. For example, too rigid a sense of body boundaries tends to inhibit erotic interaction and demand unnecessary levels of security, while a highly developed self-centeredness may starve compassion. Habit here refers both to overtly bodily habits—how we walk or throw a ball, whether we drive defensively, when we go to sleep and wake up—but also cognitive and emotional habits. And even if we are not caught up in the disabilities of grand trauma, the claim is that habit, in this broad sense, however necessary it is as a norm, is responsible both for a loss of pleasure, joy, and diversity and for the kind of metaphysical deprivation to which Heidegger alludes when he speaks of a crisis of dwelling.

Art, Dehabituation, and Embodiment

The significance of this discussion of habit becomes clear if we allow Heidegger's sense of art as disclosing truth to broaden into a more general capacity for dehabituation. On this account, then, art is centrally engaged in dehabituation, allowing us to see things anew, reopening the congealed field of embodied dispositions. This helps save the earth to the extent that it is our suboptimal habits that are destroying it.

In this light, Richard Long's walking practices are ways of reminding us of atrophying modes of bodily dispositions. There are many sculptors and painters working in this area—Antony Gormley, Richard Deacon, Joseph Beuys, Francis Bacon, Barbara Hepworth, Magdalena Abakanowicz—the list goes on and on. Art as bodywork operates through displacement, distortion, reconstruction, and transformed representation of the actual fleshy human body. By such means, it reopens what we might call the underlying schematizations and relationalities of embodiment and facilitates our release from at least the taken-for-grantedness of these schemes and relations. It may well not be enough. We have known since Freud that the effects of trauma and our investments in suboptimal patterns of behavior are not reversed just by self-awareness. But we might hope that the value of art is precisely what Hegel thinks of as its limitation—that it is not on par with reason or science. It might precisely, for that reason, be able to intervene in breaking loose locked-down dispositions, even if there are no guarantees of better replacements.

This specific reference to art as a surrogate site for exploring alternative shapes of embodiment is meant to make a more general point. With reference to film and earth art, I have argued that complicity with the market and commodification is no fatal obstacle to art having salutary effects. The more general point is one that cuts right against any sense of the end of art. Art as bodywork may not be revolutionary in the sense of announcing a new and compelling dispositional dispensation, but it does mobilize resistance to those modes of embodiment that most support what we could call toxic dwelling. Minimally, it does so by disrupting the illusion of naturalness.

If commodification, technology or what Heidegger calls the *Gestell*, is the reigning paradigm, art may not be able to unify and lead a historical people, as Hegel lamented, but it may, across a broad front, be able to encourage and promote resistance to such a paradigm. For Heidegger, saving the earth consists of preserving the strife between earth and sky. If we were to gloss this as keeping open the play between the sustaining powers to which we are ultimately subject (earth) and the space of possibility and life-practices we create for ourselves (world), the idea of art as resistance to static, locked-down versions of the earth/world relationship would fit right in. According to what I've read, these rigidifications appear and arise at many levels and in many ways. Habits and embodied dispositions are just examples. There are many others that span the field of even the most abstract of modern art. Fried (as we have seen) decries the theatricality of minimalist art (Judd, Morris, Andre), promoting art that attends to the distinctly aesthetic experiences it generates in the course of its own activity as art. But based on our reading, this distinction just marks different *levels* at which art might "save the earth." If earth art is theatrical in that it dramatizes the relation between earth and sky, it is because it effectively engages the observer. But both geometrical and more squiggly forms of the abstract expressionism that Fried was promoting play with line, shape, and boundaries. As such, they raise questions (albeit "abstractly" and on a canvas) about reality and representation, about the relation between things and energies, foreground and background, inside and outside and so on. And these issues are connected to existential questions about how, outside art, we regulate our engagement with the world—questions of dwelling. They may not be direct connections, but they are deep. Our preferences for order, for geometry, for (en)closure, and the tension between personal

feeling and outer shape are the very issues in play at the most profound levels of the kind of dwelling that Heidegger is seeking to
redeem. And again, the fact that these are paintings with commodity values may make it easy to lose sight of their qualities as paintings, but it need not count against their deeper significance in the
disclosedness game.

Central to my argument here is that if art may be thought to save
the earth by protecting and encouraging other possibilities of dwelling, this can and does happen in various ways and at many levels. To
the extent that art deploys framing (as a painting, as a particular
installation, as a sculpture or building), it cannot help in some way
putting into play the whole question of the relation between the
things we humans shape, create, and focus on, on the one hand, and
the outside (nature, background, "away") from which we separate it.
The routinization of this relation in the form of production methods
that generate "waste" dumped into "sinks" (like the oceans and the
atmosphere) like there was no tomorrow is precisely the pattern of
subordination/spoliation that Heidegger says we will need a god to
save us from. I am arguing that, across the board, art offers opportu-
nities to contest this operation, and especially its unthinking routinization.[26]

Aesthetic Illusions

Filling out the various ways in which art might save the earth, it is
worth reminding ourselves that the aesthetic, at least, is not always
on the side of salvation. When we think about art saving the earth,
we are tempted by two kinds of aesthetic illusion: Let us call them
the illusion of the spectacular and the illusion of the spectacle. The
spectacular illusion flows from the desire for a certain kind of natural beauty—say that of a landscape painting, the sort of eco-porn
favored by the Sierra Club. I readily admit I am as drawn to these
scenes as much as the next two-legged—it may date back to the feeling of safety our Neolithic ancestors had when they could survey for
danger perched up a tree.[27] But these scenes set a false standard for
what needs protecting. Consider instead Aldo Leopold's praise of
bogs and marshes which may not please the distant eye, but if we
get down on our knees and look close we can see they are bubbling
with life and a more reticent beauty.[28] And the rolling lawns of many
a great country park are green monocultures, stunning canvases for
sculpture, perhaps, but environmentally poor.[29] If there are ecological

values, like biodiversity, that are only accidentally connected to beauty, art that itself has transcended such a narrow purview is well placed to represent them. The other temptation, that of the spectacle, is a theatrical dream—that some great event would tear the veils from our eyes and let us see. We conjure up a public scene, like the storming of the Bastille, after which nothing would be the same again. Imagine the unveiling of the Reichstag, after Christo had wrapped it, bringing some cosmic revelation, depicted à la William Blake. Or imagine Al Gore's movie *An Inconvenient Truth* directed by Leni Riefenstahl giving the world new marching orders.[30] These are aesthetic illusions, themselves reflections of a certain desire for palpable presence, for a change we can witness. When it comes to saving the earth, this desire is an understandable response to the urgency of the situation. For as much as we may come to understand that this will involve or require a different way of living, a different dispensation of dwelling in Heidegger's sense, we are acutely aware that there may well be event thresholds on the terrestrial horizon, irreversible tipping points. The earth as a planet is not in peril. But the earth as a system of life-sustaining energies tuned in anything like the current way could well be. In his *Contributions* and in his *Der Spiegel* interview, Heidegger is not just managing expectations, as the saying goes.[31] But he does insist that neither thinking nor art/poetry can do more than prepare the way for a new order, a new god, a real change. If we were to pursue this line, we should be announcing not the End of Art but the end of a certain *aesthetic* model of the power or efficacy of art.

Art, Green Jazz, and Beyond

In *Red Sky at Morning*, Gus Speth addresses the problem of global climate change without specific reference to art, while weighing up a whole basket of approaches—technological, spiritual, social, cultural, political, and so forth.[32] His name for this diverse range of approaches is green jazz. In his follow-up book *The Bridge at the Edge of the World*, he identifies the problem directly as consumer capitalism, and its obsession with growth.[33] It would be tempting to think that while art might contribute to green jazz, as one player on the stage, once the problem has been more clearly identified, there is little room for art, that what would then be needed are the heavy tanks. My argument is different. If art as a polymorphous practice opens up at many levels the shapes of our investment in boundaries, in packaging the real, in denying costs, in maintaining rigid inside/ outside distinctions, in believing that all change is reversible—in other words, a whole set of rigidly toxic dispositions—and makes these kinds of connections visible, if not making them tremble, it may be just this softening up process, and our increasing ease in playing with and around these shapes, that will make possible the shifts in patterns of dwelling necessary to "save the earth."

This prescription has two dimensions to it, and I will merely note them here. The first, as we have seen, is the idea that there are vital analogies between what we might call the schemas of human embodiment—both spatial and temporal—and those explored by various kinds of art. By virtue of various kinds of distance, art allows proxy exploration of how these modes of embodiment might be transformed and thereby the relations to the world and to others that they imply. The second dimension I would call desire, a certain sclerotic desire. I mean here, particularly, to highlight our tendency to identify with the fixed, the stable, the controlled—defenses against anxiety. The role I am attributing to art might be thought analogous to the relation between eros and thanatos. These schemas of embodiment are the sites of forms of desire, often appearing as habits, by which individuals are bound to social processes. The theorists I have in mind here would include Reich (body armor), Adorno (authoritarian personality), Heidegger (*Gelassenheit*, dwelling), Deleuze and Guattari (anti-Oedipus), John Protevi (Political Affect), and indeed Freud.[34]

It is important, with Joseph Beuys (for whom "[e]very human being is an artist"), to think of art here not as the special possession of Artists but as a widely shared capacity.[35] In terms of efficacy, what it would mean for art to save the earth is that the multileveled exhibition and performance of a whole range of practices that would contest the growth economy, even at the level of our micro-habits, might well make the difference between necessary structural transformations happening or not happening. Public sentiment is often the key factor in whether new laws get passed, for example. A general culture of art as disturbing of schemas and desires might be a necessary condition, if not a sufficient one for the change we need. In saying this, I am echoing Heidegger's sense that art (and thinking) can at least prepare the way, even if they are not direct or first-order powers.

This account of how art can save the world could be developed in two directions. First, one could put flesh on the bones of Krauss's expanded field of art, which marks not so much "the end of art" as the end of our captivation with a certain aesthetic. Today, this includes performance art, participatory art, interactive art, installation art, video art and new media generally, art/science collaborations, innovatory forms of dance, theater, and so on. Art, typically, is understood here as an engaged process rather than as an object, and as such has a particular power to recalibrate habit. Second, one could put more stress on the conceptual dimension of contemporary art. I have given a certain privilege to the dislodging of embodied habits (e.g., rigid boundary protection), but there are deep cognitive frames that need challenging just as much. (Think of the work of George Lakoff on framing).[36] It is no accident that the most highly paid political consultants (e.g., Frank Luntz) focus on *framing* debates and issues. And conceptual art is especially good at framing and reframing. Mel Ziegler's piece *Catch and Release*, in which a US soldier is photographed "catching" air in a bottle in Iraq, subsequently to be released in the same uniform at the University of Virginia, uses images conceptually to try to break our insular bubble. We breathe the same air as our enemy. He lets us "see" it.

Imag(in)ing Otherwise

Clearly, for art to flourish in this way, it needs to be part of a broader critically lively culture, itself embedded in and reinforcing emancipatory educational practices. Moreover, art cannot claim sole ownership of this space. Political "theater" of various sorts may not be art, but it plays its part in displacing our habitual frames, as do advertising, documentaries, reports, deconstructive texts and so on.

Of course, not all works of art, or experiences of those works, operate in the same way. Art can be a stimulus to the direct pleasure it itself affords. But a work of art can take us beyond itself and reawaken us to the broader pleasures of the senses. And it can draw us, more metaphysically, to attend to certain kinds of constitutive relationality. The experience of the sublime reanimates the tension between our power and our fragility. The experience of beauty has often been thought to be edifying, to draw us toward the good. Art may bring us to wonder if anything at all exists. In short, art delights, stimulates, and reveals, all against the backdrop of the necessity of habit both for survival and for social life. In addition to stimulus and delight, art arguably models for us possibilities of ordering, and hence re-ordering, the world, allowing us to imagine wholly other shapes of life, ways of dwelling, moving, and being. Art can function at one extreme as entertainment and at the other as offering profound but temporary reminders of other possibilities, glimpses of the beyond. But art can also bring about transformation—enabling, provoking, soliciting, seducing us not just to become aware of our habits, and imagine otherwise, but to change them, or perhaps to move the line marked by the necessity of repetition, to renegotiate our lives. Art as transformation, even as revolution, gets tighter traction at the point at which we come to see that some of our habits at least are deadly, in terms of quality of life, or even its very sustainability.

I began with the thought that we might need art to help us bridge the imagination gap, to make our potentially catastrophic future vividly plausible. I end with the thought that what art can do perhaps better is to disturb the constitutive shapes of our bodily, spiritual, social, and economic investments in our commodified world, and thereby soften our resistance to change. It helps us begin to feel our way toward imag(in)ing and living otherwise. This, I believe, is what Heidegger meant by "saving the earth," even though we need a dramatically expanded and diversified version of that vision.

Landscapes of the Environmental Imagination

Ranging from NASA and Cuyahoga Images to Kiefer and O'Keeffe Paintings

Irene J. Klaver

Introduction

Why did it take until 1969 before the burning of the Cuyahoga River ignited a public outcry? For a century, since the beginning of its industrial development in the 1860s, the Cuyahoga River, flowing through a rapidly industrializing Cleveland, Ohio, caught fire basically every decade. This strange phenomenon, however, never sparked an outrage, not even much amazement, until the summer of 1969. Why was that? What had changed by then, which primed people to see a counter-elemental event of "water-catching-fire" as a matter of concern? I will trace this back to a crucial change in the American cultural imagination that had developed by the late 1960s, which I call the rise of an environmental imagination or environmental imaginary.

By the 1960s, the environmental consequences of modern development—especially the scope of pollution and the dramatic changes in the landscape—had come onto the radar screen of the general public. Various events contributed to this change, which I call the rise of an environmental imagination, not the least of which was the growing importance of mass media, including the popularization of the works of scientists such as Rachel Carson. Here I will focus on the role of images in this process. They played an active role in catalyzing an environmental imaginary. In 1968 the crew of Apollo 8 sent back the first photographs of the Earth from space. These NASA

Time Life, "Cuyahoga River Fire: Time Magazine," Teaching & Learning Cleveland, accessed October 12, 2012, http://csudigitalhumanities.org/exh. This image of the 1952 Cuyahoga River fire was a wire photo labeled United Press Telephoto; this accounts for the seeming poor quality.

images evoked a sense of fragility of our own planet in a vast universe, while pictures of the Cuyahoga River burning tapped into a sense of vulnerability of the local environment.

Besides an explicit role, images also play an implicit role: They can be read as indicators of changes in mentality and interests, tagging, so to say, a new emerging mentality and thereby furthering it. I have argued elsewhere that the rise of the so-called realistic Dutch landscape painting school in seventeenth-century Netherlands was closely related to the radical changes in the Dutch cultural and natural landscape. These profound changes awakened an interest in landscape as such. Where landscape had been a sheer background of either biblical or aristocratic scenes, now it rose to the foreground and appeared on the canvas as interesting and relevant in its own right, providing its own stage. The landscape images the painters produced further catalyzed this changing mentality—they revealed, constituted, and contributed to, what I call, an early environmental imaginary or imagination: a newly found validation, respect, and maybe even concern for the environment at the moment that it is radically altered, undermined, or polluted.[1]

In the following, I will sketch a conceptual framework of the environmental imagination through the work of literary and social theorists and philosophers such as Lawrence Buell, Benedict Anderson, Edward Said, Arjun Appadurai, and Maurice Merleau-Ponty, who all developed a notion of the imagination beyond the mental faculties of the individual subject. I will use the environmental imagination as a conceptual tool to reveal how various images signaled and catalyzed changes in perception intrinsically related to the changing place of the environment in the cultural imagination. Environmental imagination functions thus as a paradigmatic lens to show a shift in mentality, and images function as a barometer for change in environmental relations. I zoom in on two photographs that marked this process explicitly. I also show the more implicit workings of this process through landscape paintings of two exemplary twentieth-century landscape painters, Georgia O'Keeffe and Anselm Kiefer. Their landscape paintings traced—in radically different ways—implicitly a changed relation to the land.

These photographs and paintings fulfill multiple interpretative roles. I am not addressing them here as an art historian or media scholar. As a cultural and environmental philosopher, I examine them as probes into a new cultural sedimentation of our relation to our environment (i.e., as indicators of change). They are not necessarily instruments for environmental activism or politics, but they can catalyze an environmental imagination, a new sense of imagining and experiencing a connection to the world around us. An environmental imagination evokes a new awareness of the environment and can, in that sense, contribute to changes in environmental policy, to, what Michel Serres calls, a new natural contract.[2]

Old World, New World

It is hard to imagine two painters more different than Georgia O'Keeffe (1887–1986), a quintessential American painter, and Anselm Kiefer (born in 1945), a profoundly German painter. O'Keeffe's thinly painted, a-historical landscapes seem at the opposite end of the spectrum from Kiefer's heavy, history-laden paintings, literally loaded with lead and straw. For a long time, I have been intrigued by how they seem to represent, at least at first face value, a most stereotypical American-European differentiation: superficial surface versus cultural depth. Attempting to problematize this stereotype, I decided to explore the nature of their similarities. Despite their differences, they both were—at least for a period in their career—landscape painters. They both paint a uniquely culturally mediated relation to the land; both are drawn to landscape as a mode of mediation, and in that sense lift landscape out of a taken-for-granted state. For that reason, I would argue, they both reveal implicitly an environmental imagery.

I took the 2011 Environmental Philosophy Conference in Nijmegen, the Netherlands, with its theme "Old World and New World Perspectives on Environmental Philosophy," as an occasion to explore further the potential relation between Kiefer, the "Old World" painter, and O'Keeffe, the "New World" painter. I examined them as paradigmatic representatives of European and American culture who paint their cultural relation on the specific canvas of landscape, foregrounding the importance of landscape as such. Different as their landscape paintings may be, they thus, both, catalyze an environmental imagination.

I use the conference's distinction between "Old World" and "New World" somewhat tongue in cheek. There are many old worlds in the "New World" and, vice versa, there are manifold new worlds in the "Old World"; most importantly, "worlds" constantly infuse each other.

In fact, the complex intertwinement between the "Old World" and the "New World" is already manifest in the very rise of landscape painting in nineteenth-century America as a crucial marker of cultural and national American identity and could be seen as an early indication of an environmental imagination. Again, as in the seventeenth-century Dutch landscape painting school, a relation emerges between a landscape lost and a landscape perception gained. This time, the "lost landscape" refers to the declining place of natural landscapes in the "Old World," which turned the representation of the "sublime wild" lands of the "New World" into a unique and cultural advantage. It is precisely this change in perception (i.e., the "landscape perception gained," the renewed value of the other-than-human landscape) that became formative for the "New World's" self-perception, if not self-esteem. The young American nation had suffered a sense of cultural inferiority vis-à-vis Europe because of a presumed lack of national and cultural history. The landscape painters of the Hudson River School (1825–1875) provided America with a sense of self in celebrating its pristine, "virginal" landscapes and rivers running sinuously through wide, open lands, wild woods, and rocky mountains—something Europe had all but lost. Thomas Cole, Sanford Gifford, Frederic E. Church, and Albert Bierstadt—to name just a few of the Hudson River School painters—consolidated, nationally and internationally, an American artistic identity through its sublime imagery of the wild American landscape.[3]

This imagery has an abiding power, still influential for the experience of the rise of American cultural identity: In 1997 the U.S. Congress declared the Hudson River Valley National Heritage Area to be the "Landscape that Defined America." The area has been nominated to be the country's next National Park. The nature of the "definition" of the "Landscape that Defined America" is cast precisely in the light that America still had something which Europe had long lost. The self-definition implied in the declaration does not refer to a uniquely American style of painting but to its subject matter of a wild, untamed, sublime nature.

I might add that by 1997, the very area of the Hudson Valley had another unique trait, which was not invoked in the declaration of the "Landscape that Defined America"—but very well could (and maybe should) have been. Modern industrial developments of the late nineteenth and the major part of the twentieth century had produced serious environmental pollution in the Hudson Valley through industrial disposal, urban sewage, an intensely used transportation infrastructure, and electric power production, including nuclear. In the 1960s broad-based protests turned the Hudson Valley into the birthplace of the modern environmental movement and the first River Keeper organization, the Hudson River Keepers. A new legal landscape ensued with the National Environmental Policy Act (NEPA), signed into law by President Nixon in 1970; a "Landscape," I would say, "that re-defined America." We could say that that a "New World" began in the 1960s, one of an environmental imagination, an awakening of an environmental awareness, leading to radical changes in environmental policies.

What Is an Environmental Imagination or Imaginary?

Philosophically, the imagination has run the gamut from a faculty of the mind, connected to a flight of fancy, a far inferior mental process than the faculty of reason, to the seat of creativity, at the root of science and art. It has gained increasingly philosophical attention since the last decades of the twentieth century.[4]

In environmental philosophy, the imagination has not gained much traction yet, defined as the field has been by environmental ethics. Still, it has been taken up occasionally. In his 1986 book

Respect For Nature, environmental philosopher Paul Taylor, working from a biocentric egalitarian approach to other species, was one of the first to attribute a crucial role to the imagination in providing "genuine understanding" of other species by "imaginatively" placing oneself in the position of the other organism so that one can look at the world from its standpoint.[5] Sara Ebenreck thematizes explicitly the important potential of the imagination in her 1996 article "Opening Pandora's Box: The Role of Imagination in Environmental Ethics" and points at the powerful influence of metaphorical constructs of nature.[6] As did Paul Taylor, Ebenreck sees the activity of the imagination as a vehicle to envision the perspective of other-than-human beings. She broadens the workings of imaginative empathy by referring to the imaginative visions of indigenous cultures. However, despite a larger cultural connotation, Ebenreck ultimately sees the work of the imagination as an activity of the individual, just like the work of reason. Her important contribution lies in the fact that this work is no longer considered to be inferior to the work of reason but occupies a complementary status. Roger King also foregrounds the imaginative power of metaphors and narratives in his 1999 article "Narrative, Imagination, and the Search for Intelligibility in Environmental Ethics." He explicitly adds the significance of narratives for the articulation of environmental ethics and the creation of "discursive spaces" for environmental discourse.[7]

The formative relation between space or place and narratives or metaphors has been most carefully examined by literary scholar Lawrence Buell, who coined the very term "environmental imagination" in his 1995 *The Environmental Imagination: Thoreau, Nature Writing, and the Formation of American Culture*.[8] The book became a seminal text for environmental literature, or ecocriticism, one of environmental philosophy's sister disciplines in the humanities. In detailed literary analyses, Buell shows how deeply intertwined human history and the environment are—the latter not just a framing or staging for the first. According to Buell, a writer's imagination is profoundly influenced by the specifics of a place, such as its geological, biological, geographical, historical, and ecological characteristics. Where his focus was initially on Anglo-American imagination, ecocriticism has expanded its horizons over the years to include global, postcolonial, and environmental justice themes.

Here I set out to further this expanded sense of environmental imagination by connecting it to a social political body of literature around cultural imagination, beginning with Benedict Anderson's work on the imagination in the context of the nation state. In his influential 1983 book *Imagined Communities*, Anderson defines the nation as an "imagined political community."[9] He calls it *imagined* "because the members of even the smallest nation will never know most of their fellow-members, meet them, or even hear of them, yet in the mind of each of them lives the image of their communion." That is, they experience themselves to have similar interests and they identify themselves as being part of the same nation. According to Anderson, the nation-state became a powerful master narrative or imaginary in the Western world in the modern age, replacing the two previous central imaginaries of the religious community and the nobility. Nationality, nation-ness, and nationalism became powerful "cultural artefacts . . . once created, they became 'modular,' capable of being transplanted . . . to a great variety of social terrains, to merge and be merged with a . . . wide variety of political and ideological constellations."[10]

Edward Said develops a similar sense of the "imagined" in his concept of "imagined geographies," which does not refer to "fake" or "false" senses of space but to the spaces that are created through certain discourse, texts, and images. In his book *Orientalism*, he critiques the way Western culture has created an image of the "Orient" as a feminized territory without the capacity to govern itself in an organized fashion.[11] It is a clear example of what Said calls "imagined geography." It reveals how the constructed colonial view of the Orient based upon popularized images and travel writings functions as a structure of power. The negative image, a stereotype of inadequacy—the feminized territory—functions as tool to control and subordinate certain geographical areas.

As with Buell's imagination, Anderson and Said's imaginaries are not simply located in the individual subject but are part of a larger dynamic. Where for Buell this is primarily a place-related (or *nature*-based) dynamic, for Anderson and Said it bespeaks a social-political (or *culture*-based) field. This nature-culture difference seems to reflect the old debate between natural determinism versus social constructivism in the social sciences and humanities. However, the picture is a bit more complex: For Buell and other ecocritics, the experience of place is also culturally (and historically and politically, etc.) mediated,[12] and, vice versa, social-political-cultural analyses do note that events take place *somewhere*. Still, one could say that the latter have a tendency to underestimate the significance of the natural environment, while the former might tend to over-emphasize it.

I want to explicitly broaden the notion of environmental imagination with theories of the cultural imagination and social imagery. A thorough understanding of how the environmental imagination works needs both a place perspective and a social-cultural perspective at the same time. Bringing these perspectives together facilitates seeing them on a continuum rather than in a dualistic or dichotomous fashion. It accentuates their deeply co-constitutive relation.[13]

This focus on the *workings* of the imagination brings me to the last theoretical perspective I add here to the understanding of environmental imagination, namely the imagination as a *practice*. For this, I will take recourse to the writings of Appadurai and Merleau-Ponty.

Anthropologist Arjun Appadurai explores the imagination as a property of collectives, instead of as a faculty of the gifted individual. Collective representations, according to Appadurai, are not subjective inventions, fantasies, or desires but objective facts, leading to a plurality of imagined worlds. He takes Anderson's sense of imagined communities from the nation-state to a globalized world, emphasizing the active workings of the imagination as a social practice.

> The image, the imagined, the imaginary—these are all terms that direct us to something critical and new in global cultural processes: the imagination as a social practice . . . a form of work (in the sense of both labor and culturally organized practice), and a form of negotiation between sites of agency (individuals) and globally defined fields of possibility. This unleashing of the imagination links the play of pastiche (in some settings) to the terror and coercion of states and their competitors. The imagination is now central to all forms of agency, is itself a social fact, and is the key component of the new global order.[14]

In our contemporary era of mass mediation, migration, and globalization, the imagination works, according to Appadurai, through constructing landscapes of "collective aspirations," which he calls *ethnoscapes, mediascapes, technoscapes, financescapes,* and *ideoscapes*. These "scapes" form the building blocks of "imagined worlds"; they are the works of the imaginary, or the imagination as a "social practice." They form the cultural dimensions of globalization, "deeply perspectival constructs, inflected by the historical, linguistic, and political situatedness."[15] Appadurai's "scapes" are deeply embedded in social construction. Through Merleau-Ponty, I will bring the natural place-related aspects of the environmental imagination back into play.

In the "Preface" of the *Phenomenology of Perception*, Merleau-Ponty invokes Husserl's concept of "operative (*fungierende*) intentionality," that he does not further explore at that point, but which will pervade his latest work, the *Visible and Invisible* and return explicitly in its "Working Notes," where he describes his own philosophy as developing "the *fungierende* [operative, I.K.] *or latent* intentionality which is the intentionality within being."[16] Intentionality is not simply located in the subject, neither in the object, but operative between the two. For example, seeing a picture of a glass of water makes me realize I am thirsty. It shifts the attention from the individual subject as agent to, what I would call, a situational agency, in other words, the co-constitutive force of larger cultural and material patterns (of being), the embedded practices that codetermine how we experience things. Similarly, I see the environmental imagination as an *operative* imagination, understanding operative in Merleau-Ponty's sense of the word. Images are not just "signs" waiting to be interpreted by us; they have an existence and power of their "own." Here we can invoke W. J. T. Mitchell's writings and ask: *How do pictures work and "what do they want?"*

Images and Environmental Imagination

Mitchell has probed the question of the image deeply and systematically. His work has spanned more than thirty years of analyses of the way pictures and images work in the cultural imagination.[17] In *What Do Pictures Want?*, Mitchell explores why people have such strong attitudes toward images and media, as if they were alive and want things from us, seduce us. Of course, he hastens to add that this way of talking "has overtones of animism, vitalism, and anthropomorphism," and, of course, it is "only" a metaphor. However, the main point remains: Images have an immensely powerful presence in our world. To understand the modalities of visual culture, our own prejudices, iconoclastic inclinations, or idolatrous convictions, we have to understand how images and imagination work together, how they co-constitute each other. Here I look specifically at the co-constitution of environmental imagination and images.

Imagination is not formed or maintained in a vacuum; it needs seeds; it needs means of transmission. The Hudson River School and government survey teams brought the look of the new lands and waters to people who might never see any such features in person but now knew they were part of an "America." That is, images showed people and places not seen, and then the constructed, imagined environment gave rise to particular choices of what to image and how to image that. We saw the new, we imagined, then we further imaged from within our imagined and with the help of our images.

In the last three decades of the twentieth century, a new image of human community had emerged, one of humanity on its home base, the Earth. This image began to function as a complementary image to the nation state, in some cases overriding it but usually working on the level/scale of the nation state. What were the emergent factors that gave rise to this image? How did this image influence the art of landscape? How was it influenced by the art of landscape?

Two images played an important role in this shift, the first images of the earth taken from space and the catching fire of the Cuyahoga River in Cleveland, Ohio. They powerfully framed the age of modernity and gave rise to new political institutions such as the Environmental Protection Agency.

The NASA Apollo 8 Earthrise photograph, the first color picture of our planet from the perspective of lunar orbit, showed us an unseen of cosmic proportions—our whole planet, seemingly suspended above the surface of the Moon. As had the nineteenth-century geological survey photographs and the Hudson River School landscape paintings, the Earthrise image showed us what had been our entire sphere of influence. The Earthrise photographic image might be said to have expanded Benedict Anderson's notion of the imagined community. We might now say, "[B]ecause the members of even the smallest [planet] will never know most of their fellow-members, meet them, or even hear of them, yet in the mind of each of them lives the image of their communion." The photographs appeared for the first time in print in January 1969 and became instantaneously popular and appeared on a United States postal stamp the same year.

Half a year later, another iconic picture engraved itself into the popular imagination. The Cuyahoga River in Cleveland, Ohio, caught fire in June 1969. Interestingly enough, it was far from the first time the river had burned and this one was in comparison a minor fire, lasting only about half an hour.

The river had caught fire virtually every decade for the hundred years leading up to 1969, from the time of Cleveland's industrial

NASA image "Earthrise"—Apollo 8. The photograph was made during the spacecraft's orbiting of the Moon on December 24, 1968. Note that the original orientation of the image was vertical: NASA GRIN Data Base Number: GPN-2001-000009 http://www.nasa.gov/mission_pages/LRO/news/apollo8-retrace.html (October 5, 2012).

development in 1868. Earlier river fires barely made the national press. This one did. A widely read and quoted article appeared in *TIME* magazine in August 1969. The fire became Cuyahoga's shadow, catapulting Cleveland to the national forefront of environmental exploitation. The sparks of the passing train, setting the Cuyahoga afire, also ignited an environmental movement. The dual image of the Earth rising over the Moon with the image of a river on fire touched a nerve in the American imagination.

In the 1970s a broad-based interest in environmental issues emerged in American culture. It represents a rupture in the modern story of progress. Instead of a simple celebration of technological innovation, a more complex sentiment appears at the horizon, questioning the destructive forces and "un-intended consequences" of technology, and a plea for a precautionary principle arises. This new-born perspective was then hallmarked by president Nixon's signing of the Clean Water Act in 1970 and the first Earth Day on April 22, 1970, in which an unexpected nearly 20 million Americans participated, giving voice to a growing concern about the environment.

Photographic images as the Earthrise or the Cuyahoga River afire became powerful agents in the emergence of an environmental imagination in the 1960s and 1970s. In the following, I explore the more implicit effects of images upon the rise of an environmental imagination.

Environmental Imagination and Kiefer and O'Keeffe

Kiefer is a distinctively German landscape painter and O'Keeffe is a profoundly American one. Landscape painting is not simply a representation of a landscape but a cultural—if not theatrical—setting of elementary forces, be they historical or natural. The works of both artists bespeak clearly the cultural imagination of their time and place and are in that sense radically different. However, we could say that on a meta-level there is an unexpected similarity: The very choice of painting landscapes reveals in each artist a nascent environmental imagination. How does this work?

Georgia O'Keeffe was the quintessential New World painter. She was celebrated by American pop icons such as Andy Warhol and Joni Mitchell, who both admired her work and visited her—Warhol took one of his famous "Polaroids" of her in 1980, when she was ninety years old.

As we saw earlier, America had defined itself vis-à-vis Europe in terms of its wilderness and natural landscape, as in the paintings of the Hudson River School. Implied in this self-definition is a celebration of the frontier life—a frontier mentality with a concomitant myth of rugged individualism. Ralph Waldo Emerson's transcendentalism was the philosophical framing of this tenet, with its focus on individual freedom and the self-realization. Where the Hudson River School represented the cultural and artistic symbol of American independence from Europe, Emersonian transcendentalism symbolized its intellectual independence. As contemporary philosopher John Rajchman states: Self-reliance introduced "a mythology of America itself . . . the mythology of constant renewal with no fixed tradition, of an endless youth . . . , always starting afresh."[18] O'Keeffe is a perfect embodiment of this. She regularly left New York, reinventing herself in the stark New Mexico desert landscape, where she finally settled down. She was a loner, taking off on solitary desert trips in her Ford Model A, collecting rocks and bones, and painting them against the blue sky and painting the barren mountains, the rather pristine Chama River. The American mythology of

O'Keeffe's painting *East River from the Thirtieth Story of the Shelton Hotel*.
Georgia O'Keeffe, 1928. Photograph from WikiPaintings at www.wikipaintings.
org/. Retrieved October 12, 2012.

self-reliance is very different—as we will see—from the European
blood and soil Nazi mythology Anselm Kiefer invokes. The "self" in
Emersonian self-reliance does not refer to a search for a so-called
authentic self, tied to the spirit, blood or destiny of a people, but to
the adaptive, skeptic, and creative sense of self-experimentation.
Stanley Cavell sees Emerson's skepticism as the American counterpart to Heidegger's return to the everyday lifeworld.

O'Keeffe was part of the avant-garde in New York City, the first
woman with a retrospective at the Museum of Modern Art in New
York organized by James Johnson Sweeney, a major figure in the art
world. From the late twenties onward, O'Keeffe regularly visited the
desert of New Mexico and moved to Abiquiu, NM, in 1949. The
choice is reflected in the way she paints her rivers. O'Keeffe's New
York East River shows all the impacts of urban rivers in modernity.
The East River was heavily industrialized; booming with economic
activity; lined by factories, slaughterhouses, refineries, busy piers and
power plants, and poor folks tenement slums along the filthy waters.
Robert Moses finalized the cutting off of the East River from
Manhattan's FDR Drive (officially called the Franklin D. Roosevelt
East River Drive). O'Keeffe's Chama River in New Mexico is devoid
of any human impact—despite the thousand-year settlements of
pueblo Indians and hundreds of years' inhabitation of Spanish-
speaking populations.

Chama River, Ghost Ranch, New Mexico (Blue River), 1935. Georgia O'Keeffe. "Art review: 'Georgia O'Keeffe in New Mexico' at the Montclair Art Museum," by John Zeaman, October 2, 2012. www.northjersey.com/ arts_entertainment/art/172228781_Art_review___Georgia_O_Keeffe_in_ New_Mexico__at_the_Montclair_Art_Museum_to_the_Southwest_are_ spotlighted_in_exhibit.html.

Anselm Kiefer, the profoundly German painter, was the first one who thematized the Nazi period of his country, painting how the Second World War ravaged through the soil of his country. Blood and soil, crucial images for the Reich, became one in Kiefer's images: the soil saturated with blood, wounded and dead bodies, the Old World devastated, lost its horizon, its way of looking forward, meshed into myths of heavy histories.

Anselm Kiefer was born in Donaueschingen in March of 1945, a couple of months before the end of World War II. Donaueschingen, in the southern Black Forest, lies at the confluence of the Breg and Brigach rivers, the two tributaries that form the source of the Danube. It is the place of the "Donaueschinger Musiktage": the oldest music festival for contemporary music in the world (founded in 1921), even visited by the renowned modern composer Arnold Schoenberg. This annual October event forms a stark contrast to the close-by *Oktoberfest* in Munich, Bavaria, Germany, the largest annual beer festival in the world. It is an important element in Bavarian culture, originated to celebrate the marriage between Crown Prince Ludwig and Princess Therese in 1810. Their grandson was Ludwig II, the King of Bavaria and patron of Richard Wagner, who eternalized the river Rhine in his *The Ring of the Nibelungs*. In the German cultural imagination, the river Rhine was superior to the Danube, which flows to the Black Sea, connecting the West with the East. The Danube's waters mix and pollute the blue-eyed, blond German race with the brown-eyed, black-haired East Europeans. The Rhine, in contrast, stayed pure and Germanic.

Kiefer's paintings resonate and invoke these mythologies, these cultural imaginations. There is barely air in Kiefer. His painted lands are compact; the soil is suffocated by layers of history, encased in grids of myth.

One can look at Kiefer's use of myth through the lens of Philippe Lacoue-Labarthe and Jean-Luc Nancy, for whom Nazism is characterized as the myth of myths. Nazism is a myth whose power derives not from its content but from its structure. As they say in their essay "The Nazi Myth":

That is why we will not speak here of Nazism's *myths*, in the plural, but only of the myth of Nazism, or of the National-Socialist myth *as such*. We will speak, in other words, of the fashion by which National Socialism constitutes itself, with or without the use of myths, in a dimension, for a function, and

A portion of *Der Rhein*, Anselm Keifer, 1982. Retrieved from Tumblr, October 12, 2012. http://www.tumblr.com/tagged/anselm-kiefer?before=1350329408.

with a self-assurance that all three can be properly called mythic.[19]

Andrew Hewitt comments,

> For Lacoue-Labarthe and Nancy, *the* myth of Nazism concerns not the content of mythology, but the very performative function of myth. The specificity of Nazism lies not in its ideological material, but in its belief in the efficacy of mythic narrative in the construction of national identity. It is not what is believed that is specifically fascist, but the belief in belief itself as the generator of historical subjectivity, as the foundation of the *Volk*.[20]

Kiefer's land is leaden land, dead land, often constituted by soldier's bodies whose forms are painted over and over into one single earth-like mass, just as their real bodies decomposed into the massive collective of the army and ultimately in the German soil. On many levels, abstract collectivity resonates in his landscapes.

Where Kiefer's land is leaden, O'Keeffe's land is light. His heavy earth is tilled with dead soldiers' bodies, her clear blue sky framed by white bones. Kiefer's canvas contains layers of paint, straw, lead, burnt paper—O'Keeffe's is thin, taut, and smooth as plastic around a well-wrapped sandwich. She refused all the interpretations of her abstract work; she preferred the sheer descriptive.

Both painters prompt the ways we reimagine our relation to the modern(ist) landscape in which we live, which we create. Is there a political potential in this art? Wherein lies this potential? It troubles our sense of place: Kiefer by loading the landscape with layers of history; O'Keeffe by painting the radical other landscape rather than the modern industrialist landscape of the East River—in a sense, unloading layers of history.

Anselm Kiefer's German places are burdened with the heavy history of the conflagration of Nazi Germany; its decay is expressed in decomposing paintings, heavily loaded with lead and straw. In contrast, Georgia O'Keeffe's smoothly painted "thin" work conveys in all its bright colors the immediacy and lightness of New Mexico's deserts—its scorching heat turns death into crisp, white bones against a blue sky. In its broad diversity, the axis Kiefer-O'Keeffe covers elemental representations and experiences, from the layered depths of history and myth to the profoundness of the surface. They do not simply represent scenes from nature or culture, but they stage elemental forces of political and earthly nature.

Both Kiefer and O'Keeffe retrieve death in a culture of individualism, which sought to overcome mortality by eternalizing its heroes into an eternal life in history. In a way, mortality itself is eternalized—death in its many manifestations: the rotting decay of land consisting of dead bodies or the white bones against the blue sky.

Landscape is a natural as well as a cultural phenomenon. The suffix -scape is etymologically rooted in *skap*, which means to create, ordain, or appoint.[21] One could say that both O'Keeffe and Kiefer *stage* landscapes; they foreground them into our consciousness. The move in O'Keeffe from painting the East River to the Chama River environment is a move from cityscape to landscape. We can say that O'Keeffe's desert paintings reveal a rise of an environmental imaginary. She makes visible what concerns us.

Discourse about imagined communities that Benedict Anderson developed around the nation state in the twentieth century is in the twenty-first century broadened in the direction of the environmental imagination. Neither Kiefer nor O'Keeffe is simply a landscape painter. Neither Kiefer nor O'Keeffe is an environmentalist. Neither Kiefer nor O'Keeffe is an environmental artist. Still, an environmental imagination elucidates their work, shines through their work, and co-creates a sense of our time as an environmental time.

In a final scene in a film about his work, Kiefer states: "The Bible constantly says everything will be destroyed—and grass will grow over your cities. I think that's fantastic. And grass will grow here too. It already is, everywhere."[22]

"I have tried to paint the Bones and the Blue," Georgia O'Keeffe writes in "About Painting Desert Bones."[23] "They were most wonderful against the Blue—that Blue that will always be there as it is now after all man's destruction is finished."

This might sound apocalyptic, but for both Kiefer and O'Keeffe these are ultimately positive statements: The landscape is our backbone, the Earth with which we must try to find a more reciprocal relation in Michel Serres' *Natural Contract*. The landscape is the bare minimum, the -scape in Appadurai's sense of the word; it is what is left over after the battle is over, it is the Earth where our life takes place—the Earth we saw from space as the Blue Marble.

The New World

The Old World is one of the imagined communities of the nation-state and the New World is one of the landscape, the river, the Earth, in all its modernity infused with an environmental imagination.

Paintings and photographs come to serve the power of the environmental imagination, to catalyze the environmental imagination.

I suggest that the Cuyahoga River fire photograph and the Earthrise photograph, too, have their abiding presence. In 2010, commenting on the BP oil spill, Nobel Economics Laureate and *New York Times* columnist Paul Krugman referred to the Cuyahoga fire as the beginning of the environmental movement and went on to note that recent environmental difficulties have been less "photogenic" and, so, passed out of the public imagination.[24] Comedian Stephen Colbert in October 2012 introduced a satiric segment on the environment with the Cuyahoga River fire tugboat picture, sixty years after it was made.[25]

The NASA Earthrise photograph has been seen in numerous venues. It has been on a United States postal stamp in 1969 and is one of only about three thousand "Featured Pictures" on Wikipedia. Earthrise is the central cover photograph on *LIFE* magazine's *100 Photographs That Changed the World*. Celebrated wilderness photographer Galen Rowell asserted Earthrise was "the most influential environmental photograph ever taken."[26,27]

In the twenty-first century, the Cuyahoga River is cleaned up, and Cleveland calls for a boardwalk along the river with restaurants and bars, a five-star boutique hotel, condos, office space, and apartments.

In the twenty-first century, both the Rhine and the Danube are part of the European Water Framework Directive. The river is managed as a river basin—the natural geographical and hydrological unit—overriding the administrative and political boundaries of nation-states. The image is the image of a river—a powerful photogenic image that inspires an environmental imagination of the future.

Imag[e]ine that.

PART

IV

Wind Farms, Shopping Malls, and Wild Animals

CHAPTER

10

Beauty or Bane

Advancing an Aesthetic Appreciation of Wind Turbine Farms

Tyson-Lord Gray

Introduction

In 2009 the American Wind Energy Association conducted a survey of small wind turbine sales aimed at assessing the market's rate of incline or decline from the years 2007 to 2009. The final report, "AWEA Small Wind Turbine Global Market Study," published in April 2010, concluded that U.S. megawatt sales had increased 15 percent from 2008 to 2009 and that global megawatt sales had increased 10 percent.[1] A closer look at the report, however, revealed that although wind turbine megawatt sales in the United States had grown, the actual wind turbine unit sales had suffered a 5 percent decline.

An article published three months later in July 2010 by *EPC Engineer* reported similar findings. It stated that Gamesa Corporacion Tecnologica SA, one of the top ten suppliers of wind turbines in the nation, had suffered a significant decline in their wind turbine sales during the first half of the year. The article "Gamesa First Half Net Profits Drop 65 percent, Cut 2010 Turbine Sales Goal" stated that Gamesa's net profits fell to 22.5 million euro in the first six months of the year, down from 65 million euro the year prior.[2]

Then in April 2011, *Venture Beat* published the article "GE: Wind Turbine Demand Fell Last Year," reporting that General Electric, one of the top three wind turbine suppliers in the nation, saw a drop in their demand for wind power turbines to around half of their 2009 sales.[3] The article reported that although wind power deployment in the United States has consistently grown for the last three years, GE had only added 5,116 megawatts' worth of wind turbines in 2010, a considerable decline from the more than 10,000 megawatts in 2009.

The declining rate of wind turbine sales demonstrated by these reports is perplexing. Current research regarding climate change has indicated that fossil fuel usage must be reduced in order to mini-mize future tragedies.[4] Subsequently, many countries have begun to invest in renewable energy. China has increased their diesel car pro-duction, and in 2010 the European Union (EU) set new targets for its members to obtain 10 percent of their energy for transportation from biofuels.[5] Each of these developments has given the illusion that societies are becoming more aware of the dangers of nuclear and fossil fuel energy and more intentional about promoting sus-tainability. This is not without sufficient cause.

In 2010 the explosion of the Deepwater Horizon Rig killed eleven workers and gushed 4.9 million barrels of oil into the Gulf of Mexico, destroying the coastal habitat of the surrounding area and killing countless mammals, birds, and sea life in the process. There have been countless coal mine explosions, such as the one in New Zealand's Pike River mine that killed twenty-nine men and the one in the Baluchistan, Pakistan, coal mine that killed forty-five.[6] And few will forget the Fukushima Daiichi nuclear plant explosion in Japan that resulted in the evacuation of more than fifty thousand people from the city who feared potential radiation poisoning.[7] If these disasters have not been sufficient enough to encourage an increase in wind turbines, one has to ask, what is?

The *Venture Beat* article actually indicated that power companies are turning to natural gas as an alternative to wind power. Of course, the dangers posed to human health and the environment from natu-ral gas drilling is also troubling. The process of hydraulic fracturing contaminates ground water used for drinking, and leaks can result in deadly explosions or carbon monoxide poisoning. Natural gas is also composed primarily of methane, which traps heat at a rate twenty times greater than that of carbon dioxide, contributing to global warming. Consequently, natural gas is not an acceptable alternative to wind power among avid environmentalists.

The explanation for this decision was attributed to two main factors. First, wind turbines carry enormous upfront costs, which can take up to several years for power companies to recover in profit. This makes natural gas a cheaper and more appealing option. Second, wind turbines carry a negative stigma and can be seen as eyesores by some residents who fear a windfarm in close proximity to their home will reduce their property value. Given the profit-driven nature of most companies, the first factor is not surprising. However, the second presents a case for further questioning and investigation. Although the threat of one's property value declining is a legitimate fear, is it credible?

In examining this concern, I looked at three studies which each assessed the sale prices of residential properties located near windfarms. A 2003 study conducted and funded by the Renewable Energy Policy Project examined over twenty-four thousand residential home sales located within five miles of ten windfarms and compared them to nearby sales that were out of view of those farms.[8] This study found that sales prices actually rose at higher rates closer to the windfarms, and where prices in the region declined, the prices near the windfarms declined less.

A second study published in 2009 by the Ernest Orlando Lawrence Berkley National Laboratory looked at the sales transactions of seventy-five hundred single-family homes situated within ten miles of twenty-four wind facilities throughout nine different states.[9] This report, funded by the U.S. Department of Energy, concluded that neither the view of wind facilities nor the distance of a home to those facilities was found to have any consistent, measurable, and statistically significant effect on a home's sale prices.

However, a third study in 2009 funded by wind-power critics found that vacant residential lot sales near wind turbines suffered an average price decline of 30 to 40 percent. This study did not involve any actual home sales presumably because of the rural location and undeveloped land within the survey area. Notwithstanding, Appraisal Group Ones' study still asserted:

> It is logical to conclude that the factors that created the negative influence on vacant land are the same factors that will impact the improved property values. Therefore, it is not a leap of logic to conclude that the impact of wind turbines on improved property value would also be negative.[10]

Although the final report appears to be more conjecture than pure statistical findings, the data from the first two studies at least disproves the ad hoc fear that windfarms always lower property value. The third study is perhaps more significant because of the comments made by Kurt Kielisch, president of Appraisal Group One. He stated that in comparison to other studies he has done which examined the impact of transmission lines and gas pipelines on property value, wind turbines have the biggest impact. The main objection, he said, is aesthetics.[11]

This suggests that if windfarms actually do lower property value, it is certainly not due to concerns leveled by opponents such as health-risks or danger to birds. If so, these concerns would extend to transmission lines and gas pipelines as well. *Venture Beat's* assertion then that windfarms carry a negative stigma and are an eyesore to residents appears to strike at the foundation of declining wind turbine sales.

Opponents of windfarm projects often claim that windfarms are ugly and destroy the beauty of nature. These accusations are leveled without taking into consideration the benefits windfarms offer in terms of supplying clean energy and reducing dependency on fossil fuels. Even environmentalists and nature lovers often oppose their construction in spite of data showing windfarms to have one of the lowest environmental impacts out of all energy sources.

In 2008 plans to erect three wind turbines on Warwick Hall Farm in the United Kingdom would have provided six to nine megawatts of additional energy to the region. Yet this project was met with resistance by local residents of West Cumbrian Village, who complained that the wind turbines would "detract from the lovely landscape."[12] In 2010 the residents of Kythera, Greece, launched a campaign in protest against nine windfarm proposals which would have generated a total of 321 megawatts of renewable energy for the islands of Greece. Among their complaints, "Wind power stations are no parks. They are industrial and commercial installations. They do not belong in areas of natural beauty."[13] And a proposal in 2011 to build a sixty-four-turbine windfarm at the foothills of Pumlumon along the Cambrian Mountain Range prompted a protest by the Cambrian Mountain Society, who complained that the windfarm would "destroy this spectacular and unique area of Wales."[14]

These and other windfarm projects suggest that the main issue with wind turbines is aesthetic. Philosopher Yuriko Saito addressed this reality in her defense of a proposed windfarm off the coast of Cape Cod. She wrote, "The possible negative environmental impact, such as disturbance to area fish as well as to migrating birds, and interference with seafaring route and airplanes' flight paths, seems to have been adequately answered. So what is the source of the opposition? Aesthetics."[15] In "Machines in the Ocean," Saito offered four strategies aimed at mitigating these aesthetic concerns: imaginative comparison, historical precedents, analogy to art, and civic environmentalism. Although Saito seemed to endorse civic environmentalism, I see my endeavor here as closer to what she termed "imaginative comparison."

Imaginative comparison first requires moving the aesthetic evaluation of an item beyond simply its "thin" qualities such as color, shape, and texture to including its "thick" life values such as its environmental impact. Second, it asks the individual to imaginatively compare a proposed windfarm project with that of a nuclear power plant in the same location. Although each reaction may be negative, the case could be made that the windfarm is less bad than the nuclear power plant because of its positive environmental benefits. Saito conceded that such a strategy would amount to choosing the lesser of two evils and ultimately would not transform the negative aesthetic value of windfarms into a positive one. At its best then, imaginative comparison will promote a tolerance for windfarms but will fail to cultivate an aesthetic appreciation for these structures. The primary goal of this chapter, however, is just that—to move beyond tolerance toward an aesthetic appreciation for windfarms.

Many windfarm opponents currently regard windfarms as ugly based purely on their emotional response. Such responses only judge the "thin" qualities of wind turbines and fail to take into consideration their "thick" environmental benefits. We find justification for these types of aesthetic judgments in Kant's *Critique of Judgment*, which defends purely emotional aesthetic evaluations. I contend that such judgments must be challenged. What is needed is an understanding of beauty which incorporates both emotional and cognitive components. We find this in John Dewey's *Art as Experience*, which presents aesthetic judgments not as lying within the domain of emotions alone but as being a holistic encounter with an object. I conclude that Dewey's aesthetic provides a better method of judging objects of beauty and is more beneficial toward advancing an aesthetic appreciation of wind turbine farms. I begin therefore by looking at the problems posed by a feeling-based aesthetic.

Immanuel Kant's Critique of Judgment

Immanuel Kant begins his "Analytic of the Beautiful" in *Critique of Judgment* by stating,

> If we wish to decide whether something is beautiful or not, we do not use understanding to refer the presentation to the object so as to give rise to cognition; rather, we use imagination (perhaps in connection with understanding) to refer the presentation to the subject and his feeling of pleasure or displeasure.[16]

Here Kant drew the boundaries of all aesthetic judgments around feeling of pleasure or displeasure. Consequently, if we wanted to know if an object was beautiful or not, we were not to look to the object for understanding but to the viewing subject for feelings of pleasure or displeasure. In this regard, Kant understood all aesthetic judgments to be wholly subjective, meaning they were determined and validated by the subject. This was unlike cognitive judgments, which referred back to the object. Although these judgments were each derived from the same representation, one was aesthetic and the other logical; one was based on feelings and the other on understanding. This separation maintained a clear distinction between judgments that were aesthetics and those that were cognitive. Yet this also left aesthetic judgments to the individual mercies of subjective feelings with no grounds for external agreement or dissent. Kant therefore determined four characteristics necessary for pure aesthetic judgments: (1) disinterestedness, (2) universality, (3) finality, and (4) necessity.

First, Kant argued that judgments of beauty must be disinterested. This meant that in judging whether an object was beautiful or not, I could have no personal interest or desire for that object. A "pure judgment of taste" was completely free of desire. This did not mean that I could not desire a beautiful object, yet, it did mean that I could not judge an object as beautiful because I desired it. At a certain point, the argument begins to resemble the question of which came first, the chicken or the egg. Kant contended that a "judgment on the beautiful which is tinged with the slightest interest, is very partial and not a pure judgment of taste."[17] This is because Kant believed that to desire an object implied knowledge of the object as either good or agreeable. In either case, a concept of the object was required for such knowledge, and this could only be derived from understanding in cognition. Thus Kant's characteristic of disinterestedness ensures a distinction between the object's real existence and the subject's aesthetic judgment.

Marc Lucht suggested that this idea might actually hold environmental benefits. He argued that the concept of disinterestedness can be utilized in motivating a noninstrumental and responsive attitude toward nature. "Aesthetic contemplation is indifferent to the manner in which the judged object's existence might contribute to one's well-being, and we find ourselves enraptured by something independent of its capacity to contribute to the satisfaction of our selfish interests."[18] According to Lucht, this would open up space for nature to be judged as an end in itself as opposed to something merely for human utility.

Lucht's point is well taken but only accurate in so far as two criteria apply: (1) All judgments must refer to nature and nonrational beings and (2) all judgments must be positive. The negation of either of these criteria exposes the intrinsic challenges of appropriating this concept as environmentally beneficial. It is worth pointing out that in spite of stating "aesthetic consciousness involves a love of (at least beautiful) objects for their own sake," Lucht never actually discusses objects—only nature and nonrational beings. However, some people love houses. They ride through suburban neighborhoods and appreciate two- and three-story homes with paved driveways and three-car garages. They look in admiration at in-ground swimming pools and well-manicured yards, and without desiring to live in these homes, they appreciate their beauty.

Ironically though, the massive amounts of energy necessary to power these neighborhoods is often the very reason, as wind power opponents argue, wind farms are insufficient as sole sources of energy. Jon Boone, in his opposition to the windfarm project off the coast of Cape Cod, wrote, "These windplants will contribute only a small and diminishing percentage of the region's total electricity needs because they will produce only 'a piddling amount of electricity' relative to our demand." One should ask if this is an indictment against the windfarm or against the out-of-control energy demands of society. In either case, this case demonstrates how the disinterested appreciation of houses motivates the unreflective disregard for nature.

The second criterion exposes the implications of negative aesthetic judgments resulting from feelings of displeasure. Although Lucht does not address this possibility in his essay, it is easy to imagine the problem of an aesthetic wholly validated by feelings when those feelings are negative. Namely, if disinterested feelings of pleasure lead to a noninstrumental sensitivity to natural beauty, then, in the contrast, disinterested feelings of displeasure would lead to a noninstrumental insensitivity toward aberrations. This would explain why many windfarm projects are met with such hostility and disdain; individuals are blinded by their emotional reactions and disinterested in the potential environmental benefits.

Kant's second and fourth categories are similar enough that I treat them here in unison. Kant argued that judgments of beauty carry the claim of universality. Kant believed that since the statement "this is beautiful" carried with it no interest or cognitive understanding of the object, the claim must view beauty as being an intrinsic quality of the representation of the object. Beauty, for Kant then, was not in the eye of the beholder, but rather it was in the representation of the beautiful thing.

Consequently, Kant also felt that judgments of beauty carried with them a claim of necessity. He wrote, "In all judgments by which we describe anything as beautiful, we tolerate no one else being of a different opinion."[19] Although the claim to necessity did not imply that everyone will agree with our judgments of beauty, it did state that everyone ought to. Thus disagreements were thought to be derived from a subjective error in judgment as opposed to differing opinions. The implication was that anyone with common sense would experience the same feelings of pleasure or displeasure as I do.

Before considering that such an idea is absurd, consider the actions of windfarm opponents who argue that windfarms are ugly without ever actually qualifying that claim. It's as if they, too, believe that everyone ought to feel the same. Some make reference to wind turbines' height or their obtrusiveness onto natural land-scapes as justification; yet many buildings are tall and roads are visible from almost every place on Earth. Few areas remain purely "natural" and certainly not the "backyards" of communities that oppose windfarm projects. One has to wonder where these defenders of the "natural" environment were when trees were being cut down to build the communities in which they now reside.

In Jon Boone's article, "The Aesthetic Dissonance of Industrial Wind Machines," he somewhat undertook this task by comparing windfarms to other structures such as the Great Wall of China and the Eiffel Tower. He concluded that "only the US highway system has the scope and scale to match the aesthetic pretensions for industrial wind power."[20] In spite of the fact that roads' functional success has allowed them to become an accepted part of the natural environment, Boone stated that environmentalists should also have problems with the way in which they scar the earth, diminish ecosystems, and corrupt economies. I was, however, unable to find any articles Boone had written on the aesthetic dissonance of roads; nevertheless, the type of aesthetic justification he attempts to provide against windfarms is precisely what should be required of other opponents of windfarms projects. Unfortunately, many opponents are content with making the universal claim that windfarms are ugly because they are ugly.

Kant's third characteristic required that an object of beauty exhibit finality without an end. Although the finality in an object implies an end, Kant contended that an aesthetic judgment could not take into consideration the object's end since again this would include cognitive understanding. Knowing the object's purpose would incline the viewer to base her aesthetic judgment on either the object's utility or its conformity to an ideal. One should ask, then, "How can a viewer find pleasure in an object exhibiting finality and at the same time disassociate it from its end?" Kant would say that the pleasure derived from viewing a river is a result of the harmony and free play of intuition in the subject and the intuitive purposiveness of the river's form. However, understanding the "literal" purposiveness of the river would taint its aesthetic judgment since "every purpose, if it be regarded as a ground of satisfaction, always carries with it an interest—as the determining ground of the judgment—about the object of pleasure."[21]

The difficulty of performing such a separation is obvious. A river to an approaching swimmer would be a welcomed sight and perhaps even beautiful because for her it represents recreation and delight. To a man who experienced nearly drowning, however, it would evoke feeling of anxiety and fear. Thus what is beautiful to the woman would be loathsome to the man. Although Kant would argue that a "true" aesthetic judgment of the river would require both subjects to free their minds from these cognitions, it is difficult, if not impossible, to imagine anyone who, upon approaching a river, would be able to successfully remove all prior knowledge of a river from their mind in order to make a purely emotional judgment.

The disservice of attempting to perform such a separation is evident in windfarm opponents' refusal to consider environmental benefits of windfarms as justification for their beauty. In the United Kingdom, figures show that almost half of the windfarms planned for the countryside are rejected before they can get off the drawing board. Attorney Jacqueline Harris noted that issues such as the visual impact of wind turbines are being given special precedence, and there is little willingness to consider the benefits of renewable energy.[22] In spite of research that shows that windfarms occupy less land area per kilowatt-hour of electricity generated than any other renewable energy conversion system (apart from rooftop solar energy), they generate the energy used in construction in just months of their operation, and they have zero emission or pollution in operation, they are still regarded by "NIMBYs" as just another industrial park.[23]

Opponents to the wind turbine project on Kythera Island stated, "Even the approval of one wind-park on Kythera will make it easier for the rest of Kythera to be re-zoned for industrial use. You might then see wind-towers and factories and dumps spoiling the view from your spitaki."[24] The concept of finality without an end then implies that all objects which evoke the same feelings are the same. This promotes a disregard for the distinctions between windfarms and factories and justifies generalizations which are harmful to the development of an aesthetic appreciation for windfarms.

John Dewey's *Art as Experience*

Dewey began his philosophy of aesthetic vastly different from Kant. He argued that the current isolation of works of art from the everyday experiences which brought them into existence has led to a false separation. A wall has been built around art which renders its general significance almost opaque and isolates it from human conditions and actual life experiences. Such a perspective, he believed, was problematic. Dewey wrote, "Mountain peaks do not float unsupported; they do not even just rest upon the earth. They are the earth in one of its manifest operations."[25] He then goes on to argue that it is the role of geographers and geologists to make this fact evident so that individuals can experience the mountain peak as a part of Earth's geological process (i.e., earthquakes, erosion, and tectonic plate shifting). Likewise, the real and actual experiences that bring a work of art into existence are also an intrinsic part of the object which cannot be disavowed from it, and the theorist who deals philosophically with fine art must expose this reality. Dewey's aesthetic, then, is an attempt to relocate aesthetic experience back within the context of human activity.

By integrating perception and contemplation in aesthetic judgments, Dewey presented a holistic theory of beauty. It expanded the realm of aesthetics beyond merely those of feelings and opened up space for individuals to reflect on the purpose of an object's development. Dewey understood the aesthetic experience as touching every aspect of human life, and thus art was not relegated to a field of classification. Art, he wrote,

> is a quality that permeates an experience; it is not, save by a figure of speech, the experience itself. Esthetic experience is always more than esthetics. In it a body of matters and

meanings, not in themselves esthetic, become esthetic as they enter into an ordered rhythmic moment towards consummation. The material itself is widely human.[26]

In this regard, anything could be considered art, artistic, or aesthetic. Science, politics, and even thoughts could comprise and exhibit an aesthetic quality. In many ways, then, where we see beauty says more about us than it does about the object.

By placing Dewey's aesthetic in contrast to Kant's, we are able to identify critical points of divergence. Whereas Kant's aesthetic helps to explain the current aesthetic perspective held by windfarm opponents, Dewey's aesthetic pushes the conversation forward by challenging those judgments. In an age where the exploitation of nonrenewable resources is rampant, where oil fuels not only cars but wars and where the negative effects of climate change are more pronounced than ever, the lack of an aesthetic appreciation of windfarms can only be seen as negligent. In Dewey's *Art as Experience*, I suggest that we can find the case for such an appreciation.

Dewey believed that the process of aesthetic judgment involved more than merely judging an object. He wrote, "For to perceive, a beholder must create his own experience."[27] This meant the beholder had to have an experience with the object similar to the one had by the artist in creation. However, the experiences were not the same. Each determined what was significant and ordered the particulars into a whole: "[T]he artist selected, simplified, clarified, abridged and condensed according to his interest. The beholder must go through these operations according to his interest."[28]

This meant that aesthetic judgments were more than just about the object and the artist. They were also about the interests of the viewer, what he brought to the encounter, and how he synthesized the experience within his mind. Objects were comprised of practical, emotional, and intellectual properties, and, according to Dewey, it was impossible to divide these properties from each other as one experienced an object. Aesthetic judgments were no easy task, but ultimately the object demanded a holistic encounter. Those who only focus on the emotional, however, are left with only a partial judgment of the object, one that is deficient and lacking.

A genuine aesthetic experience was one that gave a consummatory experience and afforded continuous renewed delight. It was one which had the ability to exhibit the experience of production and consummation for viewers over and over again. For this reason,

Dewey believed that fine art should be both enjoyable and useful. What was often regarded as fine art he referred to as self-indulgent, self-expressions of egotism. In contrast, Dewey referred to things which were merely useful as routine.

In the case of windfarms, their utility is undeniable, even by opponents who would want to diminish their significance. In addition, others have commented on the "graceful lines" wind turbines exhibit in motions.[29] Yet these characteristics alone are insufficient to advance an aesthetic appreciation of windfarms. Individuals with a genuine interest for the natural environment must view wind turbines in light of those interests. An aesthetic evaluation which privileges sustainability will inevitably find beauty in windfarms for the role they play in this endeavor. As Maine resident Harold Clossey expressed, "Wind turbines are becoming more and more a source of pride, not only because so many of the people of Maine have played a part in bringing these projects to bear, but also because we believe in clean, renewable energy sources that do not pollute our rivers, lakes and streams."[30]

Kant's second and fourth categories were that beauty is universal and necessary. Dewey, however, understood the subjectivity of aesthetic judgments differently. As opposed to believing that aesthetic judgments ought to be universally shared, Dewey felt that all judgments were individualistic. Retelling the story of a man who complained of the discordant sound of church bells, he pointed out that, in fact, the sound was musical. It was later discovered that the man's betrothed had jilted him to marry a clergyman. Dewey termed this "projection."[31] That is, prior experiences transfer themselves upon the aesthetic evaluation of a present object. Such projection can lead to hostile first reactions to new modes of art.[32]

Contrary to the claim that there exists a universal subjective perception of beauty, Dewey actually argued that individual experiences and even psychical influences infuse our perception of what is beautiful. David Suzuki's recounting of a conversation with Mostafa Tolba, former executive director of the United Nations Environment Programme, demonstrated this reality. He shared with Suzuki that growing up in Egypt, smokestacks belching out smoke was considered a sign of progress. After becoming an adult and learning about pollution, it took him a long time to get over the instinctive pride he felt when passing a tower pouring out clouds of smoke. Notice that for Tolba these feelings were not deliberate or conjured up, rather they were instinctive. He demonstrates how our sense of beauty is influenced by our individual experiences.

As Justin Good pointed out in "The Aesthetics of Wind Energy," "projections" can explain why many environmentalists are opposed to windfarms. He stated that from a traditional modernist point of view, nature has no intrinsic value unless it is valued by an intelligent being with rational interests. Naturalists and ecologists who love nature and spend time there recoil at this idea. For them, the "industrial look" of wind farms is connected to modernist thought and carries with it an ideology of progress which they perceive as unnatural and ugly.[33] Dewey's understanding of how "projections" influence individual aesthetic judgments provides the opportunity for windfarm supporters and opponents to discuss these barriers. Dewey also wrote,

> [E]sthetic experience is a manifestation, a record and celebration of the life of a civilization, a means of promoting its development, and is also the ultimate judgment upon the quality of a civilization.[34]

Dewey believed then that by understanding the aesthetic experiences of a civilization, we could come to understand their culture. Art was not merely an aspect of culture, but it was the ultimate judge. As we appreciate a work of art, then, we are also appreciating the civilization from which it emerged. Though the artist may have passed away, his act of producing provides us with insight into his life and community.

As opposed to attempting to detach the ends of objects from their aesthetic judgments, it would behoove us, at in the case of windfarms, to ask what our aesthetic expressions will say about us to the next generation. Some have presumed that windfarms will become a blight on nature. Columnist Ted Smith wrote, "History tells us that all technology becomes obsolete and when technology that involves massive concrete pads and blades the size of airplane wings becomes obsolete and abandoned we will have another Tar Creek."[35] The comparison suggests that windfarms will hold no aesthetic quality when viewed from the vantage point of time and perhaps might even become comparable to a Superfund site.

It is worth noting, however, that Smith's argument here is a practical one and not aesthetic. His concern is instances in which developers, for any number of reasons, abandon windfarm projects. Often what is left behind is a wind turbine junkyard as opposed to an operating windfarm. Practically, I agree with Smith that developers should be held accountable to restore these locations to their pre-windfarm condition. A nonoperative, dilapidated wind farm would hardly be considered beautiful regardless of whether one was deploying Kant's or Dewey's aesthetic. However, I would disagree with the assumption that the mere inactivity of a windfarm would negate its beauty.

If one were to make a visit to the Smithsonian National Air and Space Museum in Washington, D.C., it would include the original 1903 Wright Flyer displayed alongside the stopwatch the Wright brothers used to time the first powered flight. Also on display would be the command module for Apollo 13, the vessel that held the first three humans to make a journey to the moon. Although these devices are no longer in use, their construction, the knowledge of their place in history, and the ingenuity behind their design all contribute to their aesthetic appeal. Furthermore, they reflect the culture of a civilization marked by technology and exploration.

As society moves forward in the face of climate change and global warming, we should begin to ask ourselves what values we want portrayed about us in the next one hundred years. If Dewey is correct that our aesthetics are the ultimate judge of our values, then the road ahead is difficult one. An article published in September 2011 indicated that Texas has nineteen coal-fired plants and plans to build nine more.[36] Dewey's aesthetic provides criteria to view such decisions as contradictory and challenges us to examine the ends of the objects and structures we create. If the ideals we seek to advance are sustainability, biodiversity, and concern for posterity, judging objects with their ends in mind will inevitably serve to expose the beauty of windfarms.

Conclusion

In conclusion, Dewey offers a response to the aesthetic concerns presented in Kant and the feeling-based aesthetic practiced by many windfarm opponents. By advancing an aesthetic which integrates interest, individuality, and purpose, we are able to understand beauty as a total experience with an object rather than simply an emotive response. And if, peradventure, Dewey's only contribution here was correction to a currently dysfunctional system, while this would be commendable, it could hardly be deemed an advance in an aesthetic appreciation of windfarms. But there's more!

The greatest benefit in Dewey's aesthetic lies in its potential to enrich future aesthetic judgments. According to Dewey, experiences are occurring continuously; however, they are not all complete experiences. Some are inchoate, meaning that they are merely part of a total experience. Every "experience," then, is not necessarily "an experience." Take, for instance, Dr. Martin Luther King's famous "I Have a Dream" speech; it would hardly be considered "an experience" if an individual heard only those four words. There would be no purposiveness, unity, or consummation; however, within the context of the entire manuscript, those words ring with artistry and bravado. Thus it is only after one has partaken in a whole experience that one can genuinely make an aesthetic judgment. While this does not preclude aesthetic judgments along the way, Dewey would say that without a total experience there is no pure aesthetic judgment.

For communities and windfarm opponents, this means that upon hearing of a proposed windfarm project, they should delay their judgment and opposition. Instead of immediately reacting from an emotional place, they should have town hall gatherings and attend city council meetings. By discussing the potential benefits/harms of a proposed windfarm project, individuals will slowly move toward having "an experience." In Boone's article "The Aesthetic Dissonance of Wind Machines," he challenged Saito's support of the Cape Cod windfarm project. He called attention to the relatively low percentage of electricity the project would produce and also questioned its location given that 33 percent of the nation's potential wind energy is located in North Dakota, South Dakota, and Kansas.[37] In response, Saito indicated that both sides were waiting for the final report of the environmental impacts study by the U.S. Army Corps of Engineers.[38]

Dewey would not only applaud this type of rigorous and engaged research but he would argue that a pure aesthetic judgment demands it. In some situations, a proposed environmental project may actually produce more harm than good, altering its aesthetic evaluation. In 1979, as the Tellico Dam was being completed to bring hydro electric power to Tellico Village in Tennessee, it was discovered that the dam would put the Snail Darter fish in danger of extinction. Consequently, the project was halted. Although the project was later completed, this is one example of how an ongoing query into environmental impacts of a project can and should affect its aesthetic judgment.

Allen Carlson wrote, "When we are actually unable to find an object aesthetically pleasing in the thick sense because of the (negative) nature of its expressive qualities, this often makes aesthetic enjoyment of this object in the thin sense psychologically difficult, if not impossible."[39] Carlson's observation points out how knowledge of the "thick" description of an object can affect its aesthetic enjoyment. Saito made a similar point when she questioned the perception of a beautiful green lawn sustained by toxic chemicals. "Such an attractive green carpet may not necessarily turn ugly with knowledge, but it may start appearing somewhat sickly and garish; at the very least, it will not remain innocently and benignly beautiful."[40] These points demonstrate that additional knowledge of an object's negative impacts can affect the sensory perception of that object. The question remains, however, if knowledge of benefits can make an object beautiful. Professor David Suzuki's article "The Beauty of Windfarms" suggests so:

Some people think wind turbines are ugly. I think smokestacks, smog, acid rain, coal-fired power plants and climate change are ugly. I think windmills are beautiful. They harness the power of the wind to supply us with heat and light. They provide local jobs. They help clean our air and reduce climate change. And if one day I look out from my cabin's porch and see a row of windmills spinning in the distance, I won't curse them. I will praise them.[41]

For Suzuki, coal-fired plants and windfarms are not simply different types of industrial parks that ruin the beauty of nature as Kythera, Greece, residents suggest. Rather, coal-fired plants are ugly because they contaminate drinking water, ruin air quality, and increase climate change, while windfarms are beautiful because they produce zero harmful emissions, are 100 percent renewable, and reduce climate change. Such an understanding integrates both cognitive and emotional judgments into an aesthetic evaluation and is indicative of hard but necessary work required for an aesthetic appreciation of windfarms.

Of course, there are limits to even Dewey's philosophy, and I am not in any way suggesting that cognitive knowledge will change aesthetic judgments in every case. That would be far too idealistic. There is undoubtedly a difference in the aesthetic appeal of two wind farms with the same degree of environmental value based on qualities like color, arrangement, size, and so forth. In this regard, Kant's aesthetic is not useless nor am I advocating the random, disorderly arrangement of clumsy wind turbine structures against a landscape. Factors such as placement, color, and configuration all serve to enhance the aesthetic appeal of a wind turbine farm and can even meet the standards of Kant's purposiveness without a purpose. The distinction between Kant and Dewey, then, is not that Kant is against wind turbine and Dewey in favor but rather their basis for judging beauty. Dewey's aesthetic asks a lot of individuals in the way of conceptual knowledge and requires that individuals move beyond a mere knee-jerk reaction toward being informed, aware, perceptive, and engaged. This is not impractical. As Saito pointed out, "[W]e engage in conceptually-based aesthetic appreciation with works of art all the time—by taking courses in music, art history, and literature. . . . It is just that we have not developed an equivalent formal discipline or discourse guiding our aesthetic appreciation of nature, environment, and designed objects."[42]

If the current decline in wind turbine sales along with Kant's feeling-based aesthetic is going to be overcome, this work is essential. For although it is far from my intention to lay the environmental woes of society at the feet of Immanuel Kant, his philosophy is not blameless. It is therefore the responsibility of philosophers and environmentalists to take the lead in redirecting renewable energy conversations beyond merely emotional responses toward a more holistic understanding.

CHAPTER

11

Thinking Like a Mall

Steven Vogel

In a famous passage in *A Sand County Almanac*, Aldo Leopold tells of the time he and some others, "young and full of trigger-itch," spotted a wolf and her cubs from a rim rock and shot at them, hitting one of the cubs in the leg and mortally wounding the mother. He writes that he scrambled down in time "to watch a fierce green fire dying in her eyes," and to realize, too late, that there was something "known only to her and to the mountain" that he had heretofore not understood. This hidden truth, he says, became clear in later years, as wolf herds were extirpated from many mountains on the theory that "because fewer wolves meant more deer . . . no wolves would mean hunters' paradise," and the consequence turned out instead to be a population explosion of deer that led, in turn, to slopes denuded of low-growing brush and a deer herd decimated by starvation. We must learn to "think like a mountain," Leopold concludes, by which I take it he means to go beyond our own limited understanding and to recognize the complexity and depth, indeed the very otherness of those natural processes we hubristically think ourselves able to control.[1]

I

In 1989 the City Center Mall opened in Columbus, Ohio. It was a project supported by the city of Columbus in an effort to revitalize a downtown that had been in serious decline for many years, by attracting suburban and other shoppers to an "upscale" mall anchored by significant and popular retailers such as Marshall Field's and Jacobsen's, neither of which had ever had a store in Central Ohio. With 1.3 million square feet of retail space, the mall took up several city blocks in the traditional center of the city and was, at the time, the largest mall in the region; it included several parking garages, one underneath the mall and another just to its south, that charged only $1 for a full day's parking, as well as an enclosed pedestrian walkway over a major street connecting it to the flagship store of the biggest and most successful local department store chain, Lazarus.[2] The mall was owned by the Taubman Company, and its design was similar to that of several other malls Taubman had developed, including the Beverly Center in Los Angeles. From the street, it was a large white cube, almost windowless. Inside there were three stories, with stores on each level along the sides of the structure connected by walkways that encircled a large central atrium; part of the atrium consisted of a kind of amphitheatre where one could sit and rest, or eat, while another part included some trees, a small fountain, as well as a few statues of what were apparently supposed to be typical customers (a woman with a small child, a man in business attire holding a newspaper) in front of which one would sometimes do a double-take before realizing that they weren't alive. Two glass elevators rose from the center of the amphitheatre. There were also escalators connecting the levels, carefully placed at various ends of the mall in such a way that it was quite difficult to get from one level to any other without having to walk all the way around the perimeter, something that the designers had clearly intended so as to maximize the number of stores one would pass on the way. The result was that it was impossible to simply pop into the mall to pick up one item—the organization of pedestrian traffic was such that any trip into the cube was inevitably an extended one. The lack of windows also meant that there was virtually no connection between inside and outside; inside the mall, brightly lit and gleaming with chrome and modernistic fixtures, there was no sense of being in the heart of a gritty and economically depressed downtown, while from the surrounding streets the mall appeared as a contentless white box with only a few signs to indicate what lay within.

City Center was an immediate hit; on its opening day, sixty thousand people visited, and it quickly became the most successful mall in the area—a "destination" mall that attracted customers from all over central Ohio.[3] By 1995, its sales volume of $400 per square foot placed it among the top 10 percent of all shopping malls in the United States.[4] At its height, there were more than 150 shops in the mall, including Henri Bendel, Brooks Brothers, Cinnabon, Waldenbooks, the Body Shop, Coach, and many others. The Limited Corporation, whose headquarters are in Columbus and which at the time was in a headlong expansion mode, announced soon after the mall opened that every one of its brands (Victoria's Secret, Limited Inc., Structure, etc.) would be represented at the mall. In those days, I lived about eight blocks away, and although I hated the mall I went there much more often than I would have wanted to admit. My kids loved it there; they tell me that their memories are of a glittering place filled with toys and excitement, the first place they saw Santa Claus, the place they learned to toss coins in a fountain and make a wish. There were concerts in the atrium (Hanson played there once), parades, and parties; there were attractive decorations, nice music, and a pleasant atmosphere. It's true that in its fifth year of operation what was described by police as a gang-related shooting took place in the mall in the middle of a busy shopping day, leaving one person dead—but this seemed an anomaly and barely did anything to damage the mall's reputation as the best place to shop in the central Ohio area.[5]

And yet today, City Center is no more. In 1997 its owner, the Taubman Company, opened a second mall on the northwest side of the city, the Mall at Tuttle Crossing, which was also described as "upscale" and included a Marshall Fields and other similar stores. The suburbs northwest of Columbus are particularly wealthy ones, and shoppers who lived there now no longer had to drive downtown (and pay for parking) to shop. Taubman, perhaps filled with trigger-itch, apparently thought that if one mall meant profit, a second one meant more profit, and shrugged off concerns that City Center might lose customers.[6] And then a few years later, developers associated with the Limited opened a massive new mall northeast of the city (in an area home to a new and even more wealthy suburb) named Easton Town Center, while yet another developer opened one on the north side (near, guess what, yet more wealthy suburbs) called the Polaris Fashion Center. The consequence of the opening of these three malls—larger, more modern, with free parking—for City Center was fatal.[7] It began to lose customers, and then shops, and then more customers in a death-spiral that accelerated remarkably quickly and was not helped by the poor economic environment for big department stores in the late nineties, as Jacobsen's went bankrupt, the flagship Lazarus store closed, and Marshall Fields was sold to Kaufman's, which was then renamed Macy's after being taken over by Federated Department Stores.[8]

Ultimately, the loss of tenants was unstoppable as the mall began to resemble more and more a mountain overgrazed by deer. Vacant storefronts were rented out for corporate meetings.[9] Upscale stores were replaced by downscale ones. A big-screen television was placed in the atrium showing soap operas in a desperate attempt to bring in more customers.[10] In 2006 a tattoo parlor moved in (motto: "Put some class on your ass").[11] In 2007 Macy's, the last anchor remaining, announced it was closing.[12] In the summer of that year, the owners (no longer Taubman—the mall by this point had been sold multiple times) stopped paying rent on the land, which was owned by the city of Columbus. A candidate for mayor held a press conference inside the nearly empty mall, criticizing the incumbent for doing nothing about what he called "the world's biggest aboveground cavern" and ending by saying: "Mr. Mayor, tear down this mall!"[13] In 2008 there were no more retail chain tenants, and less than twenty tenants altogether; by 2009 that number had dropped to eight.[14] In February 2009 the nonprofit urban development group that had originally planned the mall as a way to revitalize downtown Columbus, and that now had title to it, announced—with the strong encouragement of the (reelected) mayor—that it would be closed, the fixtures sold off at auction, and the building demolished, to be replaced by a new public park.[15] Demolition began in October 2009 and was completed in March of 2010. Construction of the park, named the Columbus Commons, started soon afterward; it opened to the public on May 26, 2011.[16]

No one mourns the mall much, though some (like my children) feel nostalgic for it, and presumably there are investors who are sad about the money they lost because of its failure. Many others are glad to be rid of an eyesore and happy to have a park. Photographs of the mall are surprisingly hard to find, and when I mention this fact to fellow Columbusites—including reference librarians trained in neutrality—it's striking how frequently they say, "that's because it was so ugly!" Its demolition was ugly, too. So is the death of a wolf, of course, and so, too, usually, is a mountain overgrazed by deer. And there's the question I want to pursue: What's the difference, if any, between the death of a mall and the death of a mountain, or of a she-wolf?[17] Leopold's poignant description expresses sadness about the wolf's death, and about the destruction of the mountainside that death portended, and, of course, it expresses as well his own retrospective sense of guilt and of a kind of shame over his youthful naiveté and that of his comrades. But nobody, I suspect, feels similarly about the loss of the Cinnabon at the City Center, tasty though its products were, and although there may be some investors or developers who feel guilt, and maybe even shame, about the failure of the mall,

I doubt that those who ordered its demolition feel anything along those lines—nor do the young men, full of trigger-itch in those days themselves perhaps, who actually carried it out. (Nor will they, I suspect, as they get older.) I want to ask quite seriously about the differences here—about why we find the loss of the wolf, or of the mountain, poignant and yet feel nothing similar about the loss of a piece of the built environment. And more importantly, I want to ask what it might mean to *think like a mall*, or whether thinking like one might help us better understand our environment, at least as well as thinking like a mountain would. There were no windows at the City Center Mall, as I have noted, and yet I cannot help but wonder whether, as the final walls and girders were smashed by a wrecking ball on the last evening of demolition, one might have been able to see, in the reflection of the suddenly visible setting sun glinting off the debris of sales counters and display cases as they lay on the ground, a fierce green fire dying in the Marshall Fields. Was there something the mall knew that we did not, or that the Taubman Company did not? Is there something we might learn if we tried to *think like a mall*?[18]

We do mourn buildings, sometimes: The old Pennsylvania Station in New York is a well-known example, designed by McKim, Meade, and White and demolished in 1963 in what the *New York Times* called a "monumental act of vandalism against one of the largest and finest landmarks of its age."[19] The World Trade Center is, of course, another example. Large-scale destruction of buildings is deplorable, too: We mourn what happened to Hiroshima, to Dresden, to London during the Blitz. But in these sorts of cases, what we mourn has to do with the aesthetic or symbolic value of the buildings, or more directly still with the people inside them who died in their collapse. If there is anything like "intrinsic value" to these buildings, it might have to do with their beauty or their age or their cultural significance; nothing like a Leopoldian "land ethic" with its call to value the integrity, beauty, and stability of a biotic community is suggested by our sadness about these particular losses. That's why I choose for my example a building that no one loved (not even the Taubman Company, its "parent," apparently—they sold it as soon as it started to lose money), that no one found to be beautiful, that had no deep cultural significance (though it had an economic one), that was nobody's home, and whose demolition caused no injuries or deaths to people. Should we be sad about its loss—not because of how it looked or what it meant or who it was who loved it or how much money they had invested in it, but *for its own sake*? It's hard to imagine that we should. But then why should we be sad about the wolf, or about the mountain?

II

I am asking, I suppose, about moral considerability. Leopold's remorse about the wolf's death suggests that he thinks it deserved moral consideration; and the difference between the wolf and the mall, it seems clear, is that no one seriously thinks the same thing about malls. I don't either, I hasten to point out: I'm simply asking why not. One immediate answer is that the wolf was alive, or was sentient, while the mall wasn't. But this answer doesn't explain Leopold's suggestion that the *mountain*, too, deserved to exist and to flourish—and indeed that the death of a deer killed by a wolf is less to be regretted than the defoliation of a mountainside caused by the removal of its wolves.[20] A mountain, after all, is neither alive nor sentient; yet Leopold's call to think like one suggests we should learn to feel something like compassion for it nonetheless. But surely the idea of compassion for a mall, for the poor demolished City Center, is senseless: Why? The mountain, we're inclined to answer, is *natural*—and perhaps that's the key difference: It's the *artificiality* of the mall, the fact that it was built by human beings, that seems to remove it from the realm of the morally considerable. But why does the destruction of a natural entity such as a mountainside raise moral questions while the demolition of a building does not?

There's certainly a common intuition that objects built by humans simply don't possess the same moral status as those that are "natural," where the latter term means "unbuilt."[21] But if that intuition were right, it would seem to mean that the act of building, or the human touch itself, can actually transform the moral status of an object, as "natural" raw materials are turned into "artifacts" lacking moral significance. Such a view seems to involve a perverse sort of anthropocentrism according to which one species among all others has the metaphysically impressive ability to rob something of its moral considerability just by interacting with it.[22] Mustn't there be some particular empirical characteristics that natural objects possess and human-made ones do not that lead us to find the former morally considerable and not the latter? If so, what are they?

It has frequently been noted that criteria for moral considerability such as sentience or life involve emphasizing points of commonality between humans and certain groups of nonhumans and then extending the moral concern we unquestioningly grant each other to nonhumans to which we are significantly similar. But when Leopold speaks of thinking like a mountain, he is invoking a metaphor whose point isn't to indicate how similar mountains are to us but rather to show how different they are; we are supposed to *think like a mountain, not like a human.* The mountain's moral status thus stems from its difference from us, from its possession of a perspective nothing like our own—indeed, in Leopold's account it seems almost to derive from its *indifference to* us, from the fact that we are as little significant to it as the deer are, and, in fact, are less significant to it than are the wolves. For Leopold, that is, the moral importance of the mountain arguably has to do with its *otherness* from human beings and human purposes, its unconnectedness to the realm of human concerns and needs. And, of course, the mall does not seem to possess this kind of otherness in the slightest. It was built *by* human beings *for* human purposes, and so its very existence, even its identity as the thing it was, depended on human concerns and needs. Not other from humans at all, City Center, unlike a mountain, seems rather to have been human through and through, part of the human realm, certainly not "natural" in any sense. Natural entities, we might say, possess an existence *independent* of us, and in this sense we can speak of their *autonomy* and of our own actions as either respecting that autonomy or as violating it.[23] Buildings, on the other hand, have no such independence but only come to be because humans have chosen to build them, and in particular only come to have the characteristics they possess because humans have chosen to give them such characteristics; hence they cannot accurately be said to have any autonomy to be violated. Such an argument, I suggest, frequently stands behind our intuition that harm to a mountain is a more serious moral matter than the demolition of a shopping mall.

And yet, does this argument really make sense? Is it correct that the now-demolished City Center Mall lacked autonomy or "otherness" from human beings and human concerns? I'm not so sure. There's no question, of course, that the mall could not have come to be without humans: Humans built it, and they did so for a reason (although, in fact, there were many reasons, and not all the actors involved in the building had the same ones[24]). But does the fact that humans played a significant and intentional role in the genesis of an entity necessarily mean that the entity has no autonomous existence independently of them, no moment of otherness from them that might deserve our respect?

We need, obviously, to ask what "autonomy" means here. It surely doesn't mean, first of all, what it means in Kant—the great moral thinker in whose work the concept of autonomy plays such a significant role. For Kant, of course, it refers to the capacity of a rational moral subject to deliberate and make choices for him or herself about what to do. Surely malls are not autonomous in this sense—but neither are mountains or wolves. The sense involved in Leopold's story seems rather to be a conception of autonomy as *independence*: To speak of the autonomy of an entity is to speak of the way that it would go on, or what it would do or be, *by itself*, that is to say without the involvement of human beings. This might be meant in a stronger or a weaker sense. The stronger sense is what one might call *teleological* or *developmental autonomy*, where the entity has its own internally determined goal or trajectory, and thus a set of changes or developments that it would undergo in the absence of human interference. The cub that Leopold's group shot was growing to maturity, and presumably its being lamed by one of the hunters significantly affected that process of growth (and likely led to its fairly rapid death): In this sense, its autonomy was seriously violated. This sense of autonomy, with its appeal to Aristotelian categories, is particularly well suited to talking about biological organisms, although it certainly can be applied to larger wholes such as ecosystems or Leopold's "biological communities" as well. But there is a weaker sense of autonomy, too, in which one might speak of merely *causal* or *physical autonomy*. Here autonomy is merely a matter of an entity's being *left alone*, being allowed to undergo whatever causal physical processes it confronts; talking of autonomy in this sense does not require viewing the object as involved in some sort of internally directed teleological self-development. If whatever would happen to the entity in the absence of human involvement is permitted to happen, if whatever changes it would undergo are, in fact, undergone, then the autonomy of the entity in this weaker sense has been respected. Eric Katz uses the example of the debate about the use of metal bolts hammered into rocks to aid climbers to talk about autonomy in just this way: A "cliff without the bolts," he says, "exhibits a kind of autonomy and freedom that has been denied the modified cliff."[25] The latter has been subjected to forces that, in the absence of human involvement, would never have affected it. And, of course, the inverse case is also possible, of a rock face being *prevented* from undergoing changes that would otherwise occur so as to satisfy human purposes, as, for instance, in the—ultimately unsuccessful—attempts to maintain the Old Man of the Mountain in New Hampshire.[26] In both of these sorts of case, we might still speak meaningfully of the rock's "autonomy" being violated without needing to appeal to anything like an Aristotelian telos.

But neither of these senses of autonomy has to do with the *genesis* of the entity, nor do they clearly differentiate natural entities from those that human beings have built. With respect to the causal/physical sense, it seems clear that built objects are just as subject to the causal forces of nature as non-built ones are and that it is just as possible to "interfere" with the operation of those forces in the one case as in the other. (Think, for example, of the terrible effects of the 2011 earthquake and tsunami on the nuclear reactors at the Fukushima Daiichi plant, or of the seawalls at that plant, which, of course, themselves were built in order to "interfere" with tsunamis to protect the reactors but unfortunately failed to do so.) And autonomy in the teleological/developmental sense is similarly not limited to entities whose origin lies outside human action: Domesticated animals, hybridized plants, genetically modified organisms all owe their existence to intentional human actions and yet still possess internally guided developmental trajectories that other intentional human actions can frustrate or modify. (And arguably, this is true of abiotic artifacts, too: thermostats, automatic pilots, search engines. . . .) But there's an even clearer example of an entity produced through human action that is nonetheless capable of an autonomy (in fact, in the strongest Kantian sense) that can be interfered with but ought not to be: a human baby. Babies are surely the product of human action, and often of intentional human action, but they are surely also capable of developing autonomy—and indeed that autonomy is part of what the parents typically intend when they decide to have a child. If one objects that the actions and processes that produce a child and those that produce a mall are quite different, the answer is that, of course, they are; the point is simply that if buildings or other humanly constructed things are incapable of autonomy, it cannot be simply because they're produced by human action but because of something about the *kind* of human action that produces them—and it's not so easy to specify what it is about processes of building as opposed to those processes (some of which are nowadays highly technologized) that produce babies that makes the difference.[27]

The City Center Mall was surely subject to causal physical forces: its exterior walls were heated and bleached by the sun, in different ways and to different extents depending on their orientation; rain and snow and sometimes hail fell upon and weathered its roof; gravity and other structural forces kept it rooted to the ground and prevented it from falling in upon itself; chemical forces in the steel girders that held it up guaranteed their strength. Gamma rays pierced the mall, and an earthquake might have caused it to collapse. But it also had a developmental or teleological character, in several senses. It grew, first of all—beginning as a hole in the ground and then slowly developing both upward as it was built and also outward as connections (the skywalk, the parking garages, an underground passageway) developed between it and the surrounding buildings. It responded to changes in its environment in a way oriented toward homeostasis—its internal temperature, for example, was regulated in response to changes in the weather outside, as the heating and air-conditioning systems cycled on and off via thermostats. When one store failed and threatened the mall's profitability, another one took its place. The mall underwent repetitive transformation in accordance with diurnal, annual, and other cycles: The lighting inside went on and off according to a regular schedule, as did the music that played there; Christmas decorations appeared after Thanksgiving, and disappeared after the new year; Easter eggs and bunnies showed up in store windows a few months later; and later still the windows of the clothing stores showed bikinis and short-sleeved shirts, in a pattern that repeated itself in accordance with the motion of the earth around the sun. As the mall began to fail, its ability to maintain homeostasis faltered as well: The decorations lost their regularity and vitality, the hours of light and darkness shifted as the opening hours changed, stores disappeared and weren't replaced, and eventually the HVAC ceased to function and the internal temperature of the mall began to shift more rapidly and uncontrollably.

City Center's ultimate death, though, was swift and wasn't produced by homeostatic imbalance or failure; rather it took the form of a violent and catastrophic demolition by wrecking balls that quickly put an end to the teleological forces operative within the mall and to the causal/physical ones as well. Its demise, like that of the she-wolf Leopold killed, was not the result of its own internal development but rather occurred because its human owners were unwilling to "let it be," and instead insisted on destroying it because it no longer served their own purposes, thus imposing those purposes upon a mall whose independence and otherness from those owners were causing them mounting economic losses.

It's true that humans built the mall, situating it in a way that took sunlight and rain into account, setting the thermostats to a particular temperature, determining the opening and closing hours, and putting up Christmas wreaths and swimsuit displays on the basis of commercial considerations. Yet what is it about those facts that robs the mall of its "autonomy" in the sense that we might speak of a rock face or an oak tree as autonomous? Once it's built, doesn't a building go on *by itself*? And isn't there always more to it than those who built it intended, or could imagine? There were many things about City Center that no one planned or designed, that may have resulted from human actions but were not themselves the goal of those actions: the whining of the escalator on the ground level, the tinklings of the music boxes from a neighboring gift shop that entertained the customers of Godiva Chocolatier, the condensation that fogged the walls of the skywalk to the parking garage on a rainy day, the cracks that showed up in the concrete beams supporting the mall after a few years, the way the yells of panicked shoppers echoed back and forth after the gang member was shot.[28] It simply is not true that everything about the mall was deliberately created by human beings for human purposes: Birds enjoyed nesting on its roof, and sometimes even found their way inside; the shadow of the building's walls meant fewer pedestrians on the west side of 3rd Street; and the financial troubles of Lazarus meant less foot traffic (and fewer sales) near the upper walkway and less physical wear and tear on the carpeting there. None of these were designed into the structure or were part of the business plan.

Why does the role of human action or human intention in the genesis of something real mean that that thing lacks autonomy or otherness from humans? There were some things about the mall that were intended by its designers, while there were other things about it that no one intended, and still other things about it that some people intended but weren't themselves part of the "official" intentions of the designers: mall-walkers used it as a way to get exercise, while the gang members apparently used it as a meeting place or perhaps a turf to be fought over, and I hear it was a good place for mid-afternoon assignations as well. Late in its life, the mall was used to house several charter schools, and surely that use was not part of what the original architects had planned for.[29] Each of these uses changed the character of the place, changed the mix of people there and their behaviors, and even changed its physical structure. And the interactions among all these intentions—the developers', the customers', the shop owners', the gangs'—surely combined with each other in unexpected ways to produce results that weren't planned or predictable by anyone, and so were "other" to everyone. Isn't this a kind of autonomy, a kind of independence from human action and intention, even if produced *through* human action and intention?[30]

To say humans build something is not to say it turns out exactly the way they intended. This is something that every builder knows. To say they build it is not to say they "dominate" it or that it is not "other" to them. Nor is it to say they "see themselves reflected" in it, or that it remains "identical" to the human. The mall *was* other, *was* "nonidentical," and everyone who went there knew it: To try to get from the top level to the bottom by escalator, for instance, was to suffer the confusion and frustration one feels in an alien environment, an environment in which one is *not* reflected—even the Taubman executives whose idea it was to place the escalators at those awkward locations themselves must have experienced that same alienation when visiting the store on occasion, feeling annoyed and slightly trapped like the rest of us, despite the fact that they were the ones who designed it. To design or even to build something isn't to control it—a lesson that the designers of the Fukushima Daiichi plant recently relearned as well. The things we build are not identical to us nor have they left the realm of nature: They do things we don't expect; they have characteristics we never anticipated. They are beyond us, just as Leopold's she-wolf and mountain were. We do not, finally, know them.

But ultimately the clearest indication of the fact that the mall was other, that it had its own trajectory, its own developmental process that no humans could ever fully grasp or predict, lies in the key fact about City Center's history: It failed. The Taubman Company planned it, but they surely did not plan for it to fail. Planning and building are different—one takes place in the mind while the other is real. They *planned* a successful mall, but the mall they *built* failed, which is to say that, once realized, it did not turn out to have the characteristics they intended it to have. To build something (anything!) is to set forces into motion—the physical forces of construction, first of all, but secondly also social forces, of commerce, of human sociability, of (in this case) urbanization and suburbanization—and then to wait and see what happens. For what happens when one sets forces into motion is never entirely knowable, never predictable, never fully able to be grasped—because those forces are always other than the builder, beyond his or her control, forces he or she tries to *use* but is never fully able to master. And so the building is always other than the builder, too, always something with its own autonomy—a fact that the builder, and later the owner, frequently comes to rue. No one could have predicted what the future of the City Center Mall would be—on that first happy day in 1989 when it opened—surely not the executives of the Taubman Company, despite all their careful planning. Good capitalists that they were, they must have known even as the first customers entered that they were opening the mall up to a world of commerce that was in its very essence unpredictable; and later, of course, they must in turn have agonizingly come to realize, like the heroes of a Greek tragedy, that by opening more malls in the suburbs it had been their own hubris that had set forces in motion that led to City Center's eventual demise. But ultimately the fate of the City Center Mall was, in fact, the product of billions of individual decisions made by hundreds of thousands of consumers and store owners and highway designers and government office-holders—decisions each one of which was taken on the basis of each individual's limited and inevitably partial view of their own needs, wealth, responsibility, and of the world itself. That product was not knowable or predictable by anyone ahead of time: It occurred *autonomously*, independently of the choices and desires of any person or any corporation. This is of the essence of a capitalist economy, and it even has a name in the history of capitalist economic theory: the invisible hand. If anything controlled the mall's fate, it was that hand—but that hand is not the hand of any one of us or any group of us, and so the mall's fate was not in *our* hands. Other to every one of us, it was autonomous.

The forces that operated upon the City Center Mall were both "natural" and "human"—not that I think that that distinction is a very useful or important one—and *neither* set of forces were ones that humans could fully predict and control. There is an ecology of the market, too, just as there is of the biotic community, and the Taubman Company failed to grasp it. Like Leopold and his comrades, they lacked an adequate understanding of the environment they confronted, an environment of which they falsely believed themselves to be the master.

If thinking like a mountain means recognizing the complexity of nature, and the way in which a single action (like the killing of a wolf) has so many interlacing consequences that its ultimate impact is impossible to grasp, then thinking like a mall might mean recognizing the complexity and unpredictability of the capitalist social order as well, and recognizing that it, too, always escapes our hubristic attempts to understand and control it. The mall at City Center, both as a physical object but also as an object of commerce, was part of a built and social environment that is in principle as hard to grasp and as independent of our control as is "nature" (Hegel talked of it as "second nature"). To think like a mall would be to see that it, too, might know something that we do not, and to realize that the social world, too, can be autonomous of us, just as beyond our understanding, and beyond our wishes, as a mountain.

The tens of thousands of customers traveling through the mall each day in its heyday, each concerned with his or her own needs and responding almost unconsciously to the environment around him or her, *together* set forces in motion that caused its failure. No one intended that, or planned it, or was able to predict it. Neither natural objects nor social ones are ultimately subject to human control. Everything that is escapes us. The problem isn't that we try to impose upon nature the kind of control we exhibit in the social world; the problem is that control of this sort is impossible *anywhere*. It is not nature's autonomy that was revealed to us in the catastrophe at Fukushima Daiichi, it is the autonomy of the *built environment*, or to put it another way, the autonomy of the *real*. Nothing real fails to possess such autonomy—not the mountain, not the she-wolf, not the mall. But then it scarcely seems the basis for a criterion of moral considerability. The question is not how to learn to respect the "autonomy of nature" any more than it is how to learn to respect the autonomy of the reactors, or of the mall. The question is to think about how our practices affect and are affected by our environment, the built one *and* the natural one, in a way that takes account of the autonomy it always possesses, an autonomy we neither can nor would wish to remove.

12

Aesthetic Value and Wild Animals

Emily Brady

Introduction

Animals commonly feature in our aesthetic experience, from our interactions with companion animals to the attention given to iconic species and "charismatic megafauna," yet it is surprising how neglected they are in philosophical aesthetics. Mammals, birds, insects, and marine life are part of our everyday and not-so-everyday lives, in the flesh and featuring as subjects in the visual arts, literature, and even music. Beyond this, the aesthetic appeal of animals is widely used in animal welfare campaigns, conservation, and more generally in the media. It is certainly not an understatement to say that the polar bear has come to symbolize the catastrophic effects of climate change, serving as a noble "poster child" for motivating global action around the problem.

In this chapter, I try to make some headway toward understanding the grounds of aesthetic appreciation of wild animals (including birds). Recently, Glenn Parsons has argued that the aesthetic value of wild animals is largely down to their "functional beauty"; however, as I shall argue here, this approach disregards expressive qualities as a significant source of value.[1] After raising a key problem in Parsons' position, I carve out a place for an expressive account and reply to some worries related to anthropocentrism. My discussion will be confined to wild animals, given that is the context of Parsons' discussion, but also because other kinds of animals (companion, domesticated, feral) raise a range of issues that deserve consideration in their own right. The kinds of nonhuman and human interactions that develop in more relational contexts (e.g., the home) are likely to have particular implications for our aesthetic engagement with animals, raising questions about, for example, everyday aesthetics and the role of sentimentality.[2] My focus in this chapter does not in any way intend to privilege the aesthetic value of wild animals over other kinds of animals, but the nature of our relations as well as their contexts are likely to impact on aesthetic engagement in various ways.[3]

Animals and Functional Beauty

Parsons explores possible grounds for appreciating animals aesthetically, such as vitality, strangeness and exoticism, symbolic value, and formal properties. Although he offers insight into why humans value animals, he worries that none of these grounds address what he calls the "immorality objection": "These forms of appreciation fail to provide a robust response to the charge that aesthetically appreciating animals involves relating to them in a shallow, and hence morally inappropriate manner."[4] Parsons claims that this is so even in cases where such forms of appreciation "are explicitly intended to serve as grounds for the preservation of wild animals."[5]

To meet this objection, Parsons argues that "we should reconceive the beauty of animals, focusing upon the aesthetic quality of 'looking fit for function.'"[6] He distinguishes between weaker and stronger versions of the functional beauty thesis and favors the stronger one, which claims that there is "an 'internal' relationship between function and beauty," where beauty "emerges out" of the function of the object.[7] To illustrate this, he gives the example of a cheetah, where "it is not merely that the shape of the cheetah's body is attractive, and also happens to be functional, by allowing it to reach great speeds. Rather, the shape of its body is attractive, in part, because it is functional."[8]

Parsons' strategy is consistent with two important positions in environmental aesthetics. First, he wants to provide an account of aesthetic appreciation of nature that takes nature on its own terms. This is a laudable aim, and one that many philosophers support.[9] Second, his approach is consistent with "scientific cognitivism" as the kind of theory which can provide such an account. Parsons has developed his own version of cognitivism after Allen Carlson, which explains why there is such an intimate connection between aesthetic value and knowledge in his position with regard to animals.[10] But the functional thesis, as applied to animals, suffers from a similar type of criticism that has been raised against scientific cognitivism applied to nature more generally. Noël Carroll has argued that scientific cognitivism, as closely tied to knowledge, leaves out some common appreciative responses, in particular "being moved by nature," that is, aesthetic appreciation involving expressive qualities and our emotional reactions to them.[11] I believe the same point holds with respect to leaving out our responses to expressive qualities in animals. Although Parsons does not discuss these qualities at length, in his view it appears that valuing expressive qualities falls into the category of forms of appreciation that do not satisfy the immorality objection.

Now, I should point out that Parsons anticipates this type of objection: He says that he is only trying to articulate a form of appreciation that sidesteps the moral problem, rather than arguing that the functional thesis characterizes *all* forms of aesthetic appreciation of animals. However, first, Parsons has claimed that these other forms do not provide an adequate response to the problem; and secondly, he draws an intimate connection between beauty and function. This suggests that he is, in fact, excluding other forms of appreciation on moral grounds. In other words, there is a strong indication, just as there is with scientific cognitivism, that aesthetic responses not tied to knowledge (in this case, knowledge of function) are shallow and potentially falsify nature.

I won't examine the functional thesis in more detail here but will, rather, address what's missing from Parsons' approach. While beauty in the form of expressive qualities may, of course, be compatible with function, he does not adequately explore the range of other aesthetic qualities that contribute, justifiably, to animal beauty. In taking this line, Parsons privileges function/fitness above other grounds that may enrich aesthetic valuing. The main problem with this approach lies in putting too much weight on the immorality objection, which too swiftly leads to the view that other kinds of aesthetic valuing are problematic. Shallow responses will be a concern for any theory of aesthetic—indeed even artistic—appreciation. In light of these concerns, I will argue for a different starting point that recognizes the importance of appreciating nature within the domain of the aesthetic, that is, where a wide range of qualities are significant in aesthetic appreciation, from the formal to the expressive, imaginative, and, where contributing to aesthetic value or disvalue, the functional.[12]

Expressive Qualities in Animals

Although there has been some discussion of emotional responses to nature in environmental aesthetics, there has been less treatment of expressive qualities as such, despite the fact that these qualities play a significant role in our aesthetic responses.[13] Carroll writes, "We see the gnarled branches of barren trees and call them anguished because they call to mind the twisted appearance of human suffering."[14] We easily speak of the "raging sea" or a "peaceful scene." We judge a tiger to be mighty, a falcon's flight exciting, the call of a loon melancholy, or the song of an English robin joyous. In all of these cases, we attribute expressive qualities to nature or use terms that relate to expressive qualities. Wildlife can be appealing through manifestations of inner autonomy, surprising us with a range of fascinating physiognomic and bodily expressions. With many mammals, though, aesthetic interest is connected to affinities with humans. Animals have eyes and facial expressions; they use familiar gestures and move in ways that we recognize.[15] Imagine animals without their expressions—facial or otherwise—and try imagining humans in the same way. Aesthetic appreciation would then focus on other qualities, perhaps form, but that, I suggest, would give a much thinner account of the grounds of appreciation. Likewise, appreciating animals more narrowly in terms of their fitness or function may leave out the rich expressiveness we find in them, whether in flight, in pursuit, attack, swimming, play, or sleep. It could also be argued that many cases of appreciation involving function are less meaningful when not tied to expressive qualities. I do think Parsons recognizes this, but the connection to function is not required for these qualities to be appropriate.

Linking aesthetic appreciation of animals too closely to functional beauty also potentially ignores other forms of aesthetic value. Here, I'm thinking of the category of the sublime, which certainly applies to animals both in terms of our actual experiences and the theories to which they're connected. Interestingly, Edmund Burke places usefulness and the sublime in opposition, with wild animals appearing to have greater aesthetic value than domesticated animals in so far as they're incapable of being under our control and thus able to evoke stronger emotions: "[I]t comes upon us in the gloomy forest, and in the howling wilderness, in the form of the lion, the tiger, the panther, or rhinoceros."[16] Burke also notes how these animals, including fierce wolves rather than domesticated dogs, are frequently used in sublime descriptions found in the literary arts. More recently, in his essay "The Yosemite," John Muir describes an encounter with a bear by drawing contrasts between animal and environment: The "broad, rusty bundle of ungovernable wildness" is "framed like a picture" in a "flowery glade," sublimity situated among the pretty flowers of a peaceful meadow.[17]

In what follows, I consider some of the ways we might explain various kinds of expressive qualities, and I then discuss how they fit into appropriate aesthetic responses. My aim is fairly modest: to explore some possibilities and reflect on strengths and weaknesses. Some of my claims may extend to other natural things such as trees or people, but I will not make that argument here. As I noted earlier, I limit my argument to expressive qualities in wild mammals and birds, though in a longer chapter, it would be interesting to look at a range of other creatures such as insects, fish, reptiles, and how having fewer affinities to humans affects aesthetic appreciation.

A useful starting point is to ask what can be learned from expressive theories of art, given the extensive work devoted to this topic in aesthetics. One of the most pressing questions in this debate is just how emotion qualities (and other expressive terms not connected to emotional expression) can inhere in art forms: How is it that music can be *sad*? In the context of animals, or nature more generally, we might ask: How is it that expressive qualities can be attributed to a natural, living thing that is nonhuman? For a start, we can set aside "transmission type" theories of expression concerned with the communication of emotions, since appreciation of animals is not a standard case of expression involving an artist and transmission of emotions through an artwork to an audience. Although domesticated animal breeds are clearly bred to meet both aesthetic and functional aims, and some animals have strong elements of "design" through selective breeding, transmission theories are too art-oriented and not relevant to wild animals.

A more promising approach appeals to similarity theories of expression in music, where expressive qualities are analyzed through resemblances between musical qualities and expressive qualities in humans. To hear music as having expressive qualities is to recognize in music a resemblance to human emotional behavior through speech, gestures, and bodily movement.[18] A common claim is that expressive qualities are logically independent of acts of expression or mental states. The example often used is that a St. Bernard's face is sad-looking, but the dog is not necessarily feeling sad. When bringing the theory into the context of animal appreciation, many expressive qualities may, in fact, relate to the inner states of animals. Nonetheless, the distinction is significant because there will be cases of expressive qualities where such a correspondence does not hold. A loon's call may be described as melancholy without the bird actually being in that psychological state. With animals, we draw upon similarities between two natural forms of expression: a melancholy-sounding call and actual expressions of melancholy with which we're familiar, and we commonly use expressive qualities in humans as the reference point. There is recognition of expressive qualities linked to melancholy, and we can recognize the similar qualities in other natural forms.[19] In some cases, we make fairly customary associations or follow conventional ways of perceiving such qualities.

Additionally, we should not forget the relevance of context, which is significant for determining aesthetic qualities in environments. The loon's call, like the call of a curlew, is described as melancholy not only because it brings to mind ways melancholy people sound or behave but also because of the places where it occurs. The loon and the curlew are not often encountered in flocks and are commonly found in habitats which themselves could be described as melancholy, such as remote lakes and moors. This is something we grasp from experience and attention to the environments they inhabit.

Similarity theories are clearly helpful in cases when we can locate a resemblance between an expressive quality and some kind of behavior or other point of likeness. This applies to a range of examples such as the robin's joyous song (resemblance to uplifting sounds, behavior, or music) or the majestic lion with its ruffed mane, "proud" expression, and great roar. But what about cases where no resemblance seems to exist? There are, of course, real differences between humans and animals, and the nature of some resemblances will also be very hard to pin down. What if we're struck by something strange and wonderful that doesn't fit into our normal range of experience? In reply, we might say that new expressive qualities are just what underlie aesthetic experiences connected to wonder, fascination, and the sublime. When we take aesthetic interest in something new, it will often be caused by some highly expressive qualities not encountered before in some particular way. As we have seen, the sublime is often associated with expressive qualities, and eighteenth-century writers discussed various animals—from lions and tigers to mythical serpents and monsters. Here it is power and strength, for example, which overwhelm us in ways *beyond* comparison. The sublime shows, too, how expressive qualities in animals are not just about resemblances to human behavior. It will be natural for human appreciators to use familiarity with their own species as a reference point, but wider nature will also serve as a kind of second-order reference point for grasping expressive qualities.

A more general solution for thinking through expressive qualities is to give a causal account, where a resemblance relation doesn't have to feature in the experience *itself*. Instead, resemblance is understood as a causal property, where resemblances that exist— even small ones—cause, in the case of music, the listener to experience the music as expressive in that way. For appreciation of animals, there will be some causal property such that we experience an animal as having certain expressive qualities (e.g., thrilling or graceful). While this is a neat reply to the problem, and one that can be used to support similarity theories, it won't always give us what we want, which is an account of the nature of expressive qualities and how they're operating in aesthetic experience.[20]

However, in so far as similarity theories provide an explanation of many of our responses to expressive qualities, they provide a way to avoid the immorality objection, at least in terms of showing how we can connect a quality found in one thing to a quality found in something else. This approach helps to make the connection between expressive aesthetic qualities and the non-aesthetic qualities to which they're linked. In this way, similarity theories converge with an understanding of how expressive qualities are linked to the "aesthetic surface," or the appearance or look of things. Showing how expressive qualities relate to perceptual qualities will, in turn, make it easier to establish the reasonableness of these kinds of aesthetic judgments.

Expressive Qualities and Symbolic Qualities

While useful, we've seen that similarity theories can't explain *all* of our experiences of expressive qualities. This is also the case when our attributions of these qualities are connected to associations, beliefs, or cultural conventions operating in our appreciation. Symbolic qualities are often classified as a type of expressive quality because a specific form of expressiveness is drawn upon to symbolize some cultural characteristic. Holmes Rolston provides some interesting examples: "The British prefer the lion; the Russians the bear. States have chosen their animals; Colorado has selected the bighorn sheep—stately, powerful, nimble, free, loving the hills." In the United States, the bald eagle expresses "freedom, power, grace, lofty alertness."[21] Parsons worries, though, that symbolic qualities in animals ground dubious and arbitrary forms of aesthetic appreciation, even in cases where symbolism has some moral benefit (e.g., the preservation of a species): "Since eagles are no more free, one supposes, than are crows or sparrows, appreciating them as symbols of freedom has little, if anything, to do with eagles. Rather, it has to do with the particular constellation of associations prevalent in the human society at issue."[22] But this view seems to miss the point of why we take aesthetic interest in eagles. Bald eagles, like many other raptors, soar in open spaces, often reaching lofty heights on thermals. Besides their striking white head and tail and their majestic size relative to many other birds, their movement can reasonably be described as unconstrained and unconfined relative to the flight (and other behavior) of a crow, and especially a sparrow, which are more customarily seen in more everyday, less wild environments. Seen in this way, the symbolic qualities we ascribe are more easily connected to the expressive qualities we admire.

It has been argued that for something to function symbolically, it has to be similar in structure to what it symbolizes.[23] In this case, the eagle's symbolism is partly down to resemblance and partly down to cultural conventions and associations. There are obvious associations going on here between the quality of wildness and freedom as well as flight and freedom, so the connections made are not as arbitrary as Parsons would have it. Some cases of symbolism based on expressive qualities may therefore be appropriate and reasonable because they are, in fact, connected to the character and behavior of such animals.

Many of the "customary associations" we make between forms of expression and nature make sense to us and become part of legitimate interpretations of nature, rather than being merely arbitrary or idiosyncratic. Is this sort of symbolic representation a problem? No—if we find that the symbolism bears some structural resemblance to the animal. In relation to a lion and its majesty, we might follow Rolston, who argues: "We elevate into symbolism something of the competence, the integrity, the character of the wild life."[24] This isn't to say, however, that every form of symbolism will meet the immorality objection, but I have tried to show that expressive qualities in the form of symbolic expression should not be problematic, necessarily, where connections exist to the lives of animals. There will be other forms of expressive qualities that require analysis in terms of irrelevance or inappropriateness, such as projective and metaphorical qualities, but I will have to leave them aside here.

Expressive Qualities as Literal Expressions of Feeling

An important difference between nonsentient nature and animals is that we can identify literal forms of emotional expression in animals because they have mental states while trees and rocks do not. This distinction brings us to cases where expressive qualities are, in fact, the outward expression of mental states. Why care about these "literal" expressions, or include them as something of aesthetic interest? Most discussions of expression theory arise in the artistic context first rather than in the natural one, so literal expression is normally not of interest. Literal expression as we find it in humans or other animals simply doesn't get addressed as a problem in aesthetics; presumably the view is taken that it will be of interest only to psychology or behavioral studies.

As I see it, both human and nonhuman animal cases of literal expressions are aesthetically relevant. In the case of humans, faces are especially interesting from an expressive point of view, which explains one source of the appeal of artistic portraits.[25] Now, this claim can be made regardless of whether our attributions of particular expressions are accurate (I have more to say about this later). What kinds of aesthetic reactions might be connected to such qualities? Or, why should we think that such qualities are aesthetic? My brief answer to this question is that expressive qualities are central to experiences that we have no difficulty in describing as aesthetic, where pleasure or displeasure is taken in the look, feel, or meaning of something. New work in both everyday and environmental aesthetics has shown how aesthetic objects can be extended beyond the arts, and with that, the role of a whole range of expressive qualities in appreciation.

One worry about this type of appreciation, though, stems from the Pathetic Fallacy. Parsons cites Collingwood's claim that "the bright eyes of a mouse or the fragile vitality of a flower are things that touch us to the heart, but they touch us with the love that life feels for life, not with a judgment of their aesthetic excellence."[26] Parsons argues quite rightly that potential confusion between moral and aesthetic feeling does not entail that aesthetic judgments are impossible. I want to build on this point to suggest that the "bright eyes of a mouse" can be appreciated as expressive in relevant ways, rather than merely evoking a sympathetic response.

We can and do make aesthetic judgments which distinguish between dull, insipid or tired eyes and, say, the poise and narrowed eyes of a wild cat about to pounce. We may well find the attentive appearance of those eyes interesting for their expression of vitality and expectant look—and perhaps also for the thrilling pounce that we expect to follow from that look. It is also true that bright eyes in many species are known to be an indication of good health, and this may lead us to react with sympathetic pleasure at the expression of life in the mouse. Although it may be difficult to separate moral from aesthetic feeling in experience, in these cases it would seem that such a judgment makes perfect sense on aesthetic grounds. That is, we can make distinctions between different forms of expression based on perceiving different non-aesthetic qualities. Likewise, we may judge that a single tree growing in the midst of a vast plain is "lonely." Now we might feel a sort of misplaced sympathy for this tree—trees aren't really lonely, of course—but it is reasonable to aesthetically judge the scene in this way, given the combination of non-aesthetic qualities: an empty landscape with a single object that in some ways resembles a human figure standing alone. It is possible we would make the same judgment if the object was a large boulder instead, but the shape of the tree is certainly suggestive of human form.

The Immorality Objection and Anthropomorphism

The immorality objection demands a closer look in order to work through some worries about overly humanizing aesthetic appreciation. For Parsons, the question we must answer to meet the objection is "whether it is in fact possible for the aesthetic value of an animal to bear some significant relation to the nature of the animal itself."[27] Worries about aesthetically valuing animals generally focus on anthropomorphism, the concern being that we're not appreciating animals for the distinctive creatures they are but instead humanize them in ways that are sentimental and shallow (or worse: falsifying). However, we don't need a functional thesis to address this issue; rather we can retain a broader and richer idea of aesthetic value by articulating: (1) a robust account of anthropomorphism and (2) an account of aesthetic judgment that moves between the overly trivial and overly serious.[28]

In the account I have given of some forms of expression in nature, human expression and behavior provide the main basis for making sense of expressive qualities. This might seem like a red flag to a bull where anthropomorphism is concerned, but this worry is less serious when we consider some interesting, recent accounts of anthropomorphism that try to emphasize the importance of similarities rather than differences between humans and other mammalian species. This type of approach to anthropomorphism stresses the affinities we feel for other mammals. It criticizes scientific accounts, which so often argue that we cannot have knowledge of other minds, and that we're liable to make mistaken and distorting attributions of mental states. Mary Midgley, for instance, argues that in so far as we think our attributions of various emotions to humans are apt and at least in the right ballpark, we should have a fair degree of confidence when it comes to mammals. Moreover, importantly, why should we be so concerned about mistaken readings of animals and not of humans? We do make mistakes in the human context and will also make mistakes with animals, but Midgley denies that the gap between the two forms of experiencing emotions in others is so vastly different.[29]

This position enables us to see how we might formulate something like an ideal appreciator, where aesthetic judgments strike a balance between appreciating expressive qualities that are not anthropomorphic in the problematic sense. Midgley's chief criterion for ensuring appropriate judgments is close, careful attention, especially in cases of animals with which we are less familiar. That this also holds for humans supports the robust account of anthropomorphism; people with less experience with children will have less honed skills in reading behavior in them. This sort of account— where attributing human qualities to animals is actually more one of being carefully aware of similarities and being watchful of projection and misattributions—might usefully ground aesthetic appreciation of expressive qualities such that the immorality objection becomes much less of a worry. Midgley points out (not at all lightly) that novelists as well as ethologists can successfully grasp animal feeling.

To be sure, there are worse and better forms of anthropomorphism. Some ascriptions of symbolic qualities and their anthropomorphic expressions have real consequences for animals, and these kinds of cases will not meet the immorality objection. For example, some symbolic qualities may in some way be close to the animal's behavior but impute mental qualities that are not really there—in ways that are bad for the animal (e.g., the "wily fox" that is persecuted or the fat Friesian cow browsing among the daisies on the butter tub which bears little resemblance to the lives of real butter-producing cows).

Additionally, while we seek affinities between humans and animals for what we think are good reasons, sometimes this leads to bad consequences. James Serpell cites the problem of anthropomorphic selection: "[S]election in favour of physical and behavioural traits that facilitate the attribution of human mental states to nonhumans."[30] One of the sadder cases is the English bulldog, with its expressive qualities of strength, power, and stubbornness, which became a symbol for Britain's power in the face of its enemies in World War II. Karsh's famous photograph of Winston Churchill draws on these qualities, using them to symbolically express his leadership. Unfortunately, the breed suffers from a disabling characteristic, difficulty breathing, which is a direct result of breeding to preserve particular anthropomorphic traits.[31]

Conclusion

While these cases pose challenges, they should not ultimately deter us from valuing expressive qualities that are relevant and appropriate. We can understand a variety of aesthetic responses as appropriate by identifying types that distort or overly humanize through problematic forms of anthropomorphism. Although the aesthetic value of animals will be grounded in a range of qualities, including "looking fit for function," appreciating other qualities will not necessarily undermine moral concern. Engaging with expressive qualities can deepen appreciation and open up new avenues that are not shallow but instead support respectful aesthetic valuing. Aesthetic experience is rich and varied, and I think we're better off recognizing that richness and working with it to strike a balance between aesthetic freedom and constraint.

This kind of balance broadens the foundation of aesthetic valuing and it is also, I believe, relevant in our *artistic* interactions with animals. That is, while fitness and function no doubt motivate artistic representations of animals, expressive and symbolic qualities are significant and relevant, too. Here, we might usefully contrast the horse paintings of George Stubbs with those of Théodore Géricault, where Géricault tends to present horses in more expressive behaviors. As I see it, then, we can also learn something from art about how to locate a reasonable and proper place for expressive qualities. Our aesthetic-expressive interactions with animals can support a form of valuing nature that considers remarkable affinities and meeting points between human and nonhuman natures and cultures.

Notes

Introduction
Martin Drenthen and Jozef Keulartz

1. See, Daniel E. Berlyne, *Studies in the New Experimental Aesthetics: Steps Toward an Objective Psychology of Aesthetic Appreciation* (Washington: Hemisphere Pub. Corp., 1974). This behavioristic theory is essentially concerned with the hedonic effects of fluctuations in arousal level induced by exposure to stimuli varying along so-called "collative" dimensions such as familiar- novel, simple-complex, expected-surprising, or ambiguous-clear. These collative variables also play an important role in the sociobiological theory of Jay Appleton. See Jay Appleton, *The Experience of Landscape* (London: Wiley, 1975). According to this theory, our aesthetic perception of landscapes has its roots in human biology—we appreciate most those landscapes which display the characteristics most favorable to our survival. From related evolutionary arguments, Stephen and Rachel Kaplan have developed the so-called "Preference Matrix," which roots aesthetic preference in the adaptive value of landscape characteristics. The matrix consists of four collative variables that together have proven to be reliable predictors of public landscape preference: "coherence," "complexity," "legibility," and "mystery." See Stephen Kaplan and Rachel Kaplan, *Cognition and Environment: Functioning in an Uncertain World* (New York: Praeger, 1982).

2. Gerald C. Cupchik, "A Decade after Berlyne: New Directions in Experimental Aesthetics," *Poetics* 15 (1986): 361.

3. Douglas J. Porteous, *Environmental Aesthetics: Ideas, Politics and Planning* (London: Routledge, 1996), 22.

4. Porteous, *Environmental Aesthetics*, 23.

5. See Elwood L. Shafer et al., "Natural Landscape Preference: A Predictive Model," *Journal of Leisure Research* 1 (1969): 1–19; Elwood L. Shafer and James Mietz, "It Seems Possible to Quantify Scenic Beauty in

Photographs," Research Paper NE-162 (Upper Darby, PA: U.S. Department
of Agriculture Forest Service, 1970).

6. Allen Carlson, "On the Possibility of Quantifying Scenic Beauty,"
Landscape Planning 4 (1977): 131–172. See also Allen Carlson, "Formal
Qualities in the Natural Environment," *Journal of Aesthetic Education* 13,
no. 3 (1979): 99–114.

7. Allen Carlson, "Appreciation and the Natural Environment," *The
Journal of Aesthetics and Art Criticism* 37, no. 3 (1979): 267–275.

8. See Ronald W. Hepburn, "Aesthetic Appreciation of Nature," *British
Journal of Aesthetics* 3, no. 3 (1963): 195–209; Ronald W. Hepburn,
"Contemporary Aesthetics and the Neglect of Natural Beauty," in *British
Analytical Philosophy*, ed. B. Williams and A. Montefiore (London:
Routledge, Kegan Paul Ltd., 1966), 285–310.

9. Hepburn, "Aesthetic Appreciation of Nature," 197.

10. Ibid., 199.

11. J. Baird Callicott, "The Land Aesthetic," in *Ecological Prospects:
Scientific, Religious, and Aesthetic Perspectives*, ed. Christopher K. Chapple
(Albany: State University of New York Press, 1994), 170. For an extensive
discussion of the relation between environmental aesthetics and environ-
mental protection, see Ned Hettinger, "Allen Carlson's Environmental
Aesthetics and the Protection of the Environment," *Environmental Ethics*
27, no. 1 (2005): 57–76; Ned Hettinger, "Objectivity in Environmental
Aesthetics and Protection of the Environment," in *Nature, Aesthetics, and
Environment: From Beauty to Duty*, ed. Allen Carlson and Sheila Lintott
(New York: Columbia University Press, 2008), 413–437.

12. Emily Brady, "Environmental Aesthetics," in *Encyclopedia of
Environmental Ethics and Philosophy*, ed. J. Baird Callicott and Robert
Frodeman, vol. 2 (Detroit: Macmillan Reference USA, 2009), 313–321.

13. Recently, Marta Tafalla has compared two texts that she considers
the two foundational texts for a new age of the aesthetics of nature: Ronald
Hepburn's essay "Contemporary Aesthetics and the Neglect of Natural
Beauty" from 1966 and Theodor W. Adorno's chapter "Natural Beauty"
from his book *Aesthetic Theory*, published in 1970. The analytic and the
continental discourse that emerged from these texts have remained two
parallel worlds without much communication between them. Tafalla shows
that, despite clear differences, there are also sufficient affinities and shared
ideas to make a dialogue between analytic and continental aesthetics of
nature possible. See Marta Tafalla, "Rehabilitating the Aesthetics of Nature:
Hepburn and Adorno," *Environmental Ethics* 33 (2011): 45–56.

14. His participatory model, which collapses the dichotomy between
subject and object and stresses sensory immersion and embodied appreciation, is probably the longest-standing noncognitivist approach in environmental aesthetics. See Emily Brady, "Environmental Aesthetics," 318.

15. The discussion about their relationship has been especially vivid in
Germany philosophy, one of Dumas' most important research interests.

A case in point is Martin Seel, who has examined the ethical relevance and significance of aesthetics in general and of environmental aesthetics in particular (see Maskit in this volume). Not unlike Dumas, Seel believes that respect for the human person implies a duty to protect and preserve the natural environment. "Only an aesthetics of nature can elucidate the full meaning of a non-instrumental relationship with nature, and, in this way, justify the duty to preserve a nature that allows for such a relationship." See Martin Seel, *Eine Ästhetik der Natur* (Frankfurt am Main: Suhrkamp, 1991), 342.

16. Allen Carlson, "Is Environmental Art an Aesthetic Affront to Nature?," *Canadian Journal of Philosophy* 16 (1986): 636–650. For the heated debate that was sparked off by this article, see Emily Brady, "Aesthetic Regard for Nature in Environmental and Land Art," *Ethics, Place and Environment* 10, no. 3 (2007): 257–261.

17. Glenn Parsons, "The Aesthetic Value of Animals," *Environmental Ethics* 29 (2007): 151–169.

1. Ten Steps in the Development of Western Environmental Aesthetics
Allen Carlson

1. Richard Rorty, *The Linguistic Turn: Recent Essays in Philosophical Method* (Chicago: The University of Chicago Press, 1967).

2. Ronald W. Hepburn, "Contemporary Aesthetics and the Neglect of Natural Beauty," in *British Analytical Philosophy*, ed. Bernard Williams and Alan Montefiore, 285–310 (London: Routledge and Kegan Paul, 1966).

3. Francis Sparshott, "Figuring the Ground: Notes on some Theoretical Problems of the Aesthetic Environment," *Journal of Aesthetic Education* 6 (1972): 11–23; Mark Sagoff, "On Preserving the Natural Environment," *Yale Law Journal* 84 (1974): 205–267.

4. Jay Appleton, "Landscape Evaluation: The Theoretical Vacuum," *Transactions of the Institute of British Geographers* 66 (1975): 120–123.

5. Allen Carlson, "Environmental Aesthetics and the Dilemma of Aesthetic Education," *Journal of Aesthetic Education* 10 (1976): 69–82; Allen Carlson, "On the Possibility of Quantifying Scenic Beauty," *Landscape Planning* 4 (1977): 131–172; Allen Carlson, "Formal Qualities and the Natural Environment," *Journal of Aesthetic Education* 13 (1979): 99–114.

6. Allen Carlson, "Appreciation and the Natural Environment," *Journal of Aesthetics and Art Criticism* 37 (1979): 267–276; Allen Carlson, "Nature, Aesthetic Judgment, and Objectivity," *Journal of Aesthetics and Art Criticism* 40 (1981): 15–27.

7. Allen Carlson, "Nature and Positive Aesthetics," *Environmental Ethics* 6 (1984): 5–34.

8. Arnold Berleant, *Art and Engagement* (Philadelphia: Temple University Press, 1991); Arnold Berleant, *The Aesthetics of Environment* (Philadelphia: Temple University Press, 1992).

9. For example, Arnold Berleant, "Aesthetic Paradigms for an Urban Ecology," *Diogenes* 103 (1978): 1–28; Arnold Berleant, "Aesthetic Participation and the Urban Environment," *Urban Resources* 1 (1984): 37–42; Arnold Berleant, "Cultivating an Urban Aesthetic," *Diogenes* 136 (1986): 1–18; Arnold Berleant, "The Environment as an Aesthetic Paradigm," *Dialectics and Humanism* 15 (1988): 95–106.

10. Yrjö Sepänmaa, *The Beauty of Environment: A General Model for Environmental Aesthetics* (Helsinki: Annales Academiae Scientiarum Fennicae, 1986); Yrjö Sepänmaa, *The Beauty of Environment: A General Model for Environmental Aesthetics*, 2nd ed. (Denton: Environmental Ethics Books, 1993).

11. Salim Kemal and Ivan Gaskell, ed., *Landscape, Natural Beauty and the Arts* (Cambridge: Cambridge University Press, 1993).

12. Noël Carroll, "On Being Moved by Nature: Between Religion and Natural History," in *Landscape, Natural Beauty and the Arts*, ed. Salim Kemal and Ivan Gaskell, 244–266 (Cambridge: Cambridge University Press, 1993).

13. Allen Carlson, "Environmental Aesthetics," in *A Companion to Aesthetics*, ed. David. Cooper, 142–144 (Oxford: Basil Blackwell, 1992).

14. Stan Godlovitch, "Icebreakers: Environmentalism and Natural Aesthetics," *Journal of Applied Philosophy* 11 (1994): 15–30.

15. Holmes Rolston, "Does Aesthetic Appreciation of Nature Need to be Science Based?," *British Journal of Aesthetics* 35 (1995): 374–386. See also Holmes Rolston, "Aesthetic Experience in Forests," *Journal of Aesthetics and Art Criticism* 56 (1998): 157–166.

16. Arnold Berleant and Allen Carlson, eds., Special Issue on Environmental Aesthetics, *Journal of Aesthetics and Art Criticism* 56, no. 2 (1998).

17. Emily Brady, "Imagination and the Aesthetic Appreciation of Nature," *Journal of Aesthetics and Art Criticism* 56 (1998): 139–147.

18. Marcia Eaton, "Fact and Fiction in the Aesthetic Appreciation of Nature," *Journal of Aesthetics and Art Criticism* 56 (1998): 149–156.

19. Yuriko Saito, "The Aesthetics of Unscenic Nature," *Journal of Aesthetics and Art Criticism* 56 (1998): 101–111. See also Yuriko Saito, "Appreciating Nature on its Own Terms," *Environmental Ethics* 20 (1998): 135–149.

20. John A. Fisher, "What the Hills Are Alive With: In Defense of the Sounds of Nature," *Journal of Aesthetics and Art Criticism* 56 (1998): 167–179.

21. Cheryl Foster, "The Narrative and the Ambient in Environmental Aesthetics," *Journal of Aesthetics and Art Criticism* 56 (1998): 127–137.

22. Allen Carlson and Arnold Berleant, ed., *The Aesthetics of Natural Environments* (Peterborough, Canada: Broadview Press, 2004).

23. Kevin Melchionne, "Living in Glass Houses: Domesticity, Interior Decoration, and Environmental Aesthetics," *Journal of Aesthetics and Art*

Criticism 56 (1998): 191–200; Barbara Sandrisser, "Cultivating Commonplaces: Sophisticated Vernacularism in Japan," *Journal of Aesthetics and Art Criticism* 56 (1998): 201–210; Sally Schauman, "The Garden and the Red Barn: The Pervasive Pastoral and its Environmental Consequences," *Journal of Aesthetics and Art Criticism* 56 (1998): 181–190.

24. Berleant, "Aesthetic Participation and the Urban Environment," *Urban Resources*, 37–42.

25. Allen Carlson, "On Appreciating Agricultural Landscapes," *Journal of Aesthetics and Art Criticism* 43 (1985): 301–312.

26. Michael Mitias, ed., *Philosophy and Architecture* (Amsterdam: Rodopi, 1994), and Michael Mitias, ed., *Architecture and Civilization* (Amsterdam: Rodopi, 1999).

27. Mara Miller, *The Garden As Art* (Albany: State University of New York Press, 1993); Stephanie Ross, *What Gardens Mean* (Chicago: The University of Chicago Press, 1998).

28. Arnold Berleant, *Living in the Landscape: Toward an Aesthetics of Environment* (Lawrence: University Press of Kansas, 1997).

29. Allen Carlson, *Aesthetics and the Environment: The Appreciation of Nature, Art and Architecture* (London: Routledge, 2000).

30. Allen Carlson, "On Aesthetically Appreciating Human Environments," *Philosophy and Geography* 4 (2001): 9–24.

31. Arnold Berleant and Allen Carlson, eds., *The Aesthetics of Human Environments* (Peterborough, Canada: Broadview Press, 2007).

32. For example, Yi-Fu Tuan, *Passing Strange and Wonderful: Aesthetics, Nature, and Culture* (Washington: Island Press, 1993).

33. Yuriko Saito, "Everyday Aesthetics," *Philosophy and Literature* 25 (2001): 87–95.

34. For example, Barbara Sandrisser, "Valuing the Ordinary: The Poetics of Wood in Traditional Japan," *Journal of Value Inquiry* 28 (1994): 281–295; Arnold Berleant, "On Getting Along Beautiful: Ideas for a Social Aesthetics," in *Aesthetics in the Human Environment*, ed. Pauline von Bonsdorff and Arto Haapala, 12–29 (Lahti, Finland: International Institute of Applied Aesthetics, 1999); Carolyn Korsmeyer, *Making Sense of Taste: Food and Philosophy* (Ithaca, N.Y.: Cornell University Press, 1999).

35. Yuriko Saito, *Everyday Aesthetics* (Oxford: Oxford University Press, 2007).

36. Thomas Leddy, "Everyday Surface Aesthetic Qualities: Neat, Messy, Clean, Dirty," *Journal of Aesthetics and Art Criticism* 53 (1995): 259–268; Thomas Leddy, "Sparkle and Shine," *British Journal of Aesthetics* 37 (1997): 259–273.

37. Thomas Leddy, "The Nature of Everyday Aesthetics," in *The Aesthetics of Everyday Life*, ed. Andrew Light and Jonathan M. Smith, 3–22 (New York: Columbia University Press, 2005). Leddy's most recent contribution to this area of research is *The Extraordinary in the Ordinary: The Aesthetics of Everyday Life* (Peterborough, Canada: Broadview Press, 2012).

38. Light and Smith, eds., *The Aesthetics of Everyday Life*.

39. See, for example, some of the essays collected in Pauline von Bonsdorff and Arto Haapala, eds., *Aesthetics in the Human Environment*.

40. Malcolm Budd, *The Aesthetic Appreciation of Nature* (Oxford: Oxford University Press, 2002); Emily Brady, *Aesthetics of the Natural Environment* (Edinburgh: Edinburgh University Press, 2003); Ronald Moore, *Natural Beauty: A Theory of Aesthetics Beyond the Arts* (Peterborough, Canada: Broadview, 2008); Glenn Parsons and Allen Carlson, *Functional Beauty* (Oxford: Oxford University Press, 2008); Arnold Berleant, *Aesthetics and Environment: Variations on a Theme* (Aldershot: Ashgate, 2005); and Arnold Berleant, *Sensibility and Sense: The Aesthetic Transformation of the Human World* (Exeter: Imprint Academic, 2010).

41. Arnold Berleant, ed., *Environment and the Arts: Perspectives on Environmental Aesthetics* (Aldershot: Ashgate, 2002); Sven Arntzen and Emily Brady, ed., *Humans in the Land: The Ethics and Aesthetics of the Cultural Landscape* (Oslo: Oslo Academic Press, 2008); Allen Carlson and Sheila Lintott, eds., *Nature, Aesthetics, and Environmentalism: From Beauty to Duty* (New York: Columbia University Press, 2008).

42. Reference volume entries on environmental aesthetics include Yrjö Sepänmaa, "Environmental Aesthetics," in *Conservation and Environmentalism: An Encyclopedia*, ed. Robert Paehlke, 221–223 (New York: Garland, 1995); Arnold Berleant, "Environmental Aesthetics," in *Encyclopedia of Aesthetics*, ed. Michael Kelly, vol. 2, 114–120 (New York: Oxford University Press, 1998); Allen Carlson, "Environmental Aesthetics," in *Routledge Companion to Aesthetics*, ed. Berys Gaut and Dominic Lopes, 541–555 (London: Routledge, 2001), revised in 2004 and 2013; John A. Fisher, "Environmental Aesthetics," in *Oxford Handbook of Aesthetics*, ed. Jerrold Levinson, 667–678 (Oxford: Oxford University Press, 2002); Allen Carlson, "Environmental Aesthetics," *Routledge Encyclopedia of Philosophy Online*, ed. Edward Craig (London: Routledge, 2002), revised in 2010; Stephanie Ross, "Environmental Aesthetics," in *The Encyclopedia of Philosophy*, 2nd ed., 254–258 (New York: Macmillan, 2006); Allen Carlson, "Environmental Aesthetics," in *The Stanford Encyclopedia of Philosophy*, ed. Edward. N. Zalta (Stanford: SEP, 2008), revised in 2010, http://plato.stanford.edu/ entries/ environmental-aesthetics/; Allen Carlson, "Aesthetics of the Environment," in *A Companion to Aesthetics*, ed. Stephen Davies, Kathleen Higgins, Robert Hopkins, Robert Stecker, David Cooper, 2nd ed., 134–136 (Oxford: Wiley-Blackwell, 2009). There are also a number of entries explicitly on the aesthetics of nature, for example, Allen Carlson, "Aesthetic Appreciation of Nature," in *Routledge Encyclopedia of Philosophy*, ed. Edward Craig, vol. 6, 731–735 (London: Routledge, 1998), revised online in 2010; Allen Carlson, "Contemporary Aesthetics of Nature," in *Encyclopedia of Aesthetics*, ed. Michael Kelly, vol. 3, 346–349 (New York: Oxford University Press, 1998); Emily Brady, "Aesthetics of the Natural Environment," in *Environment and*

Philosophy, ed. Vernon Pratt with Jane Howarth and Emily Brady, 142–163 (London: Routledge, 2000); John A. Fisher, "Aesthetics," in *A Companion to Environmental Philosophy*, ed. Dale Jamieson, 264–276 (Oxford: Blackwell, 2001); Malcolm Budd, "Aesthetics of Nature," in *Oxford Handbook of Aesthetics*, ed. Jerrold Levinson, 117–135 (Oxford: Oxford University Press, 2002); Donald W. Crawford, "The Aesthetics of Nature and the Environment," in *Blackwell Guide To Aesthetics*, ed. Peter Kivy, 306–324 (Oxford: Blackwell, 2003); Glenn Parsons, "The Aesthetics of Nature," *Philosophy Compass* 2 (2007): 358–372.

43. Glenn Parsons, *Aesthetics and Nature* (London: Continuum, 2008); Allen Carlson, *Nature and Landscape: An Introduction to Environmental Aesthetics* (New York: Columbia University Press, 2009).

44. For example, Yuriko Saito, "The Japanese Appreciation of Nature," *British Journal of Aesthetics* 25 (1985): 239–251.

45. Earlier versions of this chapter were delivered at a state of the discipline session on environmental aesthetics at the American Philosophical Association and the International Society for Environmental Ethics, Eastern Division, New York, December 2009 and at the Environmental Aesthetics Panel at the Eighteenth International Congress of Aesthetics, Peking University, Beijing, China, August 2010. I thank my fellow participants, Arnold Berleant, Emily Brady, Yuriko Saito, and Yrjö Sepänmaa, and the members of the audiences at these sessions for valuable suggestions.

2. Future Directions for Environmental Aesthetics
Yuriko Saito

1. Ronald W. Hepburn, "Contemporary Aesthetics and the Neglect of Natural Beauty," in *British Analytic Philosophy*, ed. Bernard Williams and Alan Montefiore, 285–310 (London: Routledge and Kegan Paul, 1966).

2. Arnold Berleant, *Art and Engagement* (Philadelphia: Temple University Press, 1991); Arnold Berleant, *The Aesthetics of Environment* (Philadelphia: Temple University Press, 1992); Arnold Berleant, *Living in the Landscape: Toward an Aesthetics of Environment* (Lawrence: University Press of Kansas, 1997); Arnold Berleant, *Re-Thinking Aesthetics: Rogue Essays on Aesthetics and the Arts* (Hants: Ashgate, 2004); Arnold Berleant, *Aesthetics and Environment: Variations on a Theme* (Hants: Ashgate, 2005); Arnold Berleant, *Sensibility and Sense: The Aesthetic Transformation of the Human World* (Exeter: Imprint Academic, 2010); and numerous articles and conference papers.

3. I explore environmental aesthetics' effects on contemporary art in "Environmental Directions for Aesthetics and the Arts," in *Environment and the Arts: Perspectives on Environmental Aesthetics*, ed. Arnold Berleant, 171–185 (Hants: Ashgate, 2002).

4. Glenn Parsons and Allen Carlson, *Functional Beauty* (Oxford: Oxford University Press, 2009).

5. I explore this complex attitude toward the aging effect in chapter 4. Yuriko Saito, "Everyday Aesthetic Qualities and Transience," in *Everyday Aesthetics*, 149–204 (Oxford: Oxford University Press, 2007).

6. Yi-Fu Tuan lists a number of examples: "When I vacuum the carpet and create neat swatches of flattened fibers, when I look at a cleanly typed page, when the plowman strives to produce a straight furrow or the carpenter looks at the joints in his woodwork with a sense of pride, there is necessarily an aesthetic tinge to the satisfaction. All these activities are attempts to maintain or create small fields of order and meaning, temporary stays against fuzziness and chaos, which can be viewed, however fleetingly, with the pleasure of an artist." Yi-Fu Tuan, *Passing Strange and Wonderful: Aesthetics, Nature, and Culture* (Washington: Island Press, 1993), 101.

7. Ronald W. Hepburn, "The Aesthetics of Sky and Space," *Environmental Values* 19, no. 3 (August 2010): 273–288, see esp. 276.

8. Berleant, *Aesthetics and Environment*, 154.

9. Arnold Berleant, "Getting Along Beautifully: Ideas for a Social Aesthetics," in *Aesthetics and Environment: Variations on a Theme*, 147–161 (Hants: Ashgate, 2005); Arnold Berleant, "Ideas for a Social Aesthetic," in *The Aesthetics of Everyday Life*, ed. Andrew W. Light and Jonathan M. Smith, 23–38 (New York: Columbia University Press, 2005).

10. Barbara Sandrisser, *Exploring the Future of Aesthetic Value* (Tokyo: The Human Renaissance Institute, 1993); Barbara Sandrisser, *Etiquette and Courtesy . . . in the 21st Century?* (Tokyo: The Human Renaissance Institute, 1994); Barbara Sandrisser, "On Elegance in Japan," in *Aesthetics in Perspective*, ed. Kathleen Higgins, 628–633 (Fort Worth: Harcourt Brace & Company, 1996).

11. Arto Haapala explores the aesthetic ramifications of "the familiar" and "the strange" or "the unfamiliar" in Arto Haapala, "On the Aesthetics of the Everyday: Familiarity, Strangeness, and the Meaning of Place," in *The Aesthetics of Everyday Life*, ed. Andrew Light and Jonathan M. Smith, 39–55 (New York: Columbia University Press, 2005).

12. John Dewey, "Having an Experience," in *Art As Experience*, 36–56 (New York: Capricorn Press, 1958).

13. Yrjö Sepänmaa, "Aesthetics in Practice: Prolegomenon," in *Practical Aesthetics in Practice and in Theory*, ed. Marti Honkanen, 13–17 (Helsinki: University of Helsinki, 1995), 15. Sheila Lintott, in her discussion of feminist environmental aesthetics, shares the same observation, challenging the commonly held assumption that aesthetics and beauty deal with trivial matters. See Sheila Lintott, "Feminist Aesthetics and the Neglect of Natural Beauty," *Environmental Values* 19, no. 3 (August, 2010): 322.

14. I explore the relationship between the aesthetic and the moral values of care and thoughtfulness and their social significance in chapter 5. Yuriko Saito, "Moral-Aesthetic Judgments of Artifacts," in *Everyday Aesthetics*, 205–242 (Oxford: Oxford University Press, 2007).

15. Gert Groening and Joachim Wolschke-Bulmahn, "Some Notes on the Mania for Native Plants in Germany," *Landscape Journal* 11, no. 2 (1992): 116–126. Another way in which Nazi Germany designed an everyday environment to promote its political agenda was through graphics, such as posters and the choice of typography. See Steven Heller, *Iron Fists: Branding the 20th Century Totalitarian State* (London: Phaidon Press Limited, 2008). I thank Scott Cook for the Heller reference.

16. For the aesthetics of falling cherry blossoms and its appropriation by the Japanese military, see Emiko Ohnuki-Tierney, *Kamikaze, Cherry Blossoms, and Nationalisms: The Militarization of Aesthetics in Japanese History* (Chicago: The University of Chicago Press, 2002). As for the aesthetics of everyday landscapes and built structures, some of the influential writings include: Shigetaka Shiga, *Nihon Fūkei ron* [Theory of Japanese Landscape] published in 1894 during the Sino-Japan war; Kojima Usui, *Nihon Sansui ron* [Theory of Japanese Mountains and Waters] published in 1904 during the Russo-Japanese war; Uehara Keiji, *Nihon Fūkeibi ron* [Theory of Japanese Landscape Beauty] published in 1943 during WWII; Yojūrō Yasuda, *Nihon no Hashi* [Japanese Bridges], published in 1936, the nationalistic significance of which is discussed by Alan Tansman in *The Aesthetics of Japanese Fascism* (Berkeley: University of California Press, 2009).

17. Tansman, *The Aesthetics of Japanese Fascism*, 4, 12, and 3.

18. For a historical account of the development of wilderness aesthetics and the formation of American national parks, see Roderick Nash, *Wilderness and the American Mind* (New Haven, Conn.: Yale University Press, 1982), and Alfred Runte, *National Parks: The American Experience* (Lincoln: University of Nebraska Press, 1987).

19. Allen Carlson, "Contemporary Environmental Aesthetics and the Requirements of Environmentalism," *Environmental Values* 19, no. 3 (August 2010): 290.

20. I discuss various aspects of green aesthetics in chapter 2. Yuriko Saito, "Green Aesthetics," in *Everyday Aesthetics*, 69–103 (Oxford: Oxford University Press, 2007).

21. Samantha Clark points out that some contemporary art helps sensitize us to the overabundance of materials that surround us. Samantha Clark, "Contemporary Art and Environmental Aesthetics," *Environmental Values* 19, no. 3 (August 2010): 360.

22. I explore the case of the Capewind project in Yuriko Saito, "Machines in the Ocean: The Aesthetics of Wind Farms," *Contemporary Aesthetics* 2, sec. 1 (2004): http://hdl.handle.net/2027/spo.7523862.0002.006; "Response to Jon Boone's Critique," in *Contemporary Aesthetics* 3 (2005): http://hdl.handle.net/2027/spo.7523862.0003.012. The most recent aesthetic battle over wind turbines and solar plants concerns an area of the Mojave Desert. See "Desert Vistas vs. Solar Power," *New York Times* (December 22, 2009). I owe this reference to Roger Paden.

23. Kathleen A. Hughes, "To Fight Global Warming, Some Hang a Clothesline," *New York Times* (April 12, 2007). A New Hampshire–based activist organization, Project Laundry List, compiles various homeowners' association rules against laundry hanging and works on promoting "Right to Dry." http://www.laundrylist.org.

24. Tansman, *The Aesthetics of Japanese Fascism*, 19.

25. David Orr, *The Nature of Design: Ecology, Culture, and Human Intention* (Oxford: Oxford University Press, 2002), 178–179; emphasis added, 185, 25, and 26. A parallel reminder is issued by Aldo Leopold who claims that "we can be ethical only in relation to something we can see, feel, understand, love" and that it is "inconceivable . . . that an ethical relation to land can exist without love, respect, and admiration for land, and a high regard for its value"; Aldo Leopold, *A Sand County Almanac* (New York: Ballantine Books, 1966), 251 and 261. Landscape architect Joan Nassauer argues for the need to make ecologically sustainable landscape design attractive and aesthetically appealing, so that people cherish, maintain, care for, and protect it, rendering it "culturally sustainable"; Joan I. Nassauer, "Cultural Sustainability: Aligning Aesthetics with Ecology," in *Placing Nature: Culture and Landscape Ecology*, ed. Joan I. Nassauer (Washington: Island Press, 1997), 68. Finally, in her project to "make explicit a developing aesthetic criteria related to both ethics and utility," landscape architect and educator Catherine Dee observes that "this separation of art, ethics, utility and nature can leave aesthetics with an atrophied, and indeed, frivolous role in landscape education." Catherine Dee, "Form, Utility, and the Aesthetics of Thrift in Design Education," *Landscape Journal* 29, no. 1 (2010): 21.

26. Marcia Eaton, *Merit, Aesthetic and Ethical* (Oxford: Oxford University Press, 2001), 176.

27. My own view is in basic agreement with Carlson's cognitivist view, although I disagree that natural science has a monopoly on what should inform our aesthetic appreciation of nature. I regard as appropriate any human attempts to understand nature on its own terms, including mythical narratives that are motivated by trying to understand the origin and function of natural objects, environments, and phenomena, as well as Zen-like efforts to directly experience the object by transcending an all-too-human viewpoint (although I see some problems associated with this last way of experiencing nature). See Yuriko Saito, "Appreciating Nature on Its Own Terms," in *Nature, Aesthetics, and Environmentalism: From Beauty to Duty*, ed. Allen Carlson and Sheila Lintott, 151–168 (New York: Columbia University Press, 2008). Carlson's recent writings seem to argue for the coexistence of cognitivist and noncognitivist approaches, thereby supporting a pluralistic view of nature aesthetics. For example, he claims that "we do not have to choose between them, since, although the two positions have different emphases, there need be no theoretical conflict between them" ("Contemporary Environmental Aesthetics and the Requirements of Environmentalism," *Environmental Values* 19, no. 3 [August, 2010]: 306).

28. Ronald W. Hepburn, "Trivial and Serious in the Aesthetic Appreciation of Nature," in *The Reach of the Aesthetic*, 1–15 (Hants: Ashgate, 2001), see esp. 13. In "The Aesthetics of Sky and Space," Hepburn continues this challenge by questioning whether scientifically informed cosmic aesthetics should take precedence over everyday experience from the perspective of the human *Lebenswelt*. However, rather than favoring the latter experience over the former, he calls for appreciating "the ambiguity itself" as "a factor to be experientially reckoned with/assimilated in a serious aesthetic experience of the spatio-temporal cosmos," thereby acknowledging the viability of both experiences particularly in relation to one another, Ronald W. Hepburn, "The Aesthetics of Sky and Space," 285.

29. Hepburn, *The Reach of the Aesthetic*, 12.

30. The cloud example is from Ronald W. Hepburn, "Aesthetic Appreciation of Nature," in *Aesthetics in the Modern World*, ed. Harold Osborne (London: Thames and Hudson, 1968), 31, and the Virgin Mary example is from Hepburn, *The Reach of the Aesthetic*, 11. The quoted passage is from Hepburn, *The Reach of the Aesthetic*, 4.

31. Hepburn, *The Reach of the Aesthetic*, 8.

32. Emily Brady, "Imagination and the Aesthetic Appreciation of Nature," in *The Aesthetics of Natural Environment*, ed. Allen Carlson and Arnold Berleant, 156–169 (Petersborough: Broadview Press, 2004), 159.

33. Brady, *The Aesthetics of Natural Environment*, 164.

34. A good discussion of the phenomenon of "aesthetic disillusionment" is given by Cheryl Foster in Cheryl Foster, "Aesthetic Disillusionment: Environment, Ethics, Art," *Environmental Values* 1 (1992): 205–15.

35. Edward Bullough, "'Psychical Distance' as a Factor in Art and an Aesthetic Principle," *The British Journal of Psychology* 5, no. 2 (1912): 88–89.

36. To list only a few writings on laundry-hanging: Cindy Etter-Turnbull, *Fine Lines: A Celebration of Clothesline Culture* (Lawrencetown Beach, Nova Scotia: Pottersfield Press, 2006); Irene Rawlings and Andrea Vansteenhouse, *The Clothesline* (Layton, Utah: Gibbs Smith, 2002); Cheryl Mendelson, *Laundry: The Home Comforts: Book of Caring for Clothes and Linens* (New York: Scribner, 2005); Pauliina Rautio, "On Hanging Laundry: The Place of Beauty in Managing Everyday Life," *Contemporary Aesthetics* (2009).

37. I develop this point in Saito, "Response to Jon Boone's Critique."

38. David E. Cooper, "Look of Lawns," *Times Literary Supplement* 5525 (February 20, 2009): 23.

39. Arthur Danto, "The Artworld," *The Journal of Philosophy* LXI (1964): 571–584, and Arthur Danto, *The Transfiguration of the Commonplace: A Philosophy of Art* (Cambridge, Mass.: Harvard University Press, 1983).

40. Cooper, "Look of Lawns," 23.

41. Richard H. Thaler and Cass R. Sunstein, *Nudge: Improving Decisions about Health, Wealth, and Happiness* (New York: Penguin Books, 2008), 10.

42. Berleant, *The Aesthetics of Environment*, 98.

43. Berleant, *Sensibility and Sense*, 191.

44. Ibid., 193.

45. Lao Tsu, *Tao Te Ching*, trans. Gia-Fu Feng and Jane English (New York: Vintage Books, 1972). The first quote is from sec. 30 and the rest from sec. 76.

46. J. Baird Callicott, *Earth's Insights: A Survey of Ecological Ethics from the Mediterranean Basin to the Australian Outback* (Berkeley: University of California Press, 1994), 74.

47. Sim van der Ryn and Stuart Cowan, *Ecological Design* (Washington: Island Press, 1996), 116. All the passages included in this paragraph are from the same page.

48. See, for example, Pamela J. Acquith and Arne Kalland, eds., *Japanese Images of Nature*, (Richmond, Surrey: Curzon Press, 1997), and Julia A. Thomas, *Reconfiguring Modernity: Concepts of Nature in Japanese Political Ideology* (Berkeley: University of California Press, 2001).

49. I explore the discussion in this paragraph in more details in Yuriko Saito, "Representing the Essence of Objects: Art in the Japanese Aesthetic Tradition," in *Art and Essence*, ed. Stephen Davies and Ananta C. Sukla (Westport: Praeger Publishers, 2003), and Yuriko Saito, "The Moral Dimensions of Japanese Aesthetics," *The Journal of Aesthetics and Art Criticism* 65, no. 1 (2007): 85–97.

50. Kenya Hara, *White*, trans. Jooyeon Rhee (Baden: Lars Müller Publishers, 2010), prologue. Samantha Clark points out that some contemporary artists are also guided by active, sensitive listening by communicating *with* the audience rather than communicating *to* them ("Contemporary Art and Environmental Aesthetics," *Environmental Values* 19 [August 2010]: 367–369).

51. Naoto Fukasawa and Jasper Morrison, *Super Normal*, trans. Mardi Miyake (Baden: Lars Müller Publishers, 2008), 116; emphasis added.

52. I explore the moral dimension of Japanese aesthetics in Yuriko Saito, "The Moral Dimensions of Japanese Aesthetics," *The Journal of Aesthetics and Art Criticism* 65, no. 1 (2007): 85–97.

53. An earlier and much shorter version of this chapter was presented at the Eastern Division Meeting of the American Philosophical Association, 2009, and at the 8th Annual Meeting of the International Society for Environmental Ethics, 2011. An earlier version of this chapter was also published in *Environmental Values*, 19, no. 3 (August 2010).

3. On Universalism and Cultural Historicism in Environmental Aesthetics
Jonathan Maskit

1. Theodor Adorno, *Aesthetic Theory*, trans. Robert Hullot-Kentor (Minneapolis: University of Minnesota Press, 1997); Theodor Adorno,

Ästhetische Theorie (Frankfurt am Main: Surhkamp, 1970). For a recent first foray toward bringing together these two parallel histories, see Marta Tafalla, "Rehabilitating the Aesthetics of Nature: Hepburn and Adorno," *Environmental Ethics* 33 (2011): 45–56.

2. Clive Bell, *Art* (London: Chatto & Windus, 1914).

3. Allen Carlson, "Appreciation and the Natural Environment," in *The Aesthetics of Natural Environments*, ed. Allen Carlson and Arnold Berleant (Peterborough, ON: Broadview Press, 2004), 64. Since so many of the key texts in the field are collected in this volume (and its companion Allen Carlson and Arnold Berleant, eds., *The Aesthetics of Human Environments* [Peterborough, ON: Broadview Press, 2007]), I cite them from these sources rather than the originals.

4. Yuriko Saito, "Appreciating Nature on Its Own Terms," in *The Aesthetics of Natural Environments*, ed. Allen Carlson and Arnold Berleant (Peterborough, ON: Broadview Press, 2004), 141; Emily Brady, "Imagination and the Aesthetics Appreciation of Nature," in *The Aesthetics of Natural Environments*, ed. Allen Carlson and Arnold Berleant (Peterborough, ON: Broadview Press, 2004), 156.

5. Emily Brady, *Aesthetics of the Natural Environment* (Tuscaloosa: University of Alabama Press, 2003), 86; Allen Carlson and Arnold Berleant, "Introduction: The Aesthetics of Nature," in *The Aesthetics of Natural Environments*, ed. Allen Carlson and Arnold Berleant (Peterborough, ON: Broadview Press, 2004), 11–42.

6. Ronald Moore, "Appreciating Natural Beauty as Beautiful," in *The Aesthetics of Natural Environments*, ed. Allen Carlson and Arnold Berleant (Peterborough, ON: Broadview Press, 2004), 215.

7. It is true that Carlson also often says that we can substitute for science's concepts those provided by common-sense experience of nature, but this seems to make his view far less cogent. For one, science and common sense are often at odds. For example, the sun doesn't, properly speaking, rise or set, despite what common sense tells us. Second, if science is supposed to guide our judgments by telling us how things truly are, then permitting common sense also to play this role seems greatly to weaken the force of Carlson's argument.

8. One might argue that the view developed in the *Critique of Judgment* offers a third view, in which the world is encountered a-conceptually and then, via reflective judgment, we seek concepts under which we can bring this experience. I developed this reading in my doctoral dissertation: Jonathan Maskit, *Aesthetic World-Disclosure in Kant and Heidegger* (Northwestern University PhD thesis, 1996).

9. Martin Heidegger, "A Dialogue on Language," in *On the Way to Language*, trans. Peter D. Hertz (New York: Harper & Row, 1971), 1–54; Martin Heidegger, "Aus einem Gespräch von der Sprache," in *Unterwegs zur Sprache. Gesamtausgabe*, vol. 12 (Frankfurt am Main: Vittorio Klostermann, 1985), 79–146.

10. Arto Haapala, "On the Aesthetics of the Everyday: Familiarity, Strangeness, and the Meaning of Place," in *The Aesthetics of Everyday Life*, ed. Andrew Light and Jonathan M. Smith (New York: Columbia University Press, 2005), 39–55.

11. Haapala, "On the Aesthetics of the Everyday," 44.

12. Pauline von Bonsdorff, "Urban Richness and the Art of Building," in *The Aesthetics of Human Environments*, ed. Allen Carlson and Arnold Berleant (Peterborough, ON: Broadview Press, 2004), 66–78.

13. Von Bonsdorff, "Urban Richness and the Art of Building," 73.

14. William Cronon, for example, argues that one of the problems of North American thinking about wilderness is its commitment to obliterating the traces and the history of the peoples who formerly inhabited these sites. See William Cronon, "The Trouble With Wilderness or Getting Back to the Wrong Nature," in *The Great New Wilderness Debate*, ed. J. Baird Callicott and Michael P. Nelson (Athens: The University of Georgia Press, 1998), 471–499.

15. See, for example, Barbara Sandrisser, "Cultivating Commonplaces: Sophisticated Vernacularism in Japan," in *The Aesthetics of Human Environments*, ed. Allen Carlson and Arnold Berleant (Peterborough, ON: Broadview Press, 2004), 150–162.

16. A similar issue is raised by Ramachandra Guha, "Radical Environmentalism and Wilderness Preservation: A Third World Critique," *Environmental Ethics* 11 (1989): 71–83. Sandrisser is significantly more careful in her work than are Bill Devall and George Sessions in the work criticized by Guha. Nevertheless, the worry remains any time one attempts to appropriate another culture that one will fail to grasp it adequately.

17. Yuriko Saito, "Appreciating Nature on Its Own Terms," 141–155.

18. Perhaps reflecting the continuing marginality of environmental aesthetics (for both continental *and* analytic aestheticians), it is principally Seel's and Böhme's work on the philosophy of art that has been translated into English. For Seel's work on environmental aesthetics, see Martin Seel, *Eine Ästhetik der Natur* (Frankfurt am Main: Suhrkamp, 1991). See also the essays of Martin Seel, "Ästhetische Argumente in der Ethik der Natur," in *Ethisch-ästhetische Studien* (Frankfurt am Main: Suhrkamp, 1996), 201–243; Martin Seel, "Ästhetische und moralische Anerkennung der Natur," in *Ethisch-ästhetische Studien* (Frankfurt am Main: Suhrkamp, 1996), 201–243; and Martin Seel, "Aesthetic Arguments in the Ethics of Nature," trans. Catherine Rigby, *Thesis 11* vol. 32 (1992): 76–89. For Böhme, see Gernot Böhme, *Für eine ökologische Naturästhetik* (Frankfurt am Main: Suhrkamp, 1989), and Gernot Böhme, "An Aesthetic Theory of Nature: An Interim Report," trans. John Farrell, *Thesis 11* vol. 32 (1992): 90–102. For an English language review of Seel's and Böhme's monographs referenced here, see Catherine Rigby, "Beyond the Frame: Art, Ecology and the Aesthetics of Nature," *Thesis 11* vol. 32 (1992): 114–128.

19. Seel, "Ästhetische und moralische Anerkennung der Natur," 221. All translations are my own.

20. Ibid., 225.

21. Ibid., 226.

22. Ibid., 227.

23. Böhme, *Für eine ökologische Naturästhetik*, 12.

24. Ibid., 31.

25. Phenomenologists such as Edmund Husserl and Heidegger, as they sought to overcome this cleavage, often ended up reinscribing it in various ways. Maurice Merleau-Ponty was more successful, particularly in his later works, managing to rethink the subject not just as embodied but as a body whose flesh is not distinct from, but continuous with, what he calls the flesh of the world. However, I can find no references in Böhme's work to Merleau-Ponty. See, in this regard, Maurice Merleau-Ponty, *The Visible and the Invisible*, ed. Claude Lefort, trans. Alphonso Lingis (Evanston, Ill.: Northwestern Univ. Press, 1968).

26. Böhme, *Für eine ökologische Naturästhetik*, 34.

27. See Gernot Bohme, *Atmosphäre: Essays zur neuen Ästhetik* (Frankfurt am Main: Suhrkamp, 1995); Gernot Böhme, *Anmutungen: über das Ätmospherische* (Ostfildern vor Stuttgart: Edition Tertium, 1998); and "Atmosphere as the Subject Matter of Architecture," in *Herzog & de Meuron: Natural History*, ed. Philip Ursprung (Montréal: Canadian Centre for Architecture, 2002), 398–406.

28. See, for an overview of these issues, Jonathan Maskit, "Something Wild? Deleuze and Guattari, Wilderness, and Purity," in *The Wilderness Debate Rages On: Continuing the Great New Wilderness Debate*, ed. J. Baird Callicott and Michael Nelson (Athens: University of Georgia Press, 2008), 461–484.

29. Earlier versions of this chapter were presented not only at the meetings of the *International Association for Environmental Philosophy* in Nijmegen, the Netherlands, in June 2011 but also at the meetings of the *International Association for Environmental Philosophy* in Philadelphia in October 2011 as well as to my colleagues in Denison University's Department of Philosophy in September 2011 as part of our Brandt discussion series. I am grateful to all of those present at these sessions, in particular to Emily Brady, Allen Carlson, Barbara Fultner, Irene Klaver, Mark Moller, John McHugh, and David Seamon. I would like to thank an anonymous reviewer as well for suggesting that I include a discussion of Gernot Böhme's work.

4. The Cultural Aesthetics of Environment
Arnold Berleant

1. See Justus Buchler, *The Metaphysics of Natural Complexes* (New York: Columbia University Press, 1966); 2nd ed. (New York: State University of New York Press, 1990).

2. Val Plumwood, *Environmental Culture: The Ecological Crisis of Reason* (London and New York: Routledge, 2002), develops the implications of ecological thinking for philosophic rationality and ethics. The same cultural and natural embeddedness that affects our understanding of environmental aesthetics influences profoundly our understanding of environmental justice.

3. See especially Arnold Berleant, *The Aesthetics of Environment* (Philadelphia: Temple University Press, 1992).

4. Cheng Xiangzhan offers an account of the influence of my work in environmental aesthetics on the development of ecological aesthetics in China. See Cheng Xiangzhan, "Environmental Aesthetics and Ecological Aesthetics: Arnold Berleant's Impact on Ecological Aesthetics in China," *Sztuka i Filosofia* 37 (2011): 24–35 (in Polish).

5. Such work is widely scattered and is international in scope. Three environmental designers whose work combines ecological and aesthetic concerns are the American Patricia Johanson, the Brazilian Fernando Chacel, and the Chinese Yu Kongjian.

6. Genesis 1:28-29.

7. Plato, *The Republic* V, 475–480; VI–VII.

8. For example, the German *Umwelt*; the French *environs*.

9. The Orphic ideas have been traced to the fourth century B.C.E. but are likely even older. Relevant here is its mythology in which Zeus designates his illegitimate child Dionysus as his heir. His wife, Hera, incites the Titans to murder and eat Dionysus, but Zeus, when he learns of this, incinerates the Titans with a thunderbolt. Mankind is born from the ashes, which contain the bodies of the Titans and Dionysus, resulting in humans having a divine soul (Dionysus) and a body (the Titans) to which the soul is in bondage.

10. See especially Berleant, *The Aesthetics of Environment*.

11. Zeng Fanren, in particular, has developed the conception of an ecological environmental aesthetic. See Zeng Fanren, "A Conception of Ecological Aesthetics in the Perspective of Today's Ecological Civilization," *Literary Review* 4 (2005); Zeng Fanren, "A Review on the Relationship between Ecological Aesthetics and Environmental Aesthetics," *Exploration and Free Views* 9 (2008). See also Zeng Fanren, *Collected Articles on Aesthetics of Ecological Existence*, 2nd ed. (Changchun: Jilin People's Press, 2003), revised and enlarged in 2009.

5. Toward an Aesthetics of Respect: Kant's Contribution to Environmental Aesthetics
Denis Dumas

1. For a critique of classic anthropocentrism, see the well-known text by Lynn White, "The Historical Roots of Our Ecologic Crisis," *Science* 155 (1967): 1203–1207; Robin Attfield, "Social History, Religion, and Technology:

An Interdisciplinary Investigation into Lynn White's 'Roots.'" *Environmental Ethics* 31 (2009): 31–50.

2. Arne Naess, "The Shallow and the Deep, Long-Range Ecology Movement," *Inquiry* 16 (1973): 95–100. Also reproduced in a large number of collective works and anthologies. Naess's text merits mention here, given the considerable importance it has held to date in environmental ethics.

3. The imperative of prudence that I am invoking here must be carefully distinguished from the precautionary principle which has been so often discussed for more than twenty years. The imperative of prudence is much more demanding, from the normative point of view, than the precautionary principle: it enjoins us to protect the natural environment to the greatest extent possible, even where there is no question of "threats of serious or irreversible damage," as expressed, for example, in the United Nations Environment Programme, *Rio Declaration on Environment and Development.* http://www.unep.org/Documents.multilingual/Default.asp? DocumentID=78&ArticleID=1163 (accessed September 7, 2011).

4. "Only a rational being has the capacity to act *in accordance with the representation* of laws, that is, in accordance with principles, or has a *will.*" See Immanuel Kant, "Groundwork of the Metaphysics of Morals," in *Practical Philosophy,* ed. Mary J. Gregor (Cambridge: Cambridge University Press, 1996), 66 (4:412). I will cite Kant by indicating, in parentheses, the volume and page of the Akademie-Ausgabe. See Immanuel Kant, *Gesammelte Schriften,* vol. 1–23 (Akademie-Ausgabe).

5. "Instead, sensible feeling, which underlies all our inclinations, is indeed the condition of that feeling we call respect, but the cause determining it lies in our practical reason; and so this feeling, on account of its origin, cannot be called pathologically effected but must be called *practically effected,* and is effected as follows: the representation of the moral law deprives self-love of its influence and self-conceit of its illusion, and thereby the hindrance to pure practical reason is lessened and the representation of the superiority of its objective law to the impulses of sensibility is produced and hence, by removal of the counterweight, the relative weightiness of the law (with regard to a will affected by impulses) in the judgment of reason. And so respect for the law is not the incentive to morality; instead it is morality itself subjectively considered as an incentive inasmuch as pure practical reason, by rejecting all the claims of self-love in opposition with its own, supplies authority to the law, which now alone has influence. With regard to this it should be noted that, since respect is an effect on feeling and hence on the sensibility of a rational being, it presupposes this sensibility and so too the finitude of such beings on whom the moral law imposes respect, and that respect for the *law* cannot be attributed to a supreme being or even to one free from all sensibility, in whom this cannot be an obstacle to practical reason." See Immanuel Kant, "Critique of Practical Reason," in *Practical Philosophy,* ed. Mary J. Gregor (Cambridge: Cambridge University Press, 1996), 200 (5:75–76).

6. Kant, "Groundwork of the Metaphysics of Morals," 106 (4:460). See, on this subject, Ralph C. S. Walker, "Achtung in the *Gundlegung*," in *Grundlegung zur Metaphysik der Sitten: Ein kooperativer Kommentar*, ed. Otfried Höffe (Frankfurt am Main: Vittorio Klosterman, 1993), 97–116. See also Robert Theis, "Respect de la loi, respect de la personne: Kant," in *Le Portique* (November 2003), http://leportique.revues.org/index548.html (accessed September 7, 2011).

7. "The *object* of respect is therefore simply the *law*, and indeed the law that we impose upon *ourselves* and yet as necessary in itself. . . . Any respect for a person is properly only respect for the law (of integrity and so forth) of which he gives us an example." See Kant, "Groundwork of the Metaphysic of Morals," 56 (4:401). Kant writes similarly in "The Metaphysics of Morals," in *Practical Philosophy*, ed. Mary J. Gregor (Cambridge: Cambridge University Press, 1996), 531 (6:403): "Accordingly, it is not correct to say that a human being has a duty of self-esteem; it must rather be said that the law within him unavoidably forces from him *respect* for his own being, and this feeling (which is of a special kind) is the basis of certain duties, that is, of certain actions that are consistent with his duty to himself."

8. The idea of an *extended usage of the concept of respect* encapsulates the basic intuition of the present article.

9. Kant, "Critique of Practical Reason," 202 (5:76).

10. Kant, "Groundwork of the Metaphysics of Morals," 80 (4:429); italics original.

11. Kant, "The Metaphysics of Morals," 507 (6:373).

12. Immanuel Kant, *Critique of the Power of Judgment*, ed. Paul Guyer, trans. Paul Guyer and Eric Matthews (Cambridge: Cambridge University Press, 2000). Martin Seel draws partly on Kant to elaborate an aesthetics of nature. See especially Martin Seel, *Eine Ästhetik der Natur* (Frankfurt am Main: Suhrkamp, 1991); Martin Seel, "Aesthetic Arguments in the Ethics of Nature," *Thesis* 11 vol. 32 (1992): 76–89; Martin Seel, *Aesthetics of Appearing* (Stanford: Stanford University Press, 2004).

13. Here I draw the attention of readers to the works of Jean-François Lyotard, who presented an interpretation of Kantian aesthetics that is opposed to mine, insofar as it culminates in postmodern antihumanism. See on this topic, Jean-François Lyotard, *Le différend* (Paris: Les Éditions de Minuit, 1983); Jean-François Lyotard, *The Differend: Phrases in Dispute*, trans. Georges van den Abbeele (Minneapolis: University of Minnesota Press, 1988); Jean-François Lyotard, *Leçons sur l'Analytique du sublime* (Paris: Galilée, 1991); Jean-François Lyotard, *Lessons on the Analytic of the Sublime*, trans. Elizabeth Rottenberg (Stanford: Stanford University Press, 2004). See also Jean-François Lyotard, *L'enthousiasme: la critique kantienne de l'histoire* (Paris: Galilée, 1986); Jean-François Lyotard, *Enthusiasm: The Kantian Critique of History*, trans. The Board of Trustees of the Leland Stanford Junior University (Stanford: Stanford University Press, 2009).

14. Angelika Breitenbach attempts to use the Kantian theory of teleological judgment, which constitutes the second part of the *Critique of the Power of Judgment*, to found an environmental ethics. This approach seems to me to be difficult to defend. See Angelika Breitenbach, *Die Analogie von Vernunft und Natur: Eine Umweltphilosophie nach Kant* (Berlin: Walter de Gruyter, 2005). See also Angelika Breitenbach, "Kant Goes Fishing: Kant and the Right to Property in Environmental Resources," *Studies in History and Philosophy of Biological and Biomedical Sciences* 36 (2005): 488–512; Angelika Breitenbach, "Two Views on Nature: A Solution to Kant's Antinomy of Mechanism and Teleology," *The British Journal for the History of Philosophy* 16 (2008): 351–369.

15. Drawing upon Kant's aesthetics firmly entails that we opt for a subjectivist rather than a cognitivist model. Allen Carlson proposes on the contrary a cognitivist approach (the natural environment model) according to which an aesthetic appreciation of nature requires scientific knowledge. See Allen Carlson, *Aesthetics and the Environment: The Appreciation of Nature, Art and Architecture* (London: Routledge, 2000); Allen Carlson, *Nature and Landscape: An Introduction to Environmental Aesthetics* (New York: Columbia University Press, 2008); Allen Carlson and Glenn Parsons, *Functional Beauty* (Oxford: Oxford University Press, 2008); Glenn Parsons, *Aesthetics and Nature* (London: Continuum Press, 2008). On this subject, see my discussion of Carlson's theses in Denis Dumas, "L'esthétique environnementale d'Allen Carlson: Cognitivisme et appréciation esthétique de la nature." *AE: Revue canadienne d'esthétique* 6 (2001). http://www.uqtr. uquebec.ca/AE/Vol_6/Carlson/dumas.html (accessed August 21, 2013).

16. Kant, *Critique of the Power of Judgment*, 227 (5:353). "Now I say that the beautiful is the symbol of the morally good, and also that only in this respect (that of a relation that is natural to everyone, and that is also expected of everyone else as a duty) does it please with a claim to the assent of everyone else, in which the mind is at the same time aware of a certain ennoblement and elevation above the mere receptivity for a pleasure from sensible impressions, and also esteems the value of others in accordance with a similar maxim of their power of judgment."

17. The theme of the sublime (particularly its Kantian version) has been the subject of an abundant literature for over twenty years. The scope of this article does not permit me to broach the numerous problems it presents or the interpretations that have been proposed. On this topic, see Elmar Treptow, *Die erhabene Natur: Entwurf einer ökologischen Ästhetik* (Würzburg: Königshausen & Neumann, 2001).

18. Kant, *Critique of the Power of Judgment*, 140–141 (5:257).

19. Kant, *Critique of the Power of Judgment*, 180 (5:300–301). Interest does not ground a moral duty, but it does justify a normative moral judgment on our love of nature. See, on this subject, Paul Guyer, *Kant and the Experience of Freedom: Essays on Aesthetics and Morality* (Cambridge: Cambridge University Press, 1993), 311.

20. Kant, *Critique of the Power of Judgment*, 252 (5:380).

21. Kant, "The Metaphysics of Morals," 564 (6:444). See Allen Wood, "Kant on Duties Regarding Non-Rational Nature I," *Aristotelian Society Supplement* 72 (1998): 189–210.

22. It is worth mentioning that Kant himself never uses the expressions "aesthetic respect" or "aesthetics of respect." The concept of subreption merits a separate, sustained study. See, on this topic, Hanno Birken-Bertsch, *Subreption und Dialektik bei Kant: Der Begriff des Fehlers der Erschleichung in der Philosophie des 18. Jahrhunderts* (Stuttgart: Bad Canstatt, 2006); Benoît Goetz, "Le respect et le sublime," *Le portique* 11 (2003). http://leportique.revues.org/559. (accessed August 21, 2013).

23. I mention this idea briefly, being unable to discuss it here. Important studies have been devoted to it in recent years. See, for example, Arnold Berleant and Allen Carlson, *The Aesthetics of Human Environments* (Peterborough: Broadview Press, 2007); and Nathalie Blanc, *Vers une eshétique environnementale* (Paris: Éditions Quae, 2007).

24. See Arnold Berleant, *The Aesthetics of Environment* (Philadelphia: Temple University Press, 1992); Arnold Berleant, *Living in the Landscape: Toward an Aesthetics of Environment* (Lawrence: University Press of Kansas, 1997); Arnold Berleant, *Aesthetics and Environment: Variations on a Theme* (Aldershot: Ashgate, 2005); Arnold Berleant, *Sensibility and Sense: The Aesthetic Transformation of the Human World* (Exeter: Imprint Academic, 2010). Regarding this subject, see Emily Brady's discussion in Emily Brady, *Aesthetics of the Natural Environment* (Edinburgh: Edinburgh University Press, 2003), 106.

25. This is what I attempted to show in Denis Dumas, "Avons-nous un intérêt esthétique à l'égard de la nature?," in *Désintéressement et esthétique*, ed. Suzanne Foisy and Claude Thérien (Québec: Nota Bene, 2013).

26. "*Taste* is the faculty for judging an object or a kind of representation through a satisfaction or dissatisfaction *without any interest*. The object of such a satisfaction is called *beautiful*." Kant, *Critique of the Power of Judgment*, 96 (5:211).

27. On this question, see Allen Carlson and Sheila Lintott, *Nature, Aesthetics, and Environmentalism: From Beauty to Duty* (New York: Columbia University Press, 2008).

28. See Brady, *Aesthetics of the Natural Environment*, 254–260. Brady mentions the concept of "aesthetic respect" for nature (p. 260) in the context of a model she calls "integrated aesthetic," without, however, according it a primary role. Brady's model draws upon a critical reading of Kant, to which is added certain important elements of contemporary discussions. The foundation of her model seems to privilege a moderate non-anthropocentrism which seeks to go beyond modern dualism. It seems to me, however, that her subjectivist conception of aesthetic values would fit better with a humanist anthropocentrism. See also Emily Brady, "Don't Eat the Daisies: Disinterestedness and the Situated Aesthetic," *Environmental*

Values 7, no. 1 (1998): 97–114; Emily Brady, "Aesthetic Character and Aesthetic Integrity in Environmental Conservation," *Environmental Ethics* 24, no. 1 (2002): 75–91; Emily Brady, "Vers une véritable esthétique de l'environnement: l'élimination des frontières et des oppositions dans l'expérience esthétique du paysage," *Cosmopolitiques* 15 (2007): 61–72.

29. In this sense, my theory argues in favor of the *convergence hypothesis* formulated by Bryan Norton. See, on this subject, Bryan Norton, "Why I am Not a Nonanthropocentrist: Callicott and the Failure of Monistic Inherentism," *Environmental Ethics* 17, no. 4 (1995): 341–358; Bryan Norton, *Toward Unity among Environmentalists* (New York: Oxford University Press, 1991); Bryan Norton, *Searching for Sustainability: Interdisciplinary Essays in the Philosophy of Conservation Biology* (Cambridge: Cambridge University Press, 2003); Ben Minteer, *Nature in Common?* (Philadelphia: Temple University Press, 2009).

30. I thank Matthew McLennan for translating the bulk of this chapter and for helping to revise the text.

6. From Theoretical to Applied Environmental Aesthetics: Academic Aesthetics Meets Real-World Demands
Yrjö Sepänmaa

This chapter was published earlier in *Environmental Values* 19, no. 3 (2010): 393–405.

1. Ken-ichi Sasaki, "Closing Report: Stirrings of a New Aesthetics: An Essay on a Collage of Papers," in *The Great Book of Aesthetics*, ed. Ken-ichi Sasaki and T. Otabe, Proceedings XV International Congress of Aesthetics, Tokyo, Japan (August 2001) (CD-ROM).

2. Ronald W. Hepburn, "Contemporary Aesthetics and the Neglect of Natural Beauty," in *British Analytical Philosophy*, ed. Bernard Williams and Alan Montefiore, 2nd ed. (London: Routledge and Paul, 1966), 285–310.

3. Glenn Parsons, *Aesthetics and Nature* (London: Continuum International Publishing Group, 2008). See also Glenn Parsons, "From the Author's Perspective: Aesthetics and Nature," *American Society for Aesthetics Newsletter* 29, no. 2 (2009): 1–2.

4. Alexandra Koroxenidis, "Heaven," *Athens Plus* (June 26, 2009): 12–13.

5. Lars von Trier's, *Antichrist*, DVD (2009).

6. Yuriko Saito, *Everyday Aesthetics* (Oxford: Oxford University Press, 2007).

7. Emily Brady, untitled talk presented in the seminar *The Future of Environmental Aesthetics* at the University of Joensuu, Finland (March 30, 2009).

8. Charles P. Snow, *The Two Cultures and the Scientific Revolution* (Cambridge: Cambridge University Press, 1959).

9. Harold Osborne, "An Intellectual Crisis in Aesthetics," in *Crisis in Aesthetics? International conference on aesthetics*, ed. Maria Golaszewska (Krakow: Universytet Jagiellonski, Instytut Filozofii, 1979), 215–222. See also Harold Osborne, "Aesthetic Implications of Conceptual Art, Happenings, etc.," *British Journal of Aesthetics* 20 (1980): 6–22.

10. I have considered the birth and development of contemporary environmental aesthetics, particularly the relationship between theoretical and practical environmental aesthetics, among other places, in the following articles: Yrjö Sepänmaa, "The Utilization of Environmental Aesthetics," in *Real World Design: The Foundation and Practice of Environmental Aesthetics*, ed. Yrjö Sepänmaa, XIII International Congress of Aesthetics, Lahti, Finland, August 1–5, 1995. Also in *Proceedings II* (Lahti: University of Helsinki, Lahti Research and Training Centre, 1997), 7–10; Yrjö Sepänmaa, "From Theoretical to Applied Environmental Aesthetics, and Back, a Möbius Strip," in *The Great Book of Aesthetics*, ed. Ken-ichi Sasaki and T. Otabe, Proceedings XV International Congress of Aesthetics, Tokyo, Japan (August 2001) (CD-ROM); Yrjö Sepänmaa, "Home Team and Visiting Team in Applied Environmental Aesthetics," *Filozofski Vestnik* 28, no. 2 (2007): 53–64; Yrjö Sepänmaa, "Applied Environmental Aesthetics: A Preview," in *Aesthetics and Philosophy of Art: Traditions, Intersections, Perspectives. Essays in Honour of Prof. Bohdan Dziemidok*, ed. M. Bokiniec and P. Przybysz (Gdansk: Wydawnictwo Uniwersytetu Gdanskiego, 2009), 268–273.

7. Environmental Art and Ecological Citizenship
Jason B. Simus

1. A recent panel discussion at the 2006 National Meeting of the American Society for Aesthetics in Milwaukee, WI. Participants were Emily Brady, Sheila Lintott, and Isis Brook. See Emily Brady, "Aesthetic Regard for Nature in Environmental and Land Art," *Ethics, Place, and Environment* 10 (2007): 286–300; Sheila Lintott, "Ethically Evaluating Land Art: Is It Worth It?" *Ethics, Place, and Environment* 10 (2007): 263–277; Isis Brook, "Aesthetic Aspects of Unauthorised Environmental Interventions," *Ethics, Place, and Environment* 10 (2007): 307–318.

2. See Allen Carlson, "Is Environmental Art an Aesthetic Affront to Nature?," in *Aesthetics and the Environment: The Appreciation of Nature, Art, and Architecture* (New York: Routledge, 2000), 151; and Donald Crawford, "Art and Nature: Some Dialectical Relationships," *Journal of Aesthetics and Art Criticism* 42 (1983): 56–57.

3. See Adolf Gundersen, *The Environmental Promise of Public Deliberation* (Madison: University of Wisconsin Press, 1995). Gundersen's account of the value of deliberation is similar to what I present here.

4. Crawford, "Art and Nature," 56–57.

5. Carlson, "Is Environmental Art an Aesthetic Affront to Nature?," 151.

6. Crawford, "Art and Nature," 56.

7. See David Hume, "Of the Standard of Taste," in *Essays: Moral, Political, and Literary*, ed. T. H. Green and T. H. Grose, vol. 1 (London: Logmans, Green and Company, 1882).

8. Carlson, "Is Environmental Art an Aesthetic Affront to Nature?," 151.

9. Ibid.

10. The model I propose here is similar to Berys Gaut's "ethicism." See Berys Gaut, "The Ethical Criticism of Art," in *Aesthetics and Ethics: Essays at the Intersection*, ed. Noel Carroll (Cambridge: Cambridge University Press, 1998), 182–203.

11. Because, as stated earlier, there are neither necessary nor sufficient conditions governing whether something is an aesthetic affront, no calculus can be adopted that will offer a way to derive a balance of positive and negative qualities that will result in an overall evaluation.

12. Carlson, "Is Environmental Art an Aesthetic Affront to Nature?," 152.

13. Stan Godlovitch, "Offending Against Nature," *Environmental Values* 7 (1998): 144.

14. See William Cronon, "The Trouble with Wilderness: Or, Getting Back to the Wrong Nature," in *Uncommon Ground: Rethinking the Human Place in Nature*, ed. William Cronon (New York: W. W. Norton & Company, Inc., 1996), 69–90; and William Denevan, "The Pristine Myth," in *The Great New Wilderness Debate*, ed. J. Baird Callicott and Michael P. Nelson (Athens: University of Georgia Press, 1998), 414–442.

15. See S. T. A. Pickett, V. T. Parker, and P. L. Fielder, "The New Paradigm in Ecology: Implications for Conservation Above the Species Level," in *Conservation Biology: The Theory and Practice of Nature Conservation, Preservation, and Management* (New York: Chapman and Hall, 1992), 65–88; Daniel Botkin, *Discordant Harmonies: A New Ecology for the Twenty-first Century* (New York: Oxford University Press, 1990); and S. T. A. Pickett and P. S. White, eds., *The Ecology of Natural Disturbance and Patch Dynamics* (Orlando: Academic Press, 1985).

16. Allen Carlson, "Nature and Positive Aesthetics," in *Aesthetics and the Environment: The Appreciation of Nature, Art, and Architecture* (New York: Routledge, 2000), 72. Carlson adopts the same strategy in defending positive aesthetics (Berys Gaut's "pro tanto" and "all-things-considered evaluation") as I do for defending environmental art. See Gaut's explanation of this method in Gaut, "The Ethical Criticism of Art," 182. For an updated version of the positive aesthetics thesis that is consistent with the new ecological paradigm, see Jason B. Simus, "Aesthetic Implications of the New Paradigm in Ecology," *The Journal of Aesthetic Education* 42 (2008): 63–79.

17. J. Baird Callicott, "From the Balance of Nature to the Flux of Nature: The Land Ethic in a Time of Change," in *Aldo Leopold and the Ecological Conscience*, ed. Richard L. Knight and Suzanne Riedel (Oxford: University Press, 2002), 105.

18. Carlson, "Is Environmental Art an Aesthetic Affront to Nature?," 157.

19. Emily Brady states in n. 14 of her typescript "Aesthetic Regard for Nature in Environmental and Land Art" that proceeds from Christo and Jean-Claude's *The Gates* go to a charity they founded: "Nurture New York's Nature Inc." Eric Katz questions ecological restoration as a "technological fix" in Eric Katz, "The Big Lie: Human Restoration of Nature," *Research in Philosophy and Technology* 12 (1992): 321–341.

20. See V. Thomas Parker and Steward T. Pickett, "Restoration as Ecosystem Process: Implications of the Modern Ecological Paradigm," in *The Ecology of Natural Disturbance and Patch Dynamics*, ed. S. T. A. Pickett and P. S. White (Orlando: Academic Press, 1985), 17–32.

21. See Andrew Light and Eric Higgs, "The Politics of Ecological Restoration," *Environmental Ethics* 18, no. 3 (1996): 227–247; Andrew Light, "Restoration, the Value of Participation, and the Risks of Professionalization," in *Restoring Nature*, ed. Paul Gobster and Bruce Hull (Washington: Island Press, 2000); Andrew Light, "Ecological Restoration and the Culture of Nature: A Pragmatic Perspective," in *Restoring Nature*, ed. Paul Gobster and Bruce Hull (Washington: Island Press, 2000); Andrew Light, "Restoring Ecological Citizenship," in *Democracy and the Claims of Nature: Critical Perspectives for a New Century*, ed. Ben Minteer and Bob Pepperman Taylor (Oxford: Rowman and Littlefield, 2002), 153–172; and Andrew Light, "Urban Ecological Citizenship," *Journal of Social Philosophy* 34, no. 1 (2003): 44–63.

22. Dominique Leydet, "Citizenship," in *The Stanford Encyclopedia of Philosophy*, ed. Edward N. Zalta, winter ed. (2006) http://plato.stanford .edu/archieves/win2006/entries/citizenship/. For the ancients, the community was the polis.

23. S. T. A. Pickett and P. S. White, eds., *The Ecology of Natural Disturbance and Patch Dynamics* (Orlando: Academic Press, 1985).

24. Light, "Restoring Ecological Citizenship," 159.

25. Ibid., 154.

26. Ibid., 158.

27. Light, "Restoration, the Value of Participation, and the Risks of Professionalization," 164.

28. William Jordan III, "Sunflower Forest: Ecological Restoration as the Basis for a New Environmental Paradigm," in *Beyond Preservation: Restoring and Inventing Landscapes*, ed. A.D. Baldwin Jr., J. De Luce, and C. Pletsch (Minneapolis: University of Minnesota Press, 1994), 24.

29. See Light, "Restoration, the Value of Participation, and the Risks of Professionalization," 163–181.

30. Light, "Restoring Ecological Citizenship," 158.

31. Dave Foreman, *Confessions of an Eco-Warrior* (New York: Harmony Books, 1991), 27.

32. See Cronon, "The Trouble with Wilderness," 84.

33. Robert Smithson, "Conversation in Salt Lake City: Interview with Gianni Pettena," in *Robert Smithson: The Collected Writings*, ed. Jack Flam (Berkeley: University of California Press, 1996), 298.

34. See Parker and Pickett, "Restoration as Ecosystem Process."

35. See Sue Spaid, *Ecovention: Current Art to Transform Ecologies* (Cincinnati: Contemporary Arts Center Publishing, 2002).

36. Robert Elliot argues that restorations are unethical because they are artifacts, which results in a loss of "natural value," because as such they cannot restore a pristine environment back to its original condition, as if there were such a condition. See Robert Elliot, *Faking Nature: The Ethics of Environmental Restoration* (New York: Routledge, 1997). For another argument against restoration, see Katz, "The Big Lie: Human Restoration of Nature," 231–242.

37. See Max Horkheimer and Theodor W. Adorno, "The Culture Industry: Enlightenment as Mass Deception," in *Dialectic of Enlightenment*, trans. John Cummins (New York: Herder and Herder, 1972).

38. Mark Sagoff, *The Economy of the Earth* (Cambridge: Cambridge University Press, 1998), 8.

39. Ibid., 79.

40. Emily Brady argues that some environmental artworks that appear to have anti-environmental qualities may, in fact, show aesthetic regard for nature in "Aesthetic Regard for Nature in Environmental and Land Art," 291.

41. Arthur Danto, "The Artworld," *Journal of Philosophy* 19 (1964): 571–584.

42. For more on this, see Immanuel Kant's notion of the agreeable in Immanuel Kant, "Analytic of the Beautiful," in *Critique of the Power of Judgment*, trans. Paul Guyer (Cambridge: Cambridge University Press, 2000), 97. The form of our agreements regarding aesthetic judgments of this type is similar to the idea of John Rawls. See John Rawls, "Overlapping Consensus," in *Justice as Fairness: A Restatement* (Cambridge, Mass.: Harvard University Press, 2001), 32.

43. See Ludwig Wittgenstein, *Philosophical Investigations*, trans. G. E. M. Anscombe, 3rd ed. (New York: Macmillan, 1958), 256.

44. My thanks to Sheila Lintott for making me aware of this objection.

45. An example of a conceptual artwork with no location is Yves Klein's *Immaterial Pictorial Sensitivity*, which the artist sold in exchange for gold. The buyer was given a receipt that he or she was required to then burn while Klein threw the gold into the Seine. Klein insisted the work was not a performance. And while the work itself was immaterial, its documentation remains important.

46. Thanks to J. Baird Callicott, Allen Carlson, Donald Crawford, Eugene Hargrove, Glenn Parsons, and Anna-Christina Ribeiro for their helpful comments on earlier versions of this chapter. This chapter was published earlier in *Environmental Ethics* 30, no. 1 (2008): 21–36.

8. Can Only Art Save Us Now?
David Wood

1. Roland Emmerich, *The Day After Tomorrow*, DVD (2004).

2. See, for example, John Sallis, "The Elemental," in *Force of Imagination: The Sense of the Elemental* (Bloomington: Indiana University Press, 2001), where he discusses Husserl's 1934 essay on spatiality in which he famously says, "The Originary *Ark*, The *Earth*, Does Not Move." See also Giles Deleuze and Felix Guattari, "Geophilosophy," in *What is Philosophy*, trans. Graham Burchell and Hugh Tomlinson (New York: Columbia University Press, 1996). See also Martin Heidegger, "Building Dwelling Thinking," in *Basic Writings*, ed. David F. Krell (New York: Harper & Row, 1993).

3. "The most detailed model to date of the *sun's* transition to a red giant reveals that the *Earth* will be dragged to a fiery *death* in 7 billion years." Jason Palmer, "Hope Dims that Earth will Survive Sun's Death," *New Scientist*, February 22, 2008.

4. Friedrich Nietzsche, *Thus Spoke Zarathustra* (Harmondsworth: Penguin, 1978).

5. Heidegger, *Building Dwelling Thinking*.

6. Martin Heidegger, "Origin of the Work of Art," in *Basic Writings*, ed. David F. Krell (New York: Harper & Row, 1993), 172.

7. Martin Heidegger, "Der Spiegel Interview," in *The Heidegger Reader*, ed. Gunter Figal, trans. Jerome Veith (Bloomington: Indiana University Press, 2009), 325–333. "Everything functions and the functioning drives us further and further to more functioning, and technology tears people away and uproots them from the earth more and more. I don't know if you are scared; I was certainly scared when I recently saw the photographs of the earth taken from the moon. We don't need an atom bomb at all; the uprooting of human beings is already taking place. We only have purely technological conditions left. It is no longer an earth on which human beings live today. . . . [T]he uprooting of human beings which is going on now is the end if thinking and poetry do not acquire nonviolent power once again."

8. Deleuze and Guattari, *What is Philosophy?*

9. I am indebted in the following analysis to Karsten Harries, *Art Matters: A Critical Commentary on Heidegger's the Origin of Work of Art*, Series: Contributions to Phenomenology 57 (Springer, 2009). "Art no longer affords that satisfaction of spiritual needs which earlier ages and nations sought in it, and found in it. . . . Consequently the conditions of our present

time are not favorable to art. . . . In all these respects art, considered in its highest vocation, is and remains for us a thing of the past. Thereby it has lost for us genuine truth and life, and has rather been transferred into our ideas instead of maintaining its earlier necessity in reality and occupying its higher place." See Georg W. F. Hegel, *Aesthetics: Lectures on Fine Art*, vol. I (Oxford: Oxford University Press, 1968).

10. See Arthur Danto, *After the End of Art: Contemporary Art and the Pale of History* (Princeton, N.J.: Princeton University Press, 1998), 47. "[Art begins with an] era of imitation, followed by an era of ideology, followed by our post-historical era in which, with qualification, anything goes. . . . In our narrative, at first only mimesis [imitation] was art, then several things were art but each tried to extinguish its competitors, and then, finally, it became apparent that there were no stylistic or philosophical constraints. There is no special way works of art have to be. And that is the present and, I should say, the final moment in the master narrative. It is the end of the story."

11. Rosalind E. Krauss, "Sculpture in the Expanded Field," in *The Originality of the Avant-Garde and Other Modernist Myths* (Cambridge, Mass.: MIT Press, 1985).

12. Arthur C. Danto, "The End of Art," in *The Death of Art*, ed. Berel Lang (New York: Haven Publishing, 1984). It was a version of Lyotard's claim about the End of Grand Narrative. See Jean-François Lyotard, *The Postmodern Condition* (Minneapolis: Minnesota University Press, 1979).

13. Theodor Adorno and Max Horkheimer, "The Culture Industry: Enlightenment as Mass Deception," in *Dialectic of Enlightenment* (Stanford: Stanford University Press, 2002).

14. Heidegger, *The Heidegger Reader*. Derrida's references to the im-possible are rife throughout his discussions of the gift, hospitality, democracy, and so on. See, for example, his *Rogues* (Stanford: Stanford University Press, 2005), 84. For an excellent extended discussion of the im-possible, see François Raffoul, "Derrida and the Ethics of the Im-possible," *Research in Phenomenology* 38 (2008): 273.

15. Heidegger, *The Heidegger Reader*: "*Der Spiegel*: Professor . . . it cannot really be surprising that modern art has a difficult time making authoritative statements . . . Nevertheless, you call it 'destructive.' Modern art often thinks of itself as experimental art. Its works are attempts . . .

Heidegger: That is the big question. Where does art stand? What place does it occupy? . . . I do not think modern art points out a path, particularly as it remains unclear where it sees or at least looks for what is most characteristic of art. . . . *Only a god can still save us.* I think the only possibility of salvation left to us is to prepare readiness, through thinking and poetry, for the appearance of the god or for the absence of the god during the decline; so that we do not, simply put, die meaningless deaths, but that when we decline, we decline in the face of the absent god" (italics added).

16. Walter Benjamin, "The Work of Art in the Age of Mechanical Reproduction," in *Illuminations: Essays and Reflections* (New York: Schocken, 1969).

17. Lucy Lippard, *Overlay: Contemporary Art and the Art of Prehistory* (New York: Pantheon, 1983).

18. Michael Fried, "Art and Objecthood," in *Art and Objecthood: Essays and Reviews* (Chicago: The University of Chicago Press, 1998). Minimalism betrays modernism by generating a reflective detachment (theatricality) that destroys aesthetic absorption.

19. Lippard, *Overlay*.

20. See Richard Long, http://www.richardlong.org/.

21. Gary Snyder, *A Place in Space: Ethics, Aesthetics, and Watersheds* (Berkeley: Counterpoint, 1996); Wendell Berry, *A Place on Earth* (Berkeley: Counterpoint, 2001); David Abram, *The Spell of the Sensuous: Perception and Language in a More-than-Human World* (New York: Pantheon, 1996); Edward S. Casey, *Getting Back into Place: Toward a Renewed Understanding of the Place-World* (Bloomington: Indiana University Press, 1993); Edward Casey, *The Fate of Place: A Philosophical History* (Berkeley: University of California Press, 1998).

22. On "community," see Jean-Luc Nancy, *Inoperative Community* (Minneapolis: University of Minnesota Press, 1991).

23. Martin Heidegger, *Being and Time*, trans. Joan Stambaugh, ed. Dennis J. Schmidt (Binghamton: SUNY, 2010).

24. Friedrich Nietzsche, "Of Truth and Lies in a Nonmoral Sense," in *The Portable Nietzsche*, ed. Walter Kaufmann (New York: Viking Press, 1976).

25. See Mick Smith, *Against Ecological Sovereignty* (Minneapolis: University of Minnesota Press, 2011)—an exemplary critique of all such attempts at sovereignty.

26. As a philosopher, I have spent some time pondering the lessons of deconstruction, especially Derrida's persistent questioning of key philosophical oppositions—active/passive, inside/outside, copy/original, self/other, speech/writing, presence/absence. As with Heidegger's recommendation that we abandon philosophy for thinking, Derrida undermines the automatic operation of these oppositions with a view to enabling more complex responses. His texts model those kinds of response. They are not frontal assaults on a reigning ideology and in that sense might be thought weaker than such direct critical confrontation. But the argument, after Nietzsche, is that the direct approach is actually less effective in that it will just generate the opposite viewpoint without changing the game at all. I am suggesting more broadly that art can operate in a similar way. Indeed there is not only an analogy with deconstruction but real crossovers when we consider Jacques Derrida, *The Truth in Painting* (Chicago: The University of Chicago Press, 1987), and his section on "Parergon," on frames and framing.

And by and large, there is the same indirectness. Another philosophical parallel is to be found in Maurice Merleau-Ponty's (*The Visible and the Invisible* [Evanston: Northwestern University Press, 1969]) concept of hyperreflection, by which he understands a circling return from concepts to the thick perceptual matrix to which they are ultimately connected, a repeated dipping back from language to experience. Art is precisely the place where this can happen.

27. Dennis Dutton, *The Art Instinct: Beauty, Pleasure, and Human Evolution* (Oxford: Oxford University Press, 2009).

28. Aldo Leopold, *A Sand County Almanac* (New York: Ballantine, 1986).

29. Charles Jencks, *The Garden of Cosmic Speculation* (London: Frances Lincoln Limited, 2003) is an interesting anomaly, giving expression on earth to abstract physical laws governing the wider universe, and in this respect connecting earth to cosmos. And yet this all plays out on highly manicured lawns.

30. Al Gore and Davis Guggenheim, *An Inconvenient Truth*, DVD (2006).

31. Martin Heidegger, *Contributions to Philosophy (From Enowning)* (Bloomington: Indiana University Press, 2000); Heidegger, *The Heidegger Reader*.

32. Gus Speth, *Red Sky at Morning: America and the Crisis of the Global Environment*, 2nd ed. (New Haven, Conn.: Yale University Press, 2005).

33. Gus Speth, *The Bridge at the Edge of the World: Capitalism, the Environment, and Crossing from Crisis to Sustainability* (New Haven, Conn.: Yale University Press, 2008).

34. See Theodor Adorno, *The Culture Industry: Selected Essays on Mass Culture* (London: Routledge, 2000); Heidegger, *Building Dwelling Thinking*; Giles Deleuze and Felix Guattari, *Anti-Oedipus: Capitalism and Schizophrenia* (Minneapolis: University of Minnesota, 1983); John Protevi, *Political Affect: Connecting the Social and the Somatic* (Minneapolis: University of Minnesota Press, 2009).

35. Joseph Beuys, "I Am Searching for Field Character," in *Energy Plan for the Western Man: Joseph Beuys in America*, ed. Carin Kuoni (New York: Four Walls Eight Windows, 1993), 22.

36. George Lakoff, *Don't Think of an Elephant: Know Your Values and Frame the Debate* (White River Junction, VT: Chelsea Green, 2004).

9. Landscapes of the Environmental Imagination: Ranging from NASA and Cuyahoga Images to Kiefer and O'Keeffe Paintings
Irene J. Klaver

With gratitude to Brian C. O'Connor for his insightful contributions.

1. Irene J. Klaver, "Authentic Landscapes at Large: Dutch Globalization and Environmental Imagination," *SubStance* 41, no. 1 (2012): 92–108.

2. Michel Serres is one of the first French philosophers to cogently argue for a reconsideration of the relationship between nature and culture. According to him, global environmental change requires the negotiation of a natural contract between Earth and humanity. For Serres, a more reciprocal relation to the Earth, sanctioned in a natural contract, will furthermore balance a potentially oppressive social contract. See Michel Serres, *The Natural Contract* (Ann Arbor: University of Michigan Press, 1995).

3. Irene J. Klaver, "Wild: Rhythm of Appearing and Disappearing," in *The Wilderness Debate Rages On: Continuing the Great New Wilderness Debate*, ed. Michael P. Nelson and J. Baird Callicott (Athens: University of Georgia Press, 2008), 488.

4. See, for example, Edward S. Casey, *Imagining; A Phenomenological Study* (Bloomington: Indiana University Press, 1976; second edition, 2000); Richard Kearney, *The Wake of Imagination* (London: Routledge, 1988); Richard Kearney, *Poetics of Imagining: Modern to Post-modern* (New York: Fordham University Press, 1998); John Sallis, *Force of Imagination: The Sense of the Elemental* (Bloomington: Indiana University Press, 2000); the *Stanford Encyclopedia of Philosophy* gives an excellent overview of the more analytically based philosophical works on imagination, starting with P. F. Strawson's remarks in "Imagination and Perception" (1970), in *Experience and Theory*, ed. L. Foster and J. W. Swanson (Amherst: University of Massachusetts Press), to cognitive studies. See http://plato.stanford.edu/entries/imagination/.

5. Paul Taylor, *Respect for Nature: A Theory of Environmental Ethics* (Princeton, N.J.: Princeton University Press, 1986).

6. Sara Ebenreck, "Opening Pandora's Box: The Role of Imagination in Environmental Ethics," *Environmental Ethics* 18, no. 1 (1996): 3–18.

7. Roger J. H. King, "Narrative, Imagination, and the Search for Intelligibility in Environmental Ethics," *Ethics and the Environment* 4, no. 1 (1999): 23–38.

8. Lawrence Buell, *The Environmental Imagination: Thoreau, Nature Writing, and the Formation of American Culture* (Cambridge, Mass.: Harvard University Press, 1995).

9. Benedict Anderson, *Imagined Communities: Reflections on the Origin and Spread of Nationalism* (London: Verso, 1983).

10. Anderson, *Imagined Communities*, 15.

11. Edward W. Said, *Orientalism* (London: Penguin Books, 1995).

12. For excellent work on the intricacies of mediation and imaging, see Richard Grusin and Jay David Bolter, *Remediation: Understanding New Media* (Cambridge, Mass: MIT Press, 1999), and Richard Grusin, *Premediation: Affect and Mediality After 9/11* (London: Palgrave, 2010).

13. The notion of co-constitution has been a pervasive theme throughout my writing, see especially, Irene J. Klaver, "Phenomenology on (the) Rocks," *Research in Phenomenology* XXXI (2001): 173–186.

14. Arjun Appadurai, *Modernity at Large, Cultural Dimensions of Globalization* (Minneapolis: University of Minnesota Press, 1996), 31.

15. Appadurai, *Modernity at Large*, 31–33.

16. Maurice Merleau-Ponty, *Phenomenology of Perception*, trans. Colin Smith (London: Routledge and Kegan Paul Ltd., 1962), xvii–xviii. *Phénoménologie de la perception* (Paris: Gallimard, 1945), xiii. Maurice Merleau-Ponty, *The Visible and Invisible* (Evanston, Ill.: Northwestern University Press, 1968), 244.

17. See W. J. T. Mitchell, ed., *The Language of Images* (Chicago: The University of Chicago Press, 1980); *Iconology: Image, Text, Ideology* (Chicago: The University of Chicago Press, 1986); *Picture Theory: Essays on Verbal and Visual Representation* (Chicago: The University of Chicago Press, 1994); *Landscape and Power* (Chicago: The University of Chicago Press, 1994); *What Do Pictures Want? Essays on the Lives and Loves of Images* (Chicago: The University of Chicago Press, 2005); *Cloning Terror: The War of Images, 9/11 to the Present* (Chicago: The University of Chicago Press, 2011).

18. John Rajchman, *Post-Analytic Philosophy*, ed. John Rajchman and Cornel West (New York: Columbia University Press, 1985), xvii.

19. Philippe Lacoue-Labarthe and Jean-Luc Nancy, "The Nazi Myth," trans. Brian Holmes, *Critical Inquiry* 16, no. 2 (Winter 1990): 292.

20. Andrew Hewitt, *Political Inversions, Homosexuality, Fascism, & the Modernist Imaginary* (Stanford: Stanford University Press, 1996), 17–18.

21. http://www.etymonline.com (January 10, 2012).

22. Sophie Fiennes, *Over Your Cities Grass Will Grow—A Film of the Work of Anselm Kiefer*, 2010. http://overyourcities.com/.

23. Georgia O'Keeffe, "About Painting Desert Bones," in *Georgia O'Keeffe Paintings—1943* (New York: An American Place Gallery, 1944).

24. Paul Krugman, "Drilling, Disaster, Denial," op-ed column in *New York Times*, May 2, 2010. http://www.nytimes.com/2010/05/03/opinion/03krugman.html?_r=0 (accessed September 23, 2012).

In his 2010 *New York Times* op-ed column, Paul Krugman asserts: "Environmentalism began as a response to pollution that everyone could see." In his discussion of the BP Gulf disaster, he looks back to 1969 as the time when pollution and seeing came together with the oil-coated beaches of Santa Barbara and when "the Cuyahoga River, which flows through Cleveland, caught fire." He refers to these as "the photogenic crises of the 1960s and 1970s," noting that as pollution had become less and less visible, less photogenic, public interest in pollution issues waned.

25. Stephen Colbert, "Job-Killing EPA" Colbert Report on Comedy Central Network, Wednesday October 19, 2011. http://www.colbertnation.com/the-colbert-report-videos/400165/october-19-2011/indecision-2012—job-killing-epa (September 23, 2012).

The description of the segment Job-Killing EPA reads: "The Republican presidential candidates all agree on one thing: they want to end the EPA's job-murdering environmental regulations." The Colbert Report website notes the show "has garnered ratings and critical success as one of the top shows on television. Since its inception, the series has received a prestigious Peabody Award for Excellence in Broadcasting in 2008 and 18 Primetime Emmy nominations. In 2010, Colbert and his writing team won the show's second Emmy for Outstanding Writing for a Variety, Music or Comedy Program."

26. Editors of *LIFE, 100 Photographs that Changed the World*, 2003.

The review in *Publishers Weekly* noted: Nominated through online votes and selected by Life editors, the one hundred images in this compendium cover unforgettable moments in "The Arts," "Society," "War & Peace," and "Science & Nature." The photographs are all striking—whether visually or viscerally, artistically or emotionally—but many are difficult to look at. There's little here that hasn't been reprinted numerous times, but it's a stirring collection nevertheless.

27. Galen Rowell was remembered in the 2008 publication of *Galen Rowell: A Retrospective*, by the editors of Sierra Club Books. Tom Brokaw wrote the foreword. Of Rowell, the book description says: "Galen Rowell was the archetypal adventure photographer, his iconic images published in leading magazines and scores of books, exhibited in major galleries, and cherished by fans ranging from the Dalai Lama to news anchor Tom Brokaw. In Life's '100 Photographs that Changed the World,' Galen Rowell calls Earthrise 'the most influential environmental photograph ever taken,'" see http://digitaljournalist.org/issue0309/lm11.html.

10. Beauty or Bane: Advancing an Aesthetic Appreciation of Wind Turbine Farms
Tyson-Lord Gray

This chapter was previously published in *Contemporary Aesthetics* 10, no. 3 (2012).

1. Ron Stimmel, "AWEA Small Wind Turbine Global Market Study," American Wind Energy Association (April 15, 2010).

2. Juan Montes, "Gamesa First Half Net Profit Drops 65%, Cuts 2010 Turbine Sales Goal," *EPC Engineer* (July 29, 2010).

3. Matthew Lynley, "GE: Wind Turbine Demand Fell Last Year," *Venture Beat* (April 22, 2011).

4. Bill Hare, "Fossil Fuel and Climate Prevention-The Carbon Logic," *Greenpeace International* (September, 1997).

5. Rhett Butler, "Eco-friendly Palm Oil Could Help Alleviate Poverty in Indonesia," *Mongabay.com* (April 4, 2007). Alex Morales, "EU Biofuels Goals May Increase Greenhouse Gas Emissions, Lobby Groups Say," *Bloomberg* (November 7, 2010).

6. Paul Chapman, "New Zealand Miners Died 'Within Minutes' of First Explosion," *The Telegraph* (January 27, 2011). "45 Miners Killed in Pakistan Explosion," *RTE News* (March 21, 2011).

7. Barbara Demick, "Japan Evacuates 50,000 After Nuclear Plant Explosion," *The Columbian* (March 12, 2011).

8. George Sterzinger, Fredric Beck and Damian Kostiuk, "The Effect of Wind Development on Local Property Values," (May, 2003).

9. Ben Hoen, Ryab Wiser, Peter Cappers, Mark Thayer, and Gautam Sethi, "The Impact of Wind Power Projects on Residential Property Values in the United States: A Multi-Site Hedonic Analysis," (December, 2009).

10. Appraisal Group One, "Wind Turbine Impact Study" (September 9, 2009), 42.

11. Thomas Content, "Critics Say Wind Turbines Hurt Land Values," *Journal Sentinel* (September 11, 2009).

12. "Wind Turbines Would Destroy Character of West Cumbrian Village," *Times and Star* (December 9, 2010).

13. OXI Campaign, "Problems with Wind-Farms" (2010) http://www.savekythera.com/problems-with-wind-farms.

14. "Campaigners Stage Nant y Moch Wind Farm Protest," *BBC* (March 6, 2011).

15. Yuriko Saito, "Machines in the Ocean: The Aesthetics of Wind Farms," *Contemporary Aesthetics* 2, sec. 1, (2004).

16. Immanuel Kant, "Part I: Critique of Aesthetic Judgment," in *The Critique of Judgment*, trans. James Creed Meredith (eBooks@Adelaide, 2008), sec. 1.

17. Kant, *The Critique of Judgment*, sec. 2.

18. Marc Lucht, "Does Kant Have Anything to Teach Us About Environmental Ethics?" *American Journal of Economics and Sociology* (January, 2007).

19. Kant, *The Critique of Judgment*, sec. 22.

20. Jon Boone, "The Aesthetic Dissonance of Industrial Wind Machines," *Contemporary Aesthetics* 3 (2005): sec. 2.

21. Kant, *The Critique of Judgment*, sec. 11.

22. Lewis Smith and David Prosser, "Half of Planned Wind Farms Blown Away be Force of Local Protests," *The Independent* (July 11, 2011).

23. Hugh Saddler, Mark Diesendorf and Richard Denniss, "A Clean Energy Future for Australia," Clean Energy Future Group and WWF (March, 2004).

24. OXI Campaign, "The Locations" (2010), http://www.savekythera.com/problems-with-wind-farms.

25. John Dewey, *Art as Experience* (New York: Penguin Group, 1934), 2.

26. Ibid., 339.

27. Ibid., 56.

28. Ibid., 56.

29. Valerie Elliott, "Sir David Attenborough Faces Green Protests over Opera's Wind Turbine," *The Times* (February 26, 2008).

30. Harold Clossey, "Maine Compass: Windpower a Source of Pride for People in Downeast Maine," *Morning Sentinel* (May 16, 2011).

31. Dewey, *Art as Experience*, 260.

32. Ibid., 260.

33. Justin Good, "The Aesthetics of Wind Energy," *Human Ecology Review* 13, no. 1 (2006): 83.

34. Dewey, *Art As Experience*, 339.

35. Ted Smith, "Why No Plugging Bonds for Wind Turbines?" *Red Dirt Report* (January 25, 2010).

36. April Castro, "APNewsBreak: Perry Urges Obama to Halt Air Rules," *Boston.com* (September 26, 2011).

37. Boone, "The Aesthetic Dissonance of Industrial Wind Machines", sec. 3.

38. Yuriko Saito, "Response to Jon Boone's Critique," *Contemporary Aesthetics* 3 (2005).

39. Allen Carlson, *Aesthetics and the Environment* (New York: Routledge, 2000), 146.

40. Saito, "Machines in the Ocean," sec. a.

41. David Suzuki, "The Beauty of Wind Farms," *New Scientist* (April 16, 2005).

42. Yuriko Saito, "Machines in the Ocean," sec 3.

11. Thinking Like a Mall
Steven Vogel

1. Aldo Leopold, *A Sand County Almanac* (New York: Ballantine Books, 1966), 137–141.

2. *Columbus Dispatch*, August 18, 1989, "Mega-statistics Mark Mall," 4H.

3. *Columbus Dispatch*, August 19, 1989, "Shoppers' Delight—Tens of Thousands Visit Downtown Mall on Opening Day," 8D.

4. *Columbus Dispatch*, November 10, 1995, "Borrowing Success—New Indianapolis Downtown Mall Hopes to Mirror City Center's Triumph," 1H.

5. *Columbus Dispatch*, May 28, 1994, "Teen Shot to Death in City Center—2 Held," 1A.

6. "There is a mixture between the two shopping centers that gives the consumer the greatest advantage," the general manager of Tuttle Crossing was quoted as saying before it opened. "It is truly a win-win for consumers. Based on where they are and what their needs are, they now have two dynamic shopping centers to satisfy their needs." *Columbus Monthly*, August 1997, "Ralph Lauren Meets Bob Vila," 99.

7. *Columbus Dispatch*, February 4, 2009, "Downtown Site Was Death for Mall by '90s," 6A.

8. *Columbus Dispatch*, February 4, 2009, "Timeline," 6A.

9. *Columbus Dispatch*, March 22, 2002, "City Center Turns Vacant Space into Business-Services Center," 1F.

10. *Columbus Dispatch*, July 12, 2003, "Mall Hopes Soaps Will Boost Business," 1C.

11. *The Other Paper*, May 2, 2006, "Accidental Tenants," 8–9.

12. *Columbus Dispatch*, September 20, 2007, "Anchor Abandons Ship," 1A.

13. *Columbus Dispatch*, May 15, 2007, "GOP Candidate Challenges Coleman on Mall," 3B.

14. *Columbus Dispatch*, February 4, 2009, "Timeline," 6A.

15. *Columbus Dispatch*, February 4, 2009, "Goodbye City Center," 1A.

16. *Columbus Dispatch*, May 27, 2011, "Downtown Playground," 1A.

17. Does the word "death" in the first case already skew the discussion? Call it "destruction" then, and speak of the mountain's destruction, and the destruction of the wolf, as well. But note that there's a remarkable website—with a whole section about the Columbus City Center—called deadmalls. com. (See http://deadmalls.com/malls/columbus_city_center.html.)

18. Jennifer Price's essay "Looking for Nature at the Mall: A Field Guide to the Nature Company" (in *Flight Maps: Adventures with Nature in Modern America* [New York: Basic Books, 1999]) is a nice discussion of the complicated relation between "nature" and malls, understanding the latter as the central locus of modern consumerism. I am explicitly and intentionally ignoring the "cultural meanings" that malls have, as well as the roles they play within capitalist or post-capitalist social orders: What I am interested in is the way in which they, too, like mountains and like wolves, might have an autonomous existence beyond such meanings and such roles—an existence that might demand our moral consideration, just as the mountain and the wolves might.

19. *The New York Times*, October 30, 1963, "Farewell to Penn Station."

20. "Just as a deer herd lives in mortal fear of its wolves," Leopold writes, "so does a mountain live in mortal fear of its deer. And perhaps with better cause: for while a buck pulled down by wolves can be replaced in two or three years, a range pulled down by too many deer may fail of replacement in as many decades." *A Sand County Almanac*, 140. The fact that Leopold remained an avid hunter throughout his life, despite the experience described here, has often been remarked upon: See J. Baird Callicott, *In Defense of the Land Ethic* (Albany: State University of New York Press, 1989), 17–18.

21. The difficulties with defining the natural, especially when it is contrasted with the "human," are famous, and I've written about them elsewhere. But that's not (quite) the issue I'm concerned with here, and I'll assume here that somehow this distinction can be made to work. See Steven Vogel, "Why 'Nature' Has No Place in Environmental Philosophy," in *The Ideal of Nature: The Appeal to Nature in Debates about Biotechnology and the Environment*, ed. Gregory E. Kaebnick (Baltimore: Johns Hopkins University Press, 2011).

22. Or is it not the human touch in general that has this effect, but rather the *intentional* human touch—so that only things humans have planned and designed lack this sort of moral considerability? Such a view doesn't avoid the same inverted anthropocentrism, though, just giving it a (familiar) Cartesian twist, according to which it's our specifically mental, conscious, intentional capacities that have the magical (Midas-like?) ability to remove things from the realm of the morally considerable.

23. A useful set of essays on the topic of nature's autonomy is Thomas Heyd, ed., *Recognizing the Autonomy of Nature* (New York: Columbia University Press, 2005). See also my review of this volume in *Human Ecology* 36 (February 2008): 137–140. Cf. also Keekok Lee, *The Natural and the Artifactual* (Lanham, Md.: Lexington Books, 1999), and Eric Katz, *Nature as Subject* (Lanham, Md.: Rowman and Littlefield, 1997).

24. The city had one set of motivations, the Taubman Company another, the construction firm who took charge of the building a third—and each of these entities themselves consisted of various individuals each of whose motivations were likely complicated and plural themselves. So what was *the* purpose for which the mall was built?

25. Eric Katz, "The Liberation of Humanity and Nature," in *Recognizing the Autonomy of Nature*, ed. Thomas Heyd (New York: Colombia University Press, 2005), 84. For a good overview of the debate, see Matt Perkins, "Rock Climbing Ethics," *Northwest Mountaineering Journal*, issue 2 (2005). (I am grateful to George Mackaronis for pointing out to me the relevance of this debate to the concerns under discussion here.)

26. See Frances Ann Hancock, *Saving the Great Stone Face* (Canaan, N.H.: Phoenix Publishing, 1984). Compare also Martin Krieger's discussion of strategies to maintain Niagara Falls in "What's Wrong with Plastic Trees," *Science*, February 2, 1973, 446–455.

27. See Steven Vogel, "The Nature of Artifacts," *Environmental Ethics* 25, no. 2 (Summer 2003): 158–159.

28. For the cracks, see *Columbus Dispatch*, August 26, 1992, "Mall Garage Said Safe Despite Cracks," 5B.

29. *Columbus Dispatch*, September 28, 2004, "A Special Store of Knowledge," 1A.

30. It is, I'm inclined to say, the *autonomy of matter*. The view I am developing here is intended to be a robustly *materialist* one, a materialism that insists that humans—ourselves material, ourselves animals, ourselves part of nature—are never able fully to control or to predict or even to grasp the material substances with which we have to do: not the "natural" ones, and not the "artificial" or "built" ones either. This materialism, it's worth noting, is *not* the same as the "new materialism" of Jane Bennett and others for whom materialism (somehow) turns out to look a lot like traditional vitalism, emphasizing the "liveliness" of matter as opposed to the materiality of life and of human life. See Bennett's *Vibrant Matter: A Political*

Ecology of Things (Durham: Duke University Press, 2010). Nor does it have anything to do with the "panpsychism" of thinkers such as Freya Mathews, who as far as I can tell constantly emphasizes the "conative," "erotic," "enchanted" character of the natural realm without ever considering whether artificial elements of the built environment, like malls, might also be a "field of subjectivity." See Mathew's *For Love of Matter* (Albany: State University of New York Press, 2003).

12. Aesthetic Value and Wild Animals
Emily Brady

This chapter is a revised version of a guest article, "Aesthetic Appreciation of Expressive Qualities in Animals," for the *Postgraduate Journal of Aesthetics* 6, no. 3 (2009): 1–14. I would like to thank Clare Palmer and an audience at the American Society of Aesthetics Meeting, Los Angeles, 2007, for comments on an earlier version of the chapter.

1. Glenn Parsons, "The Aesthetic Value of Animals," *Environmental Ethics* 29 (2007): 151–169. Another interesting discussion of animals and aesthetics appears in Ned Hettinger, "Animal Beauty, Ethics, and Environmental Preservation," *Environmental Ethics* 32, no. 2 (2010): 115–134. Hettinger does not specifically discuss the functional thesis or expressive qualities, but he does provide an argument for the relevance of aesthetic value of wild animals to their protection and preservation.

2. See, for example, Sherri Irvin's analysis of petting her cat in, "The Pervasiveness of the Aesthetic in Ordinary Experience," *The British Journal of Aesthetics* 48, no. 1 (2008): 31.

3. Clare Palmer's work provides a rich exploration of how different dependence relations and contexts impact on our moral obligations to wild, feral, and domesticated animals. See her book, *Animal Ethics in Context* (New York: Columbia University Press, 2010).

4. Parsons, "The Aesthetic Value of Animals," 161.

5. Ibid., 161.

6. Ibid., 165.

7. Ibid., 163.

8. Ibid., 163–164.

9. See, for example, Ronald W. Hepburn, "Trivial and Serious in Aesthetic Appreciation of Nature," in *Landscape, Natural Beauty and the Arts*, ed. Salim Kemal and Ivan Gaskell (Cambridge: Cambridge University Press, 1993), 65–80; Yuriko Saito, "Appreciating Nature on its Own Terms," *Environmental Ethics* 20 (1998): 135–149.

10. See, respectively, Glenn Parsons, "Freedom and Objectivity in Aesthetic Appreciation of Nature," *British Journal of Aesthetics* 46, no. 1 (2006): 17–37; and Allen Carlson, *Aesthetics and the Environment: Nature, Art and Architecture* (New York: Routledge, 2000). Parsons and Carlson

have also, together, linked a more developed, broader theory of functional beauty to "cognitively rich" aesthetic appreciation of both artifacts and nature in Glenn Parsons and Alan Carlson, *Functional Beauty* (Oxford: Oxford University Press, 2008).

11. Noël Carroll, "Being Moved By Nature: Between Religion and Natural History," in *Landscape, Natural Beauty and the Arts*, ed. Salim Kemal and Ivan Gaskell (Cambridge: Cambridge University Press, 1993), 244–266.

12. I will not address imaginative qualities here, but for a discussion, see Emily Brady, *Aesthetics of the Natural Environment* (Edinburgh: Edinburgh University Press, 2003), 150–172; Marcia M. Eaton, "Fact and Fiction in the Aesthetic Appreciation of Nature," *Journal of Aesthetics and Art Criticism* 56, no. 2 (1998): 149–157.

13. See, for example, Jane Howarth, "Nature's Moods," *British Journal of Aesthetics* 35, no. 2 (1995); Gernot Böhme has also discussed emotions in his ecological aesthetics through the idea of "atmosphere" in *Atmosphäre: Essays zur neuen Ästhetik* (Frankfurt am Main: Suhrkamp, 1995). See also Carroll, "Being Moved by Nature"; Brady, in *Aesthetics of the Natural Environment*, 172–183.

14. Noël Carroll, *Philosophy of Art: A Contemporary Introduction* (London: Routledge, 2001), 176.

15. Holmes Rolston III, "Beauty and the Beast: Aesthetic Experience of Wildlife," in *Valuing Wildlife: Economic and Social Perspectives*, ed. D. Decker and G. Goff (Boulder, Colo.: Westview Press, 1987), 187–196.

16. Edmund Burke, *A Philosophical Enquiry into the Origin of Our Ideas of the Sublime and the Beautiful*, ed. J. T. Boulton, 2nd ed. (Notre Dame: University of Notre Dame Press, 1968), 66.

17. John Muir, "The Yosemite," in *Nature Writings*, ed. William Cronon (New York: Library of America, 1997), 231.

18. Mark DeBellis, "Music," in *Routledge Companion to Aesthetics*, ed. Berys Gaut and Dominic Lopes (London: Routledge, 2001), 531–544.

19. Evolutionary theory may be able to tell us that some of these comparisons are made the other way around, that is, our recognition of some expressions and our use of expressive terms originate from other sources (e.g., other species or natural phenomena—imagine a person "storming around"). For some early discussion of this, see Charles Darwin, *The Expression of the Emotions in Man and Animals*, ed. Paul Ekman (London: Fontana, 1999). Jane Howarth discusses similarities between human moods and nature's "moods" in Howarth, "Nature's Moods."

20. See Derek Matravers, "Art, Expression and Emotion," in *Routledge Companion to Aesthetics*, ed. Berys Gaut and Dominic Lopes (London: Routledge, 2001), 353–362.

21. Rolston, "Beauty and the Beast," 194.

22. Parsons, "The Aesthetic Value of Animals," 161.

23. John Spackman, "Expression Theory of Art," in *Encyclopedia of Aesthetics*, ed. Michael Kelly, vol. 2 (New York: Oxford University Press, 1998), 139–144.

24. Rolston, "Beauty and the Beast," 194.

25. Emily Brady, "The Expressive Face," in *Aesthetics in the Human Environment*, ed. Pauline von Bonsdorff and Arto Haapala (Lahti: International Institute of Applied Aesthetics, 1999), 70–89.

26. Robin G. Collingwood, *Philosophy and Art* (Oxford: Oxford University Press, 1963), 39–40, quoted in Parsons, "The Aesthetic Value of Animals," 154.

27. Parsons, "The Aesthetic Value of Animals," 161.

28. See Hepburn, "Trivial and Serious."

29. See Mary Midgley, *Beast and Man* (London: Routledge, 1995), 332; Bernard Rollins, "Scientific Ideology, Anthropomorphism, Anecdote, and Ethics," in *The Animal Ethics Reader*, ed. Susan Armstrong and Richard G. Botzler (London: Routledge, 2003), 67–74. For a careful analysis of anthropomorphism and the view that some forms of it are not problematic, see John A. Fisher, "Disambiguating Anthropomorphism: An Interdisciplinary Review," in *Perspectives in Ethology*, ed. Paul P. G. Bateson and Peter H. Klopfer, vol. 9 (Plenum/Springer, 1991), 49–85.

30. James A. Serpell, "Anthropomorphism and Anthropomorphic Selection: Beyond the 'Cute Response,'" *Society and Animals* 11, no. 1 (2003): 92.

31. Serpell, "Anthropomorphism and Anthropomorphic Selection," 93.

Contributors

Arnold Berleant is professor of philosophy (emeritus) at Long Island University (USA). His interests range over aesthetics, the arts, ethics, and social philosophy. He has lectured and written widely in these areas, both nationally and internationally. Berleant is the author of numerous articles as well as eight books on aesthetics, the arts, and especially the aesthetics of environment, and his work has been translated into many languages. His book, *Sensibility and Sense: The Aesthetic Transformation of the Human World*, was published in 2010, and his new book, *Aesthetics beyond the Arts*, was published in 2012. Berleant is also the founding editor of the online journal, *Contemporary Aesthetics*.

Emily Brady is reader in aesthetics in the Institute of Geography and Environment and an academic associate in philosophy at the University of Edinburgh. Her research interests include aesthetics, environmental ethics, eighteenth-century philosophy, and animal studies. She is the author of *Aesthetics of the Natural Environment* (2003) and co-editor of *Human-Environment Relations: Transformative Values in Theory and Practice* (2012); *Humans in the Land: The Ethics and Aesthetics of the Cultural Landscape* (2008); and *Aesthetic Concepts: Essays After Sibley* (2001). She is currently working on a book, *The Sublime in Modern Philosophy: Aesthetics, Ethics, and Nature*. Brady is president of the International Society for Environmental Ethics.

Allen Carlson is professor of philosophy (emeritus) at the University of Alberta in Edmonton, Canada. His research interests include environmental philosophy, aesthetics, and especially the aesthetics of nature and landscapes. He has published numerous articles and is the author of *Nature and Landscape: An Introduction to Environmental Aesthetics* (Columbia University Press), *Functional Beauty* (with G. Parsons; Oxford University

Press), and *Aesthetics and the Environment: The Appreciation of Nature, Art and Architecture* (Routledge), as well as the editor of several collections of essays, including *Nature, Aesthetics, and Environmentalism: From Beauty to Duty* (with S. Lintott; Columbia University Press) and *The Aesthetics of Natural Environments* (with A. Berleant; Broadview Press).

Martin Drenthen is associate professor of philosophy at Radboud University Nijmegen (The Netherlands). He has published about the significance of Nietzsche's critique of morality for environmental ethics, the concept of wildness in moral debates on ecological restoration, and ethics of place. He is the author of *Bordering Wildness: The Desire for Wilderness and the Meaning of Nietzsche's Critique of Morality for Environmental Ethics* (2003, in Dutch). He coedited *Ethics of Science Communication* (2005, in Dutch); *New Visions of Nature: Complexity and Authenticity* (Springer 2009); *Place, Philosophical Reflections on Connectedness with Nature and Landscape* (2011, in Dutch), and *Interpreting Nature: The Emerging Field of Environmental Hermeneutics* (Fordham University Press, 2013). His most recent research focuses on developing a hermeneutic landscape ethics, notably with regard to the relation between rewilding, cultures of place, and moral identity.

Denis Dumas is associate professor of philosophy at University of Ottawa, Canada. He published *Geschichtlichkeit und Transzendentalphilosophie. Zur Frage ihrer Vermittlung vor dem Hintergrund der Phänomenologie Edmund Husserls* (Peter Lang, 1999), and his current teaching and research interests concern environmental aesthetics and its links to ethics, from a Kantian perspective. He is equally interested in classic and contemporary German philosophy in general.

Tyson-Lord Gray is a PhD student at Vanderbilt University in ethics and society with a focus on environmental ethics and a minor in environmental law. He received a bachelor of arts in religion from Trinity International University, a master of divinity degree in practical theology from Morehouse School of Religion at the Interdenominational Theological Center, and a master of sacred theology in philosophy, theology and ethics from Boston University School of Theology. He also studied Buddhism at Harvard University and Pragmatism at Harvard Divinity School. His research interests are in the areas of pragmatism, environmental ethics, and social justice.

Jozef Keulartz is associate professor of applied philosophy at Wageningen University and Research Centre. He has been appointed special chair for Environmental Philosophy at the Radboud University Nijmegen. He has published extensively in different areas of science and technology studies, social and political philosophy, bioethics, environmental ethics, and nature policy. His books include *Die verkehrte Welt des Jürgen Habermas* [The Topsy-Turvy World of Jürgen Habermas, 1995], *Van bestraffing naar behandeling* [From Punishment to Treatment, 1996, 4th ed], *Struggle for Nature—A Critique of Radical Ecology* (1998), and *Werken aan de grens— een pragmatische visie op natuur en milieu* [Boundary-Work: A Pragmatist View on Nature and Environment, 2005]. He is editor of *Wilhelm Dilthey: Kritiek van de historische rede* [Wilhelm Dilthey: Critique of Historical Reason, 1994] and coeditor of *Foucault herdenken* [In Memory of Foucault, 1995], *Museum Aarde* [Museum Earth, 1997], *Pragmatist Ethics for a Technological Culture* (2002), *Legitimacy in European Nature Conservation Policy* (2008), and *New Visions of Nature* (2009).

Irene J. Klaver is director of the Philosophy of Water Project (www.water.unt.edu) and associate professor in philosophy at the University of North Texas. Her research and teaching focus on social-political and cultural dimensions of water. She has published and lectured widely on the topic. She is the leading coeditor of the UNESCO book *Water, Cultural Diversity & Global Environmental Change: Emerging Trends, Sustainable Futures* (Springer, January 2012). Klaver is UNESCO's water and cultural diversity advisor and co-director of the International Association for Environmental Philosophy. Irene Klaver is an award-winning documentary maker. Both "River Planet" (2011) and "The New Frontier: Sustainable Ranching in the American West" (2010) have won prestigious awards, including selection for American Documentary Showcase (ADS) of the Department of State, the CINE Award, and BEA Award.

Jonathan Maskit is visiting assistant professor of philosophy at Denison University (Ohio, USA) where he also teaches in the Environmental Studies Program. His articles on environmental aesthetics (several of which have to do with the aesthetics of postindustrial environments); everyday aesthetics; consumption, desire, and subjectivity; and the relationship between continental philosophy and environmental philosophy have appeared in journals such as *Aesthetic Pathways*; *Philosophy & Geography*; *Ethics, Place & Environment*; and *The European Journal of Geography* and in a number of edited volumes. He is currently working on a book on the role of art and culture in shaping our aesthetic appreciation of nature.

Yuriko Saito, born and raised in Japan, received her PhD in philosophy from the University of Wisconsin–Madison and is professor of philosophy at the Rhode Island School of Design, USA. Her research fields are environmental aesthetics, everyday aesthetics, and Japanese aesthetics, and she has published a number of journal articles and book chapters on these subjects, some of which have been translated into Finnish, Portuguese, and Polish. Her *Everyday Aesthetics* was recently published by Oxford University Press

(2008 hardcover, 2010 paperback). She is associate editor of *Contemporary Aesthetics*, an online, free-access, and peer-reviewed journal, and she is a coeditor of its 2012 Special Volume on "Artificiation."

Yrjö Sepänmaa is professor of environmental aesthetics at the University of Eastern Finland in the city of Joensuu. Before his present position (starting at the beginning of 2005), he held a five years' academy professorship at the Academy of Finland (2000–2005) as well as a professorship in literature (1994–2000). He was a Fulbright Scholar at the University of Georgia (USA) from 1990 to 1991 and a visiting professor at the University of North Texas (USA) in 1992. Mr. Sepänmaa's main research interests are in environmental aesthetics, especially in applying aesthetics to real-world situations. He has published numerous theoretical and practical texts on these questions, such as *The Beauty of Environment—A General Model for Environmental Aesthetics* (Helsinki 1986, second edition, 1993; transl. in Korean 2001, and in Chinese in 2006). He is working on a sequel provisionally titled *The Theory and Practice of Applied Environmental Aesthetics* and is also starting a new project on environmental aesthetic civility. Sepänmaa was the organizer of a seven-part series of international conferences on environmental aesthetics (1994–2009) in Finland; he was also the president and chair of the Organizing Committee of the XIII International Congress of Aesthetics, *Aesthetics in Practice* (Lahti, Finland, 1995).

Jason B. Simus received a doctorate in philosophy from the University of North Texas. He is now an adjunct faculty member in philosophy at Texas A&M University–Commerce and visiting research professor at the Center for Environmental Philosophy of the University of North Texas. Jason is the author of "Metaphors and Metaphysics in Ecology" (*Worldviews: Global Religions, Culture, and Ecology* 15, no. 2 [2011]: 185–202), "Aesthetic Implications of the New Paradigm in Ecology" (*Journal of Aesthetic Education* 42, no. 1 [Spring 2008]: 63–79), and *Disturbing Nature's Beauty: Environmental Aesthetics in a New Ecological Paradigm*, a book-length study currently under review for publication at SUNY Press. Topics in his current research include the ethics and aesthetics of noise pollution, the role of advocacy in teaching environmental ethics, the aesthetic value of public art, and the democratic nature of aesthetic discourse.

Steven Vogel is Brickman-Shannon Professor in the Department of Philosophy at Denison University. He is the author of *Against Nature: The Concept of Nature in Critical Theory* (SUNY Press, 1996) and of the forthcoming *Environmental Philosophy After the End of Nature* (MIT Press). He is the author of numerous articles on environmental philosophy, which have appeared in *Environmental Ethics*, *Environmental Values*, and elsewhere.

David Wood is W. Alton Jones Professor of Philosophy at Vanderbilt University, and professor of art, where he teaches nineteenth- and twentieth-century European philosophy and environmental philosophy. He is the author/editor of many books—on Kierkegaard, Levinas, Heidegger, and Derrida—including *The Deconstruction of Time*, *Truth: A Reader*, *Thinking After Heidegger*, and *Time After Time*. He is completing two books: *Trees and Truth* and *Things at the Edge of the World*. His work as an earth artist can be found at www.reoccupyearth.org.

Index

gROUNDWORKS |
ECOLOGICAL ISSUES IN PHILOSOPHY AND THEOLOGY

Forrest Clingerman and Brian Treanor, *Series Editors*

Interpreting Nature: The Emerging Field of Environmental Hermeneutics
Forrest Clingerman and Brian Treanor, Martin Drenthen,
and David Utsler, eds.

*The Noetics of Nature: Environmental Philosophy and the Holy Beauty
of the Visible*
Bruce V. Foltz

Environmental Aesthetics: Crossing Divides and Breaking Ground
Martin Drenthen and Jozef Keulartz, eds.

The Logos of the Living World: Merleau-Ponty, Animals, and Language
Louise Westling